ONE SHOE FITS ALL

Shoe

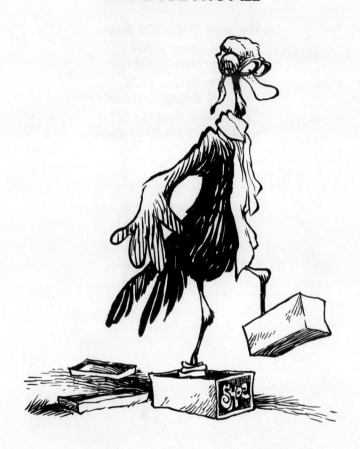

Other SHOE books by Jeff MacNelly:

The Very First SHOE Book
The Other SHOE
The New SHOE
On with the SHOE
A SHOE for All Seasons
The SHOE Must Go On
The Greatest SHOE on Earth

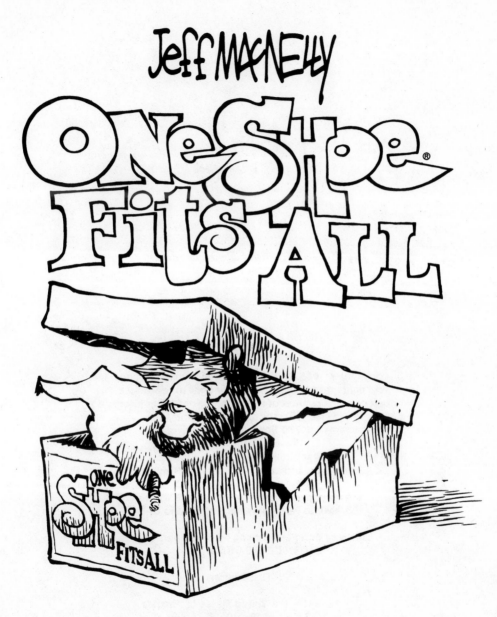

Jeff MacNelly

One Shoe Fits All

An Owl Book

HENRY HOLT AND COMPANY • NEW YORK

For further information, write Jefferson Communications, Inc.,
11730 Bowman Green Drive,
Reston, Virginia 22090.
First published in January 1987 by
Henry Holt and Company, Inc., 521 Fifth Avenue,
New York, New York 10175.
Distributed in Canada by Fitzhenry & Whiteside,
195 Allstate Parkway, Markham, Ontario L3R 4T8.

Library of Congress Catalog Card Number: 86-81206
ISBN 0-8050-0102-6 (pbk.)

First Edition

Printed in the United States of America
1 3 5 7 9 10 8 6 4 2

ISBN 0-8050-0102-6

one

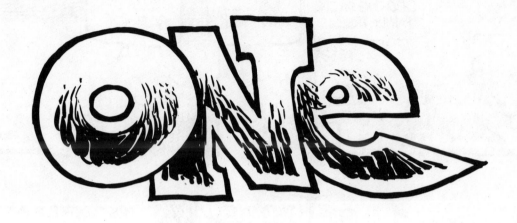

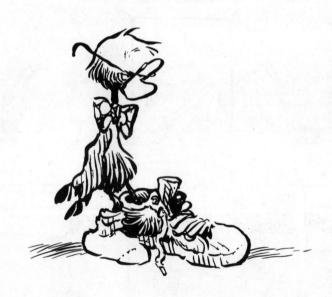

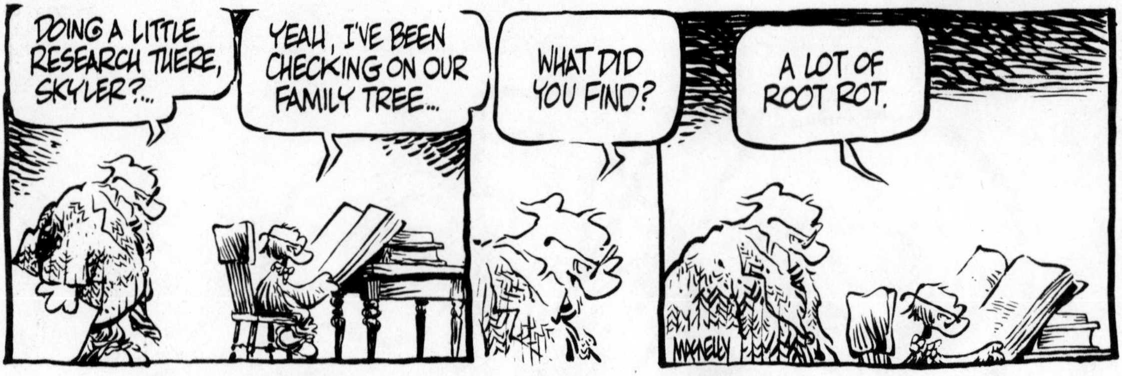
DOING A LITTLE RESEARCH THERE, SKYLER?...
YEAH, I'VE BEEN CHECKING ON OUR FAMILY TREE...
WHAT DID YOU FIND?
A LOT OF ROOT ROT.
MACNELLY

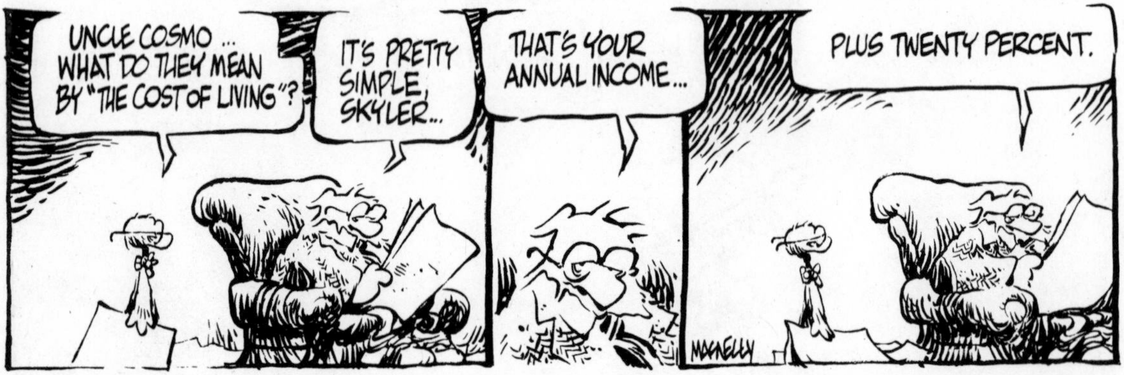
UNCLE COSMO ... WHAT DO THEY MEAN BY "THE COST OF LIVING"?
IT'S PRETTY SIMPLE, SKYLER...
THAT'S YOUR ANNUAL INCOME...
PLUS TWENTY PERCENT.
MACNELLY

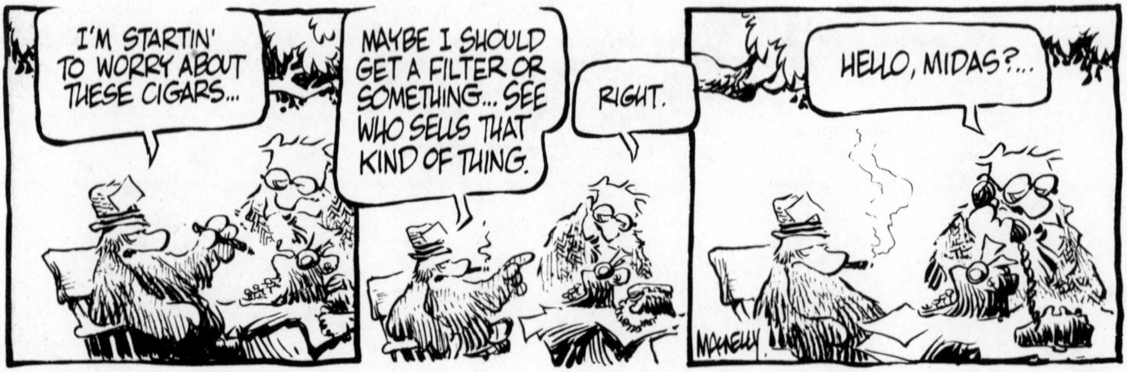
I'M STARTIN' TO WORRY ABOUT THESE CIGARS...
MAYBE I SHOULD GET A FILTER OR SOMETHING... SEE WHO SELLS THAT KIND OF THING.
RIGHT.
HELLO, MIDAS?...
MACNELLY

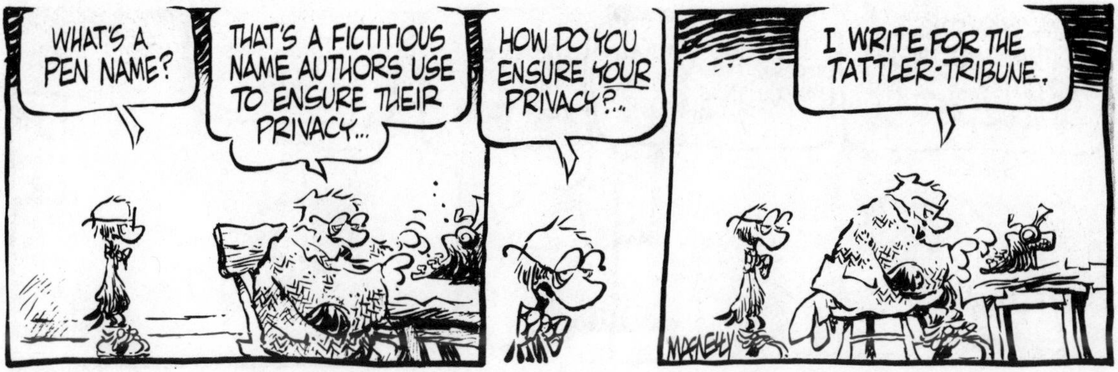
WHAT'S A PEN NAME?
THAT'S A FICTITIOUS NAME AUTHORS USE TO ENSURE THEIR PRIVACY...
HOW DO YOU ENSURE YOUR PRIVACY?...
I WRITE FOR THE TATTLER-TRIBUNE.
MACNELLY

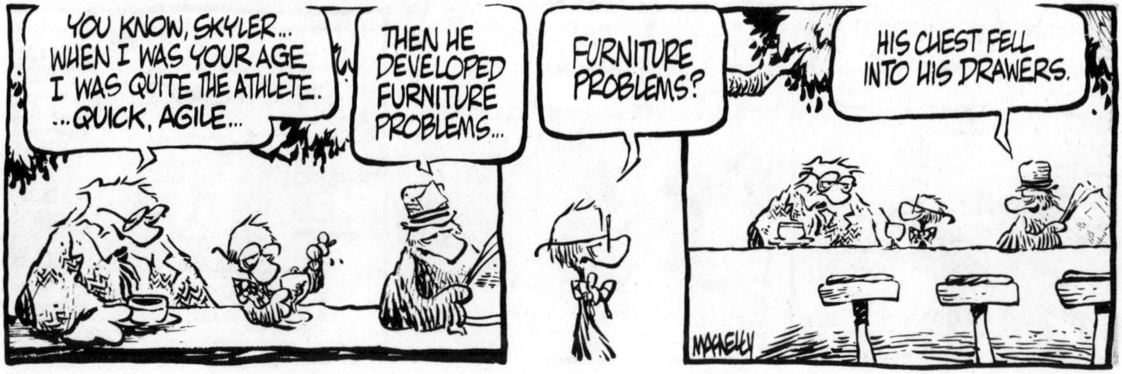
YOU KNOW, SKYLER... WHEN I WAS YOUR AGE I WAS QUITE THE ATHLETE. ...QUICK, AGILE...
THEN HE DEVELOPED FURNITURE PROBLEMS...
FURNITURE PROBLEMS?
HIS CHEST FELL INTO HIS DRAWERS.
MACNELLY

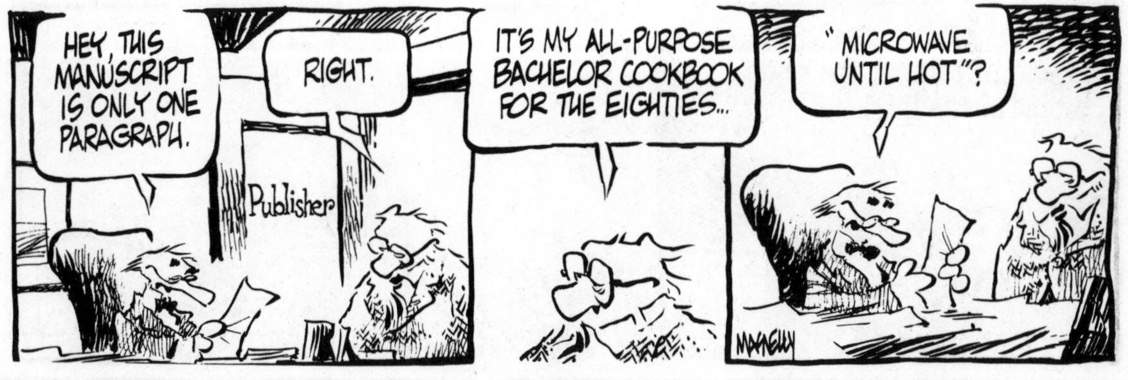
HEY, THIS MANUSCRIPT IS ONLY ONE PARAGRAPH.
RIGHT.
Publisher
IT'S MY ALL-PURPOSE BACHELOR COOKBOOK FOR THE EIGHTIES...
"MICROWAVE UNTIL HOT"?
MACNELLY

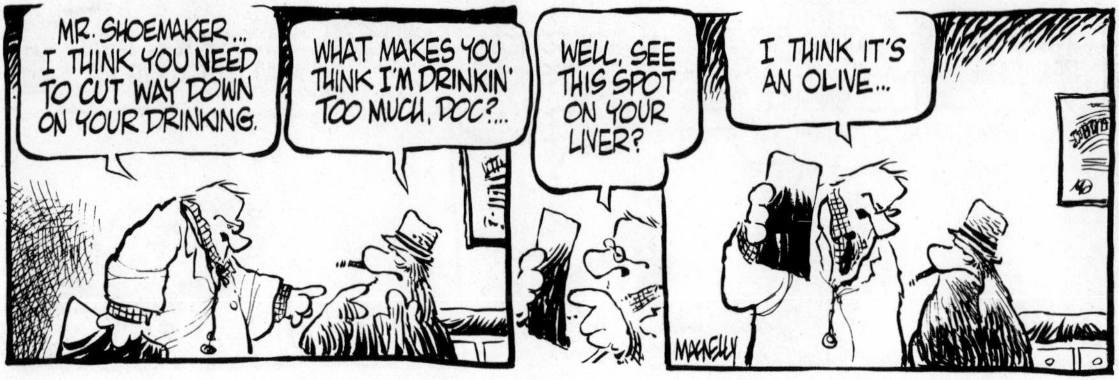
MR. SHOEMAKER... I THINK YOU NEED TO CUT WAY DOWN ON YOUR DRINKING.
WHAT MAKES YOU THINK I'M DRINKIN' TOO MUCH, DOC?...
WELL, SEE THIS SPOT ON YOUR LIVER?
I THINK IT'S AN OLIVE...
MACNELLY

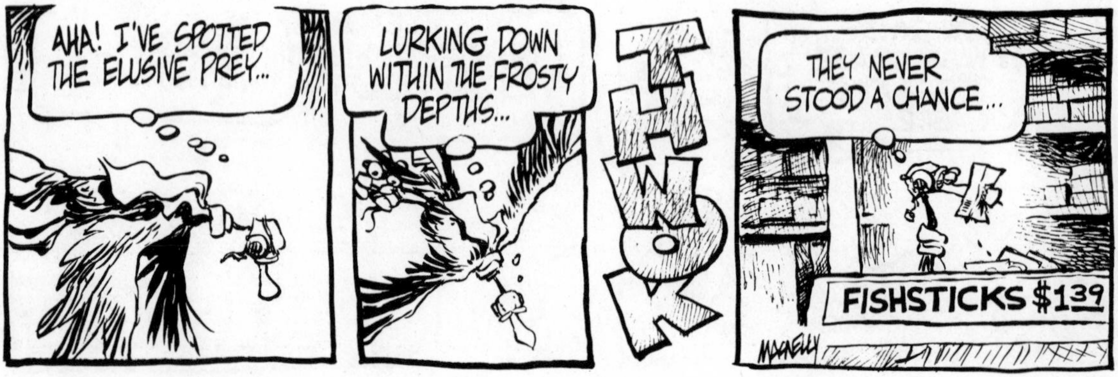
AHA! I'VE SPOTTED THE ELUSIVE PREY...
LURKING DOWN WITHIN THE FROSTY DEPTHS...
THWOK
THEY NEVER STOOD A CHANCE...
FISHSTICKS $1.39
MACNELLY

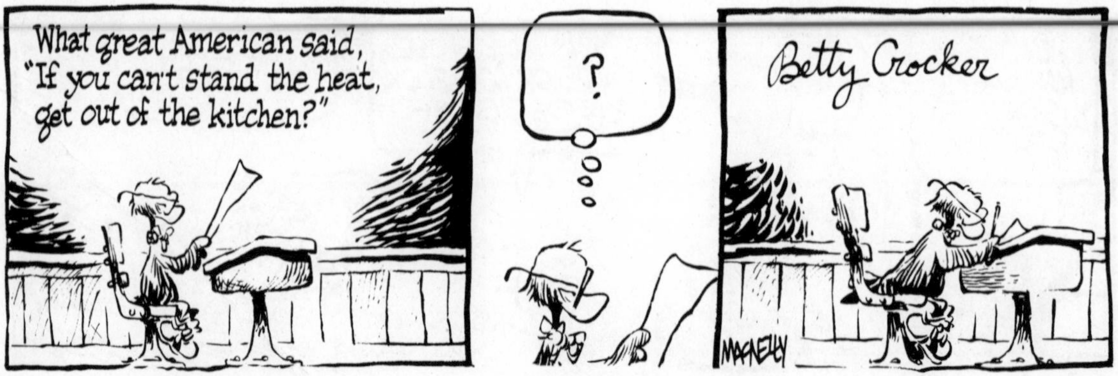
What great American said, "If you can't stand the heat, get out of the kitchen?"
?
Betty Crocker
MACNELLY

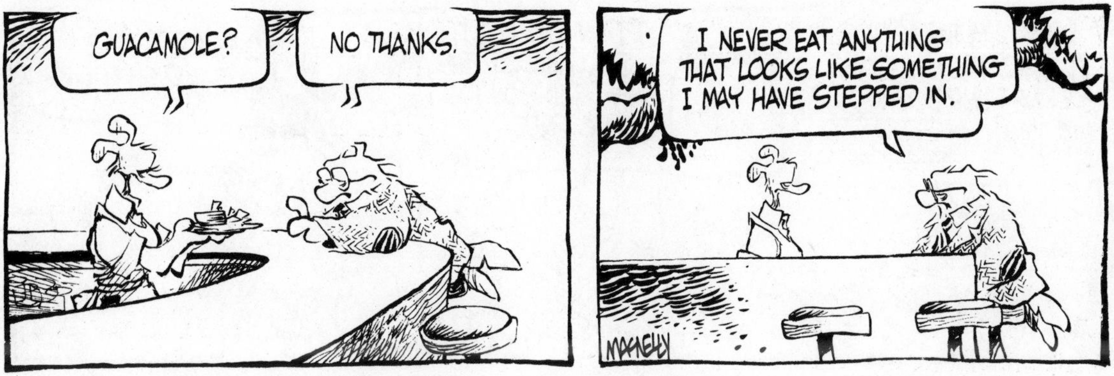
GUACAMOLE?
NO THANKS.
I NEVER EAT ANYTHING THAT LOOKS LIKE SOMETHING I MAY HAVE STEPPED IN.

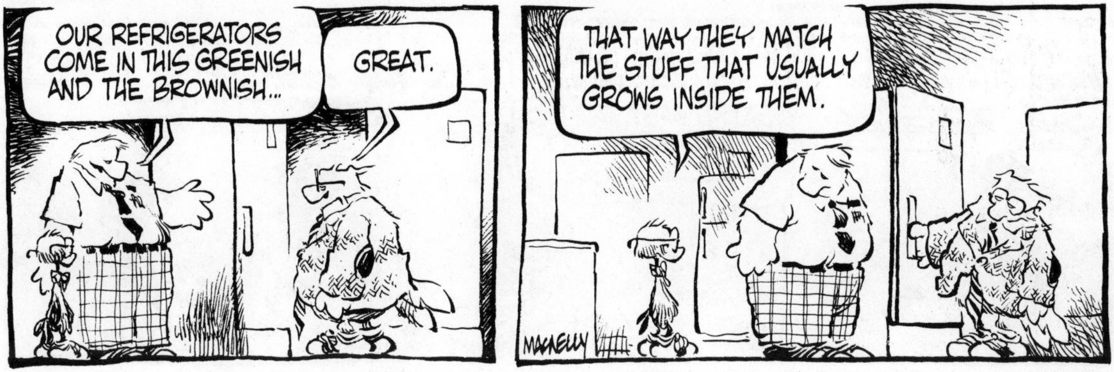
OUR REFRIGERATORS COME IN THIS GREENISH AND THE BROWNISH...
GREAT.
THAT WAY THEY MATCH THE STUFF THAT USUALLY GROWS INSIDE THEM.

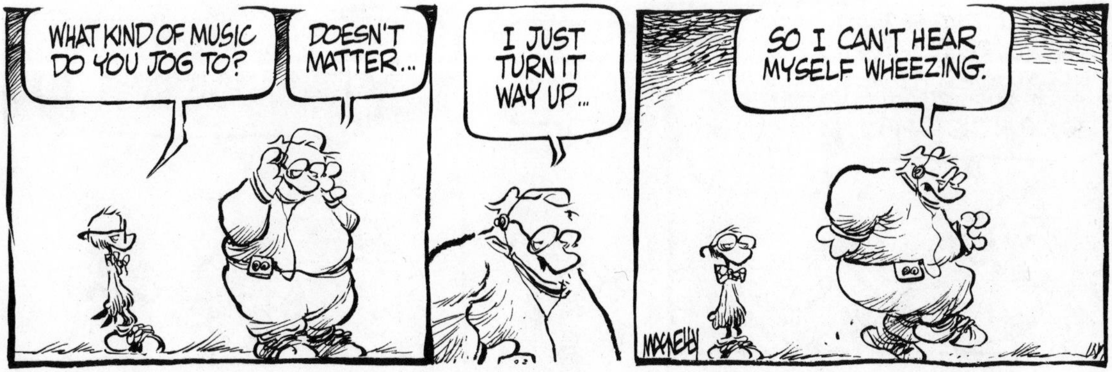
WHAT KIND OF MUSIC DO YOU JOG TO?
DOESN'T MATTER...
I JUST TURN IT WAY UP...
SO I CAN'T HEAR MYSELF WHEEZING.

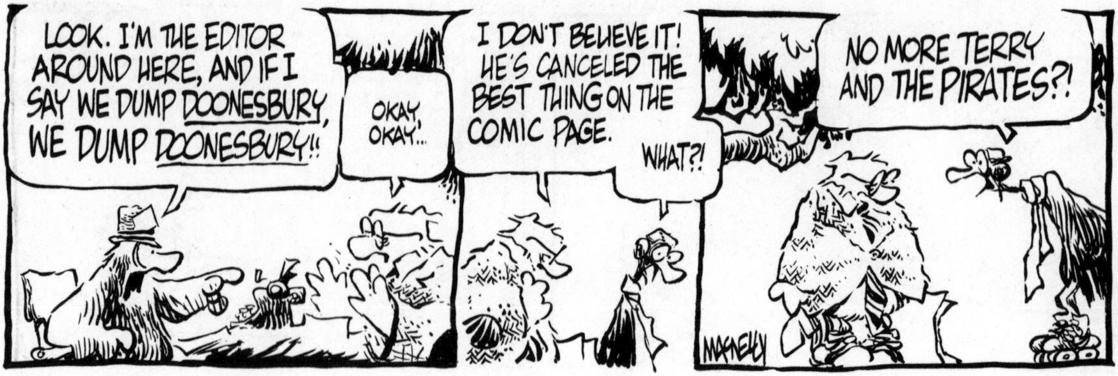
LOOK. I'M THE EDITOR AROUND HERE, AND IF I SAY WE DUMP DOONESBURY, WE DUMP DOONESBURY!!
OKAY OKAY!...
I DON'T BELIEVE IT! HE'S CANCELED THE BEST THING ON THE COMIC PAGE.
WHAT?!
NO MORE TERRY AND THE PIRATES?!
MACNELLY

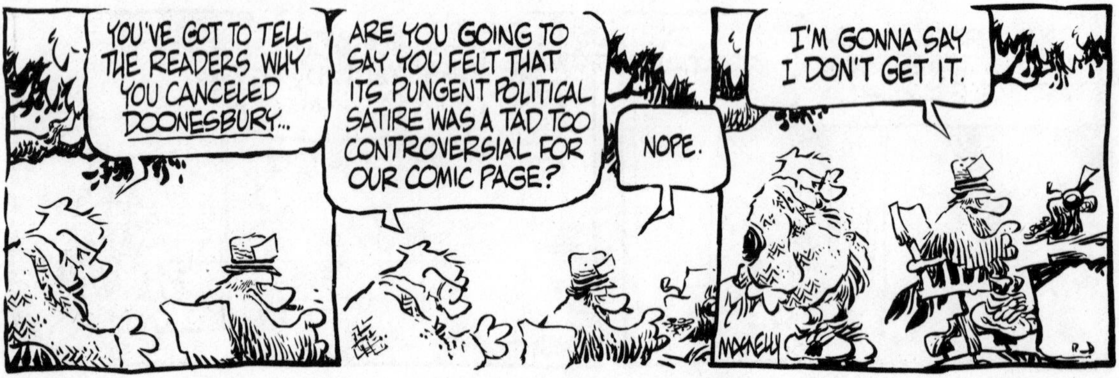
YOU'VE GOT TO TELL THE READERS WHY YOU CANCELED DOONESBURY...
ARE YOU GOING TO SAY YOU FELT THAT ITS PUNGENT POLITICAL SATIRE WAS A TAD TOO CONTROVERSIAL FOR OUR COMIC PAGE?
NOPE.
I'M GONNA SAY I DON'T GET IT.
MACNELLY

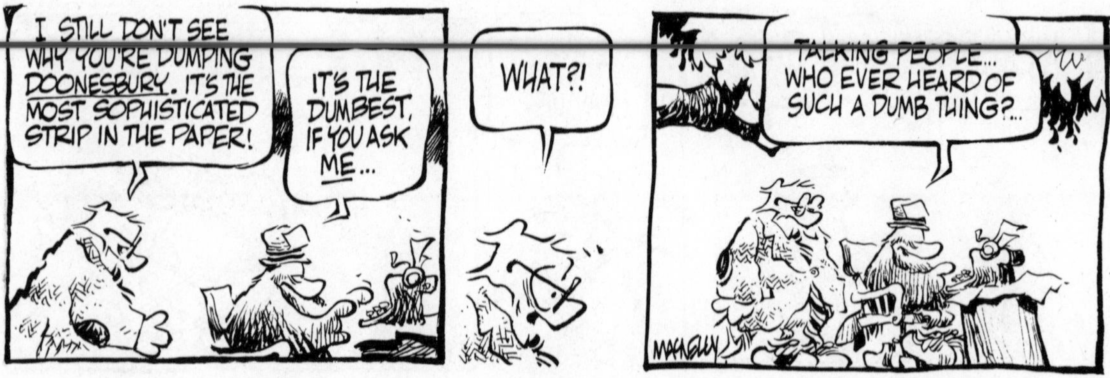
I STILL DON'T SEE WHY YOU'RE DUMPING DOONESBURY. IT'S THE MOST SOPHISTICATED STRIP IN THE PAPER!
IT'S THE DUMBEST, IF YOU ASK ME...
WHAT?!
TALKING PEOPLE... WHO EVER HEARD OF SUCH A DUMB THING?...
MACNELLY

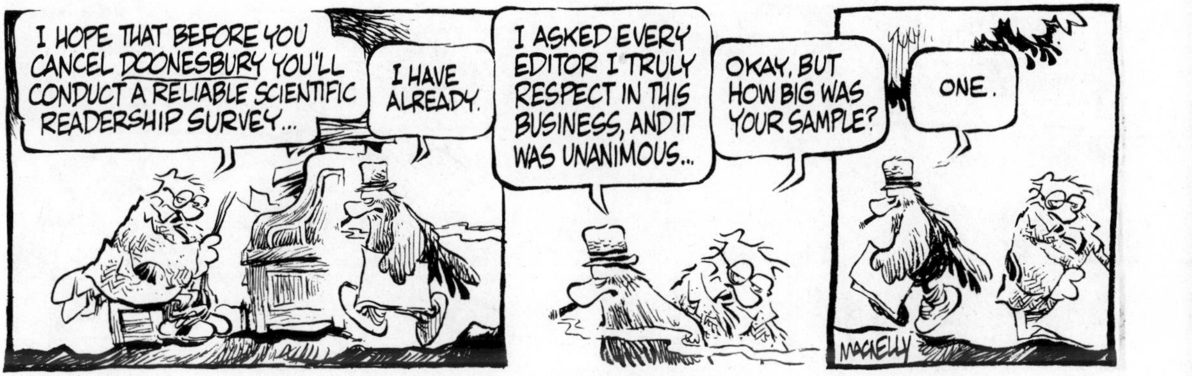
I HOPE THAT BEFORE YOU CANCEL DOONESBURY YOU'LL CONDUCT A RELIABLE SCIENTIFIC READERSHIP SURVEY...
I HAVE ALREADY.
I ASKED EVERY EDITOR I TRULY RESPECT IN THIS BUSINESS, AND IT WAS UNANIMOUS...
OKAY, BUT HOW BIG WAS YOUR SAMPLE?
ONE.
MACNELLY

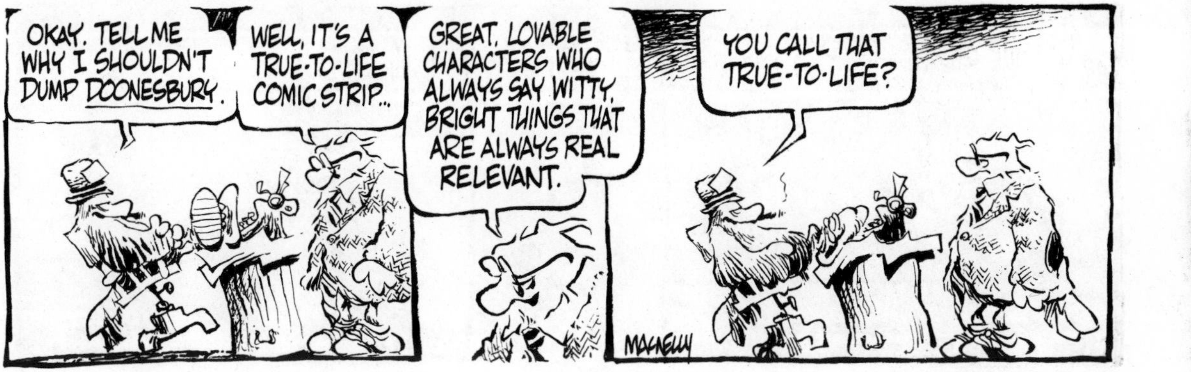
OKAY. TELL ME WHY I SHOULDN'T DUMP DOONESBURY.
WELL, IT'S A TRUE-TO-LIFE COMIC STRIP...
GREAT, LOVABLE CHARACTERS WHO ALWAYS SAY WITTY, BRIGHT THINGS THAT ARE ALWAYS REAL RELEVANT.
YOU CALL THAT TRUE-TO-LIFE?
MACNELLY

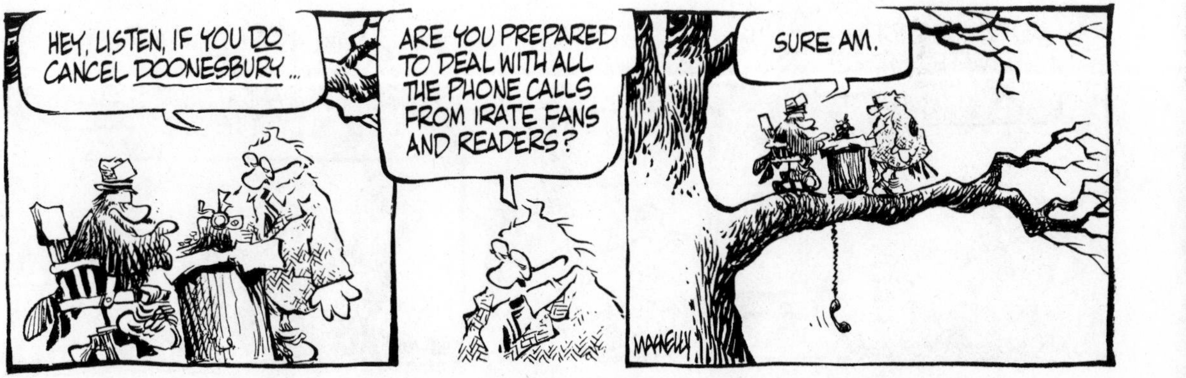
HEY, LISTEN, IF YOU DO CANCEL DOONESBURY...
ARE YOU PREPARED TO DEAL WITH ALL THE PHONE CALLS FROM IRATE FANS AND READERS?
SURE AM.
MACNELLY

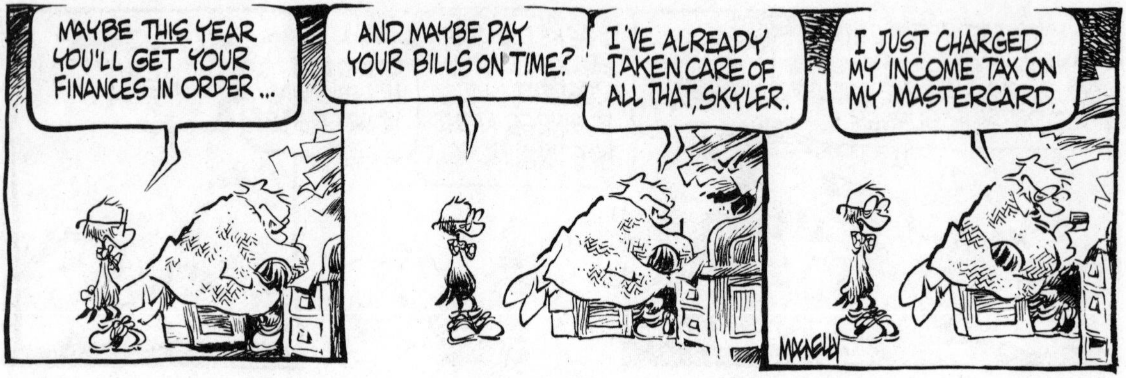
MAYBE THIS YEAR YOU'LL GET YOUR FINANCES IN ORDER ...
AND MAYBE PAY YOUR BILLS ON TIME?
I'VE ALREADY TAKEN CARE OF ALL THAT, SKYLER.
I JUST CHARGED MY INCOME TAX ON MY MASTERCARD.
MACNELLY

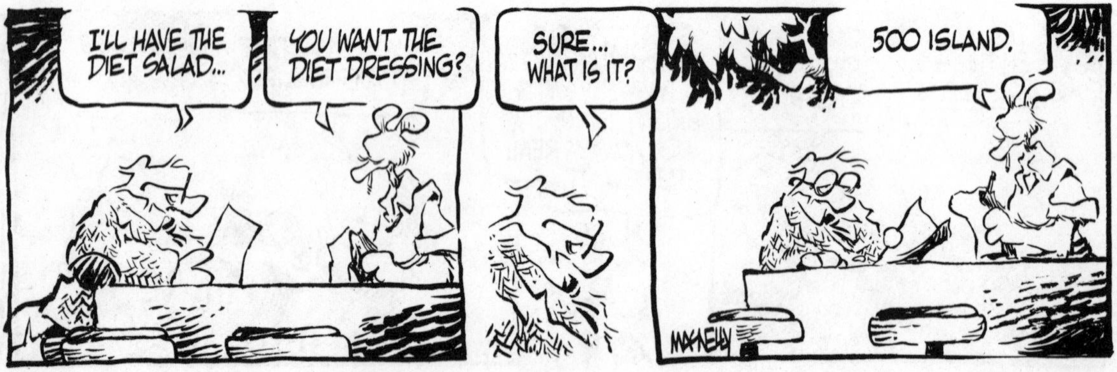
I'LL HAVE THE DIET SALAD...
YOU WANT THE DIET DRESSING?
SURE... WHAT IS IT?
500 ISLAND.
MACNELLY

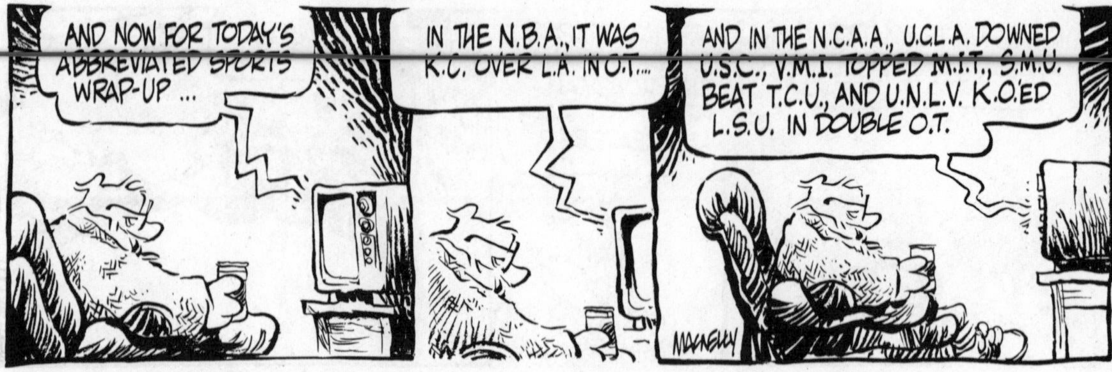
AND NOW FOR TODAY'S ABBREVIATED SPORTS WRAP-UP ...
IN THE N.B.A., IT WAS K.C. OVER L.A. IN O.T....
AND IN THE N.C.A.A., U.C.L.A. DOWNED U.S.C., V.M.I. TOPPED M.I.T., S.M.U. BEAT T.C.U., AND U.N.L.V. K.O.'ED L.S.U. IN DOUBLE O.T.
MACNELLY

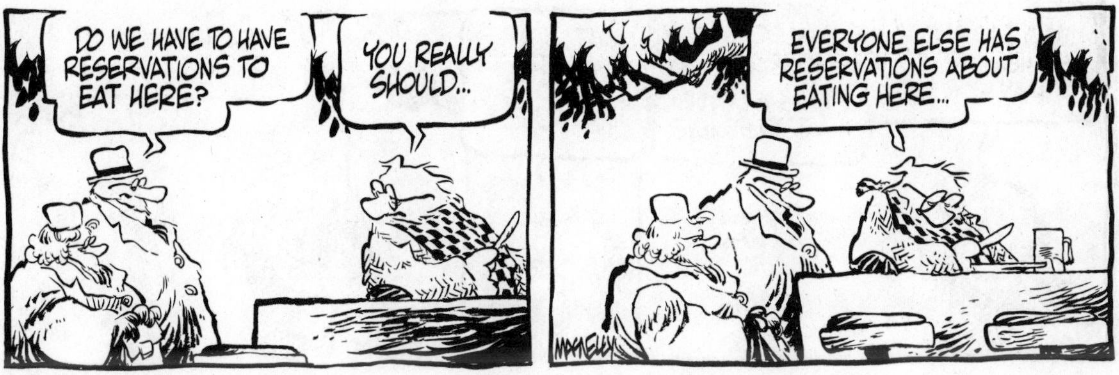
DO WE HAVE TO HAVE RESERVATIONS TO EAT HERE?
YOU REALLY SHOULD...
EVERYONE ELSE HAS RESERVATIONS ABOUT EATING HERE...
MACNELLY

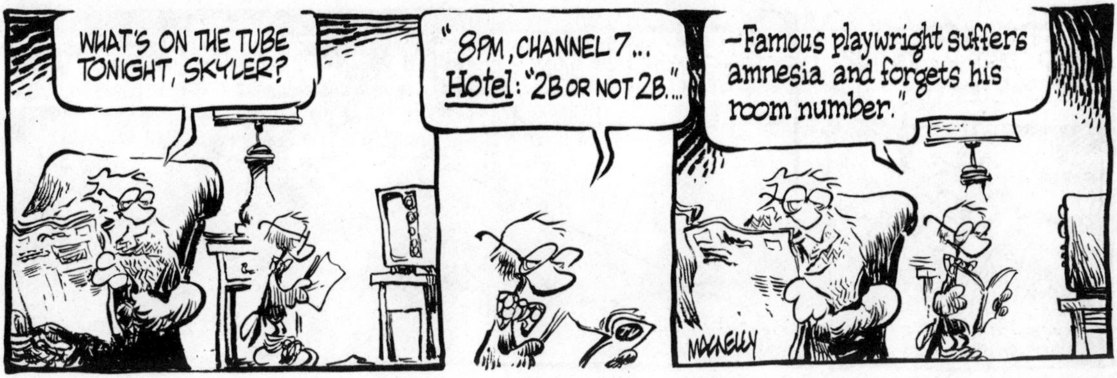
WHAT'S ON THE TUBE TONIGHT, SKYLER?
"8PM, CHANNEL 7... Hotel: "2B OR NOT 2B."...
–Famous playwright suffers amnesia and forgets his room number."
MACNELLY

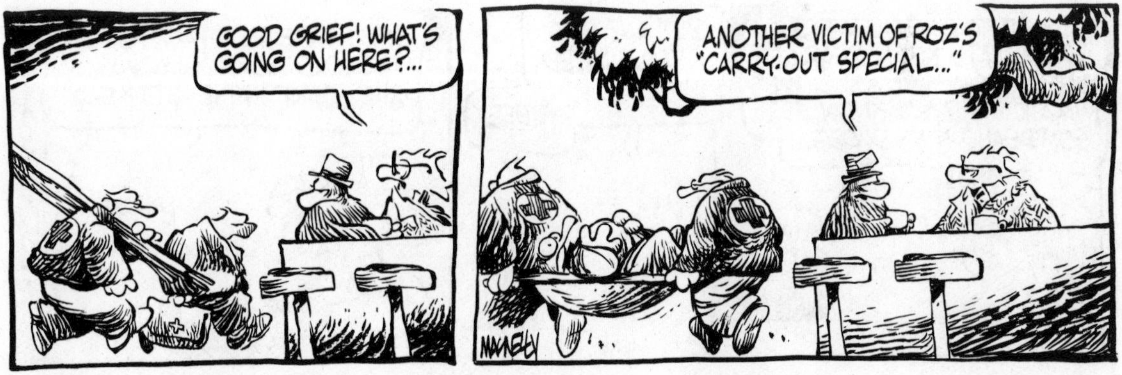
GOOD GRIEF! WHAT'S GOING ON HERE?...
ANOTHER VICTIM OF ROZ'S "CARRY-OUT SPECIAL..."
MACNELLY

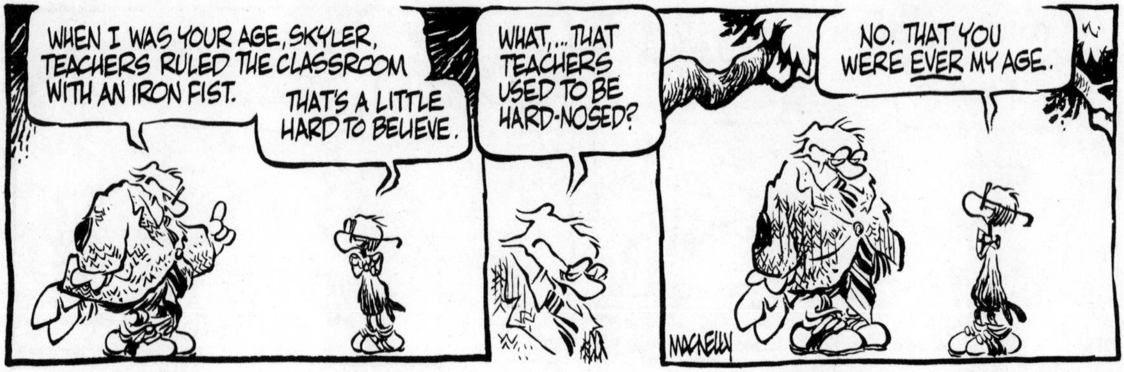
WHEN I WAS YOUR AGE, SKYLER, TEACHERS RULED THE CLASSROOM WITH AN IRON FIST.
THAT'S A LITTLE HARD TO BELIEVE.
WHAT, ... THAT TEACHERS USED TO BE HARD-NOSED?
NO. THAT YOU WERE EVER MY AGE.
MACNELLY

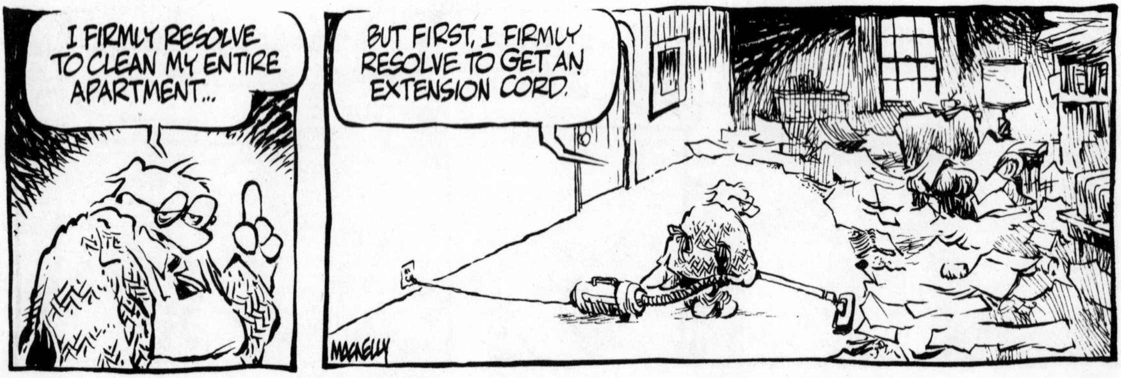
I FIRMLY RESOLVE TO CLEAN MY ENTIRE APARTMENT...
BUT FIRST, I FIRMLY RESOLVE TO GET AN EXTENSION CORD.
MACNELLY

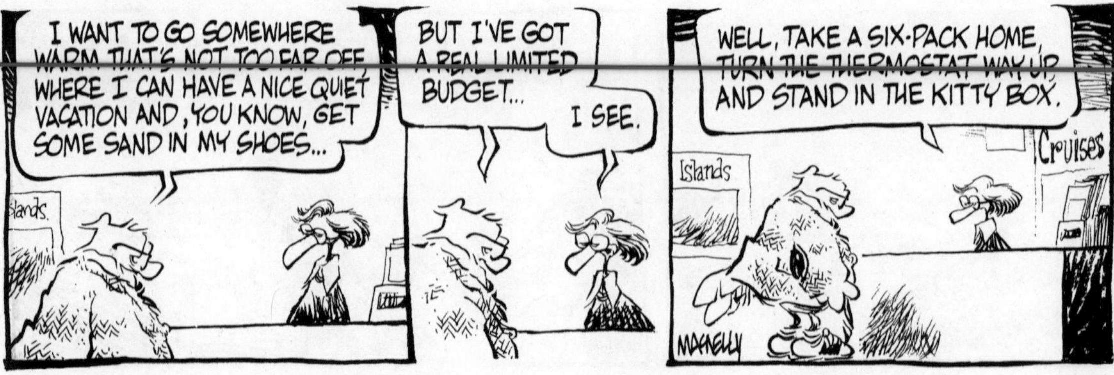
I WANT TO GO SOMEWHERE WARM THAT'S NOT TOO FAR OFF WHERE I CAN HAVE A NICE QUIET VACATION AND, YOU KNOW, GET SOME SAND IN MY SHOES...
BUT I'VE GOT A REAL LIMITED BUDGET...
I SEE.
WELL, TAKE A SIX-PACK HOME, TURN THE THERMOSTAT WAY UP, AND STAND IN THE KITTY BOX.
Islands
Cruises
MACNELLY

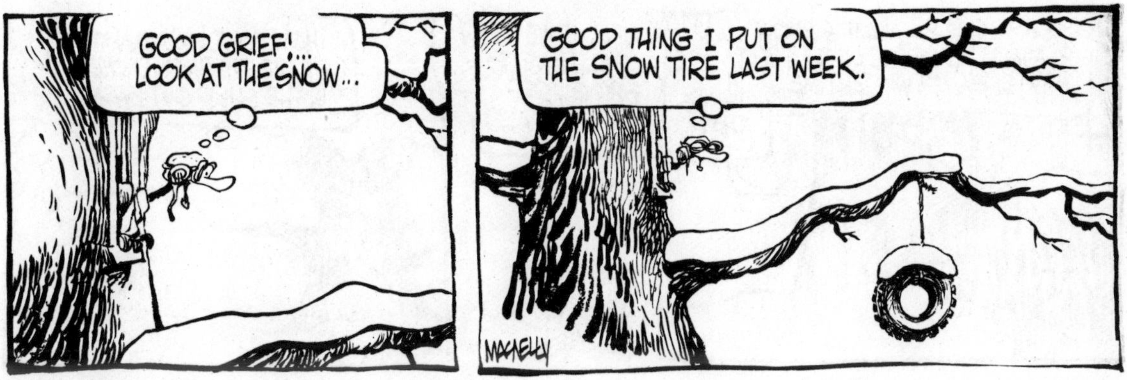
GOOD GRIEF!... LOOK AT THE SNOW...
GOOD THING I PUT ON THE SNOW TIRE LAST WEEK.
MACNELLY

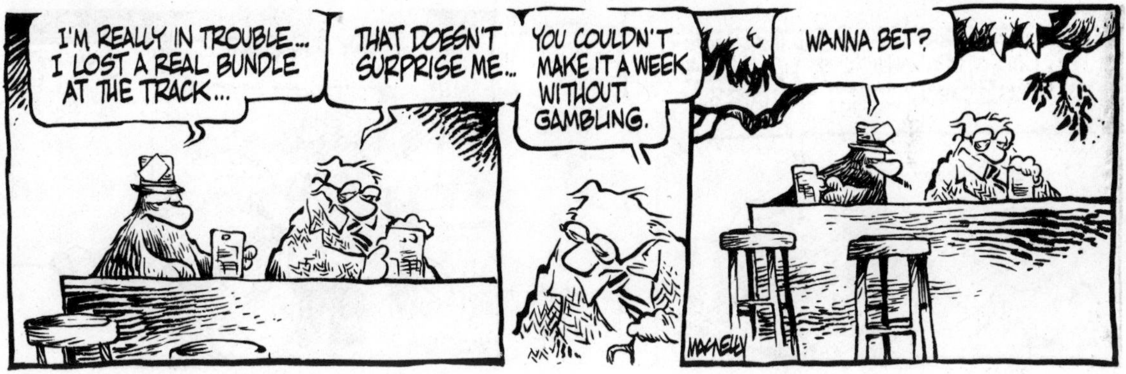
I'M REALLY IN TROUBLE... I LOST A REAL BUNDLE AT THE TRACK...
THAT DOESN'T SURPRISE ME...
YOU COULDN'T MAKE IT A WEEK WITHOUT GAMBLING.
WANNA BET?
MACNELLY

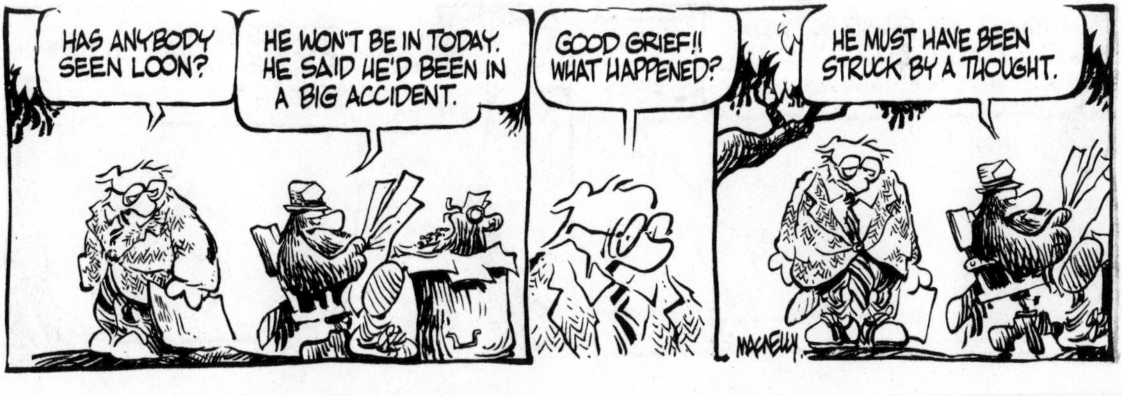
HAS ANYBODY SEEN LOON?
HE WON'T BE IN TODAY. HE SAID HE'D BEEN IN A BIG ACCIDENT.
GOOD GRIEF!! WHAT HAPPENED?
HE MUST HAVE BEEN STRUCK BY A THOUGHT.
MACNELLY

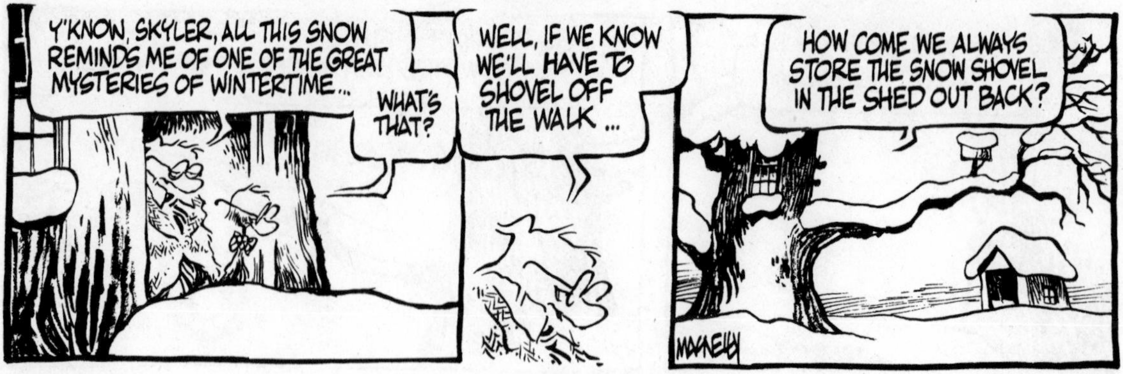
Y'KNOW, SKYLER, ALL THIS SNOW REMINDS ME OF ONE OF THE GREAT MYSTERIES OF WINTERTIME...
WHAT'S THAT?
WELL, IF WE KNOW WE'LL HAVE TO SHOVEL OFF THE WALK ...
HOW COME WE ALWAYS STORE THE SNOW SHOVEL IN THE SHED OUT BACK?
MACNELLY

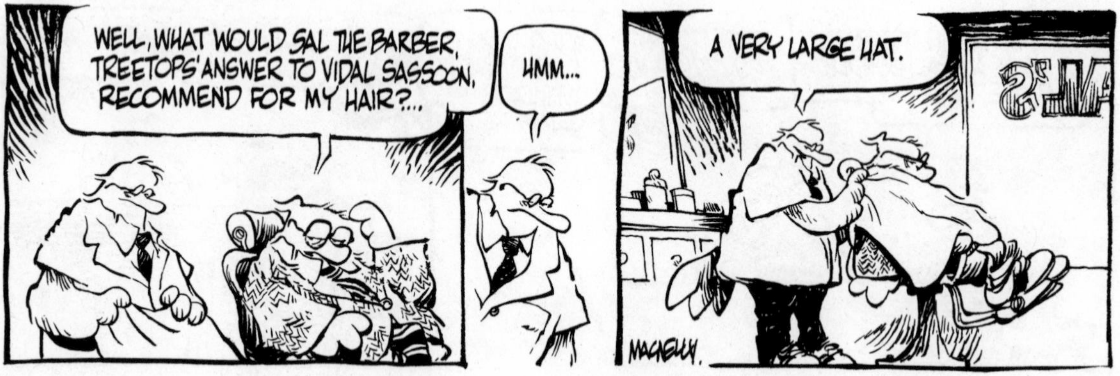
WELL, WHAT WOULD SAL THE BARBER, TREETOPS' ANSWER TO VIDAL SASSOON, RECOMMEND FOR MY HAIR?...
HMM...
A VERY LARGE HAT.
MACNELLY

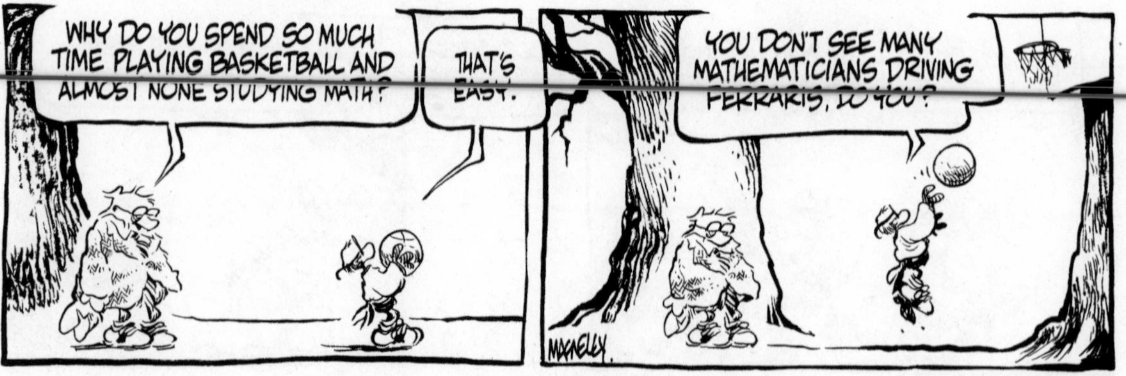
WHY DO YOU SPEND SO MUCH TIME PLAYING BASKETBALL AND ALMOST NONE STUDYING MATH?
THAT'S EASY.
YOU DON'T SEE MANY MATHEMATICIANS DRIVING FERRARIS, DO YOU?
MACNELLY

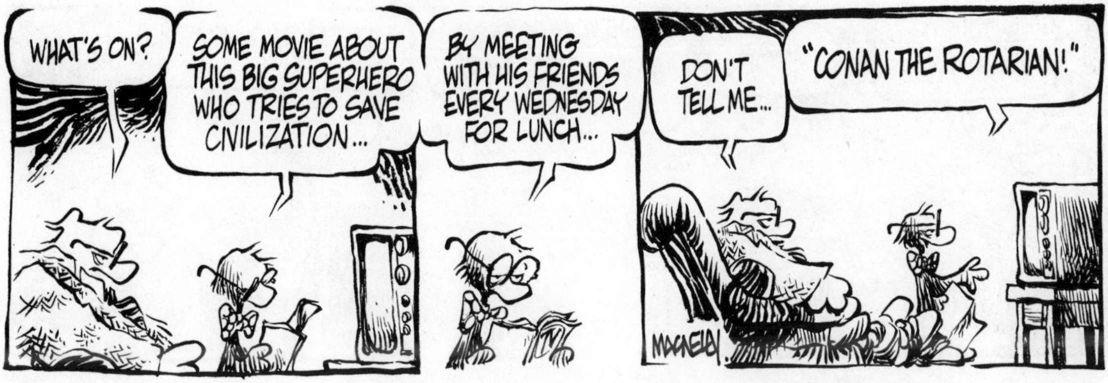
WHAT'S ON?
SOME MOVIE ABOUT THIS BIG SUPERHERO WHO TRIES TO SAVE CIVILIZATION...
BY MEETING WITH HIS FRIENDS EVERY WEDNESDAY FOR LUNCH...
DON'T TELL ME...
"CONAN THE ROTARIAN!"
MACNELLY

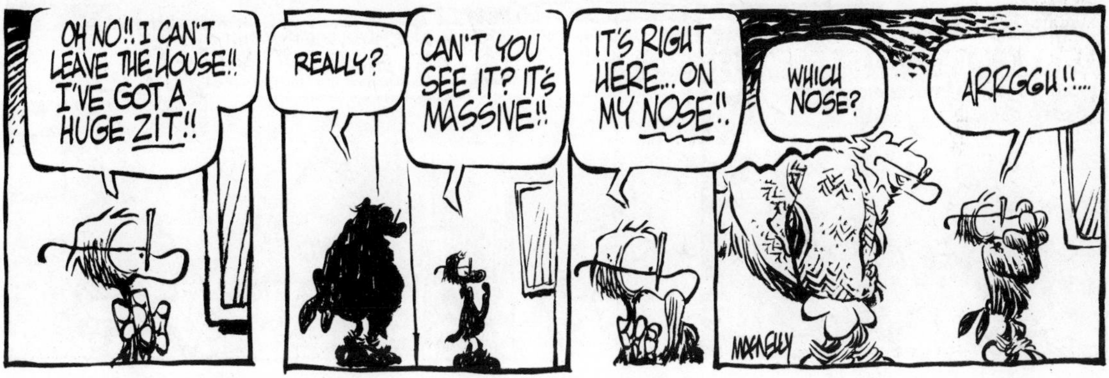
OH NO!! I CAN'T LEAVE THE HOUSE!! I'VE GOT A HUGE ZIT!!
REALLY?
CAN'T YOU SEE IT? IT'S MASSIVE!!
IT'S RIGHT HERE... ON MY NOSE!!
WHICH NOSE?
ARRGGH!!...
MACNELLY

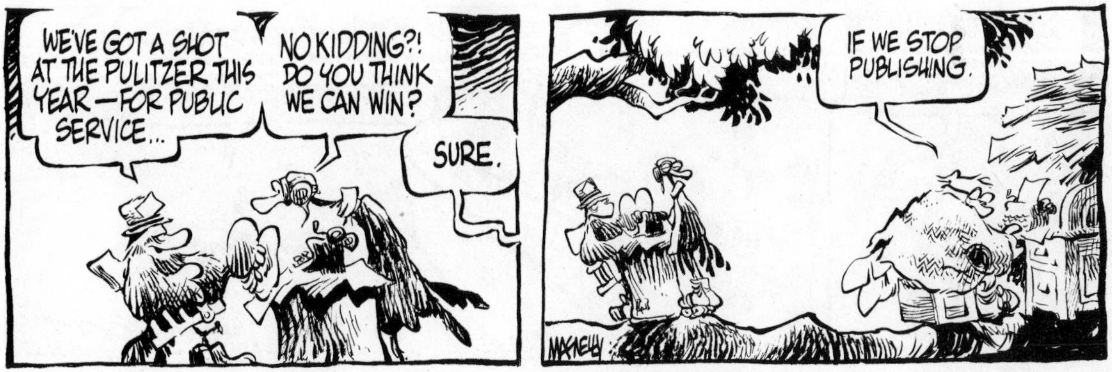
WE'VE GOT A SHOT AT THE PULITZER THIS YEAR—FOR PUBLIC SERVICE...
NO KIDDING?! DO YOU THINK WE CAN WIN?
SURE.
IF WE STOP PUBLISHING.
MACNELLY

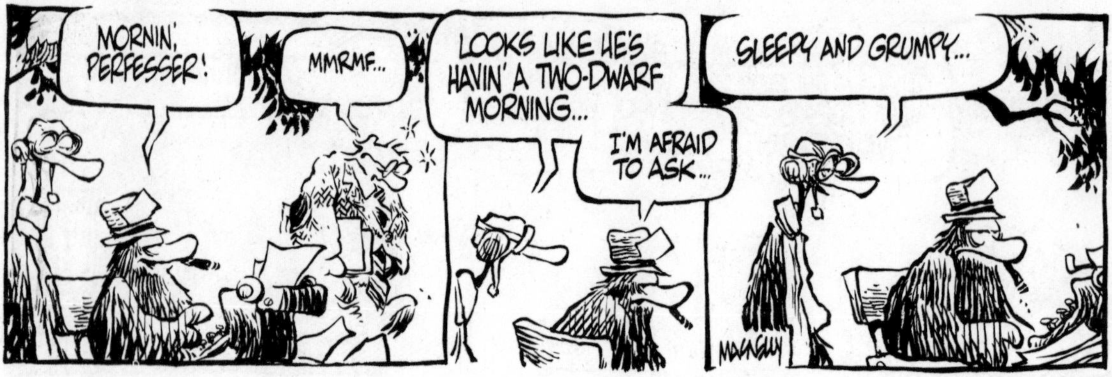
MORNIN', PERFESSER!
MMRMF...
LOOKS LIKE HE'S HAVIN' A TWO-DWARF MORNING...
I'M AFRAID TO ASK...
SLEEPY AND GRUMPY...

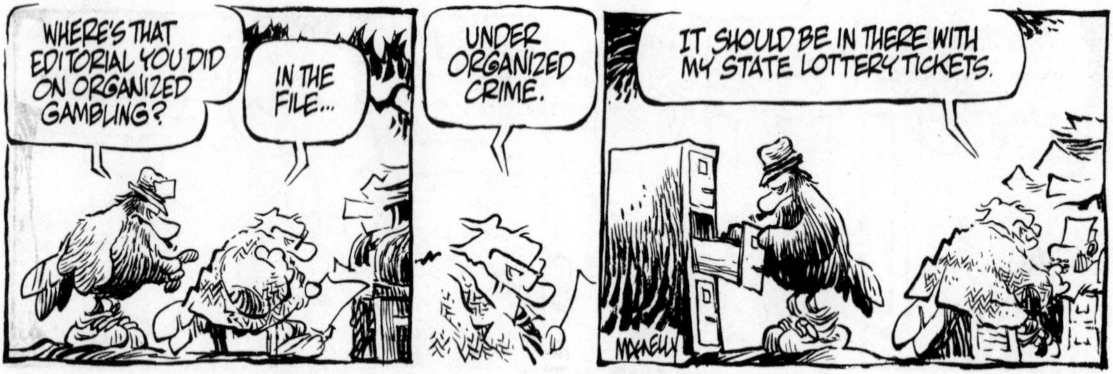
WHERE'S THAT EDITORIAL YOU DID ON ORGANIZED GAMBLING?
IN THE FILE...
UNDER ORGANIZED CRIME.
IT SHOULD BE IN THERE WITH MY STATE LOTTERY TICKETS.

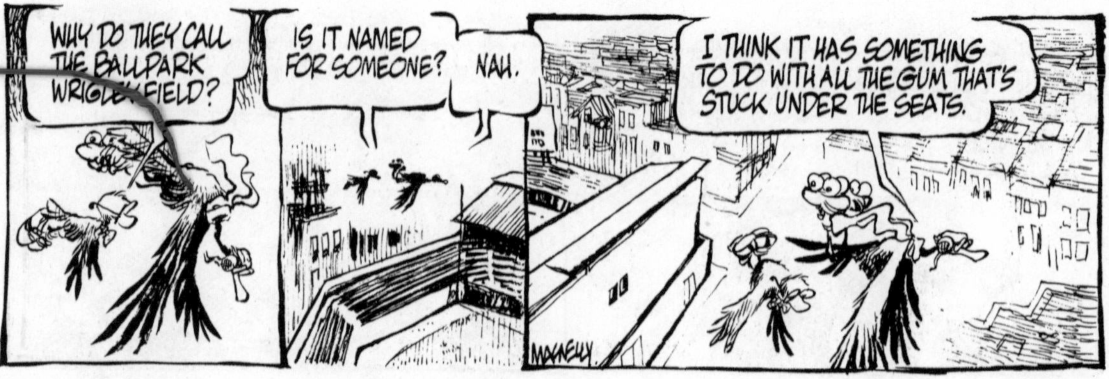
WHY DO THEY CALL THE BALLPARK WRIGLEY FIELD?
IS IT NAMED FOR SOMEONE?
NAH.
I THINK IT HAS SOMETHING TO DO WITH ALL THE GUM THAT'S STUCK UNDER THE SEATS.

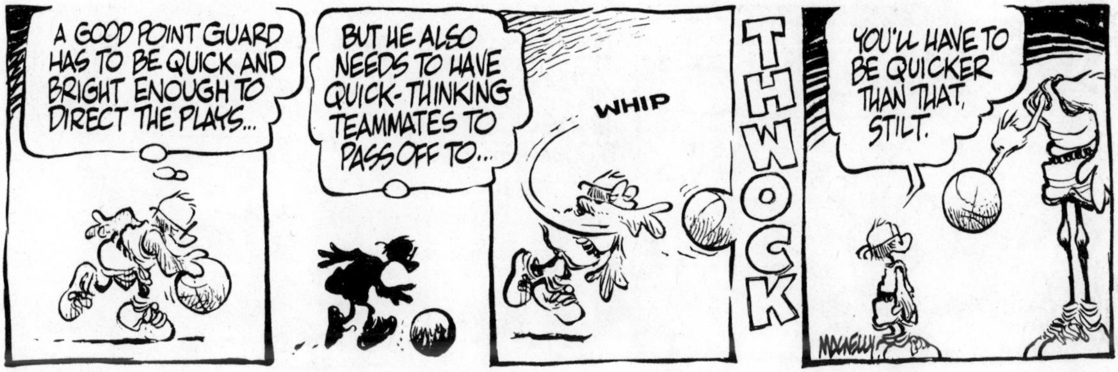
A GOOD POINT GUARD HAS TO BE QUICK AND BRIGHT ENOUGH TO DIRECT THE PLAYS...
BUT HE ALSO NEEDS TO HAVE QUICK-THINKING TEAMMATES TO PASS OFF TO...
WHIP
THWOCK
YOU'LL HAVE TO BE QUICKER THAN THAT, STILT.

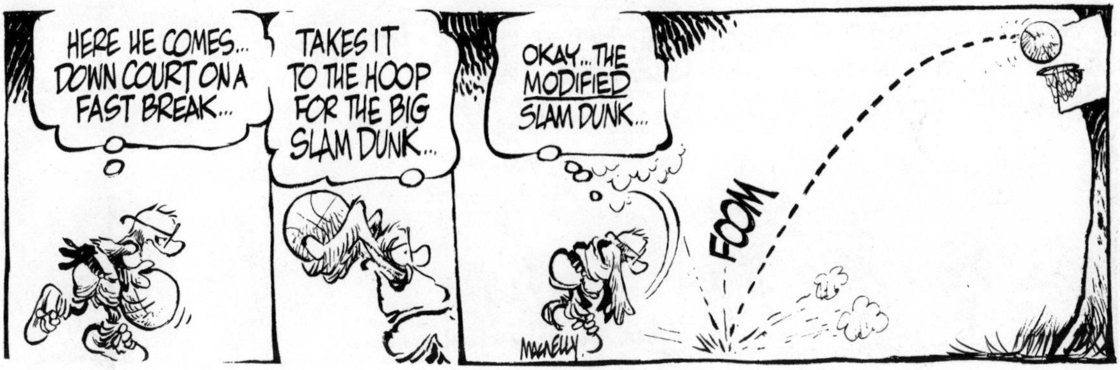
HERE HE COMES... DOWN COURT ON A FAST BREAK...
TAKES IT TO THE HOOP FOR THE BIG SLAM DUNK...
OKAY...THE MODIFIED SLAM DUNK...
FOOM

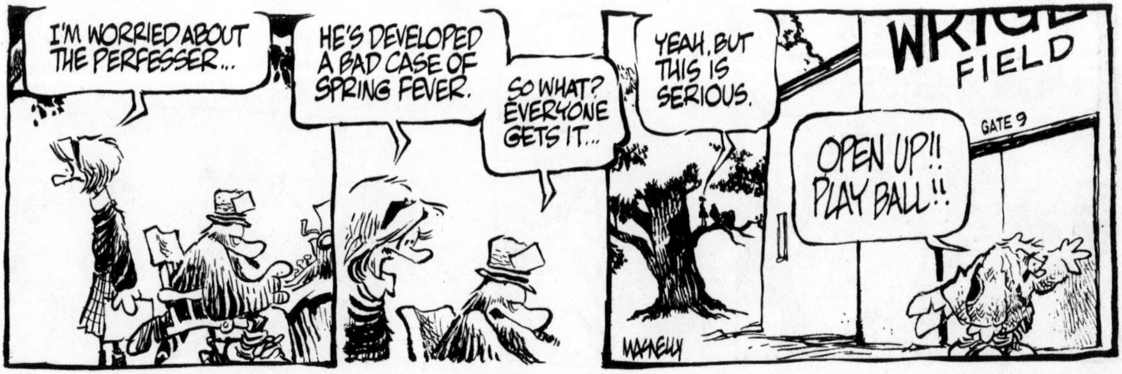
I'M WORRIED ABOUT THE PERFESSER...
HE'S DEVELOPED A BAD CASE OF SPRING FEVER.
SO WHAT? EVERYONE GETS IT...
YEAH, BUT THIS IS SERIOUS.
FIELD
GATE 9
OPEN UP!! PLAY BALL!!

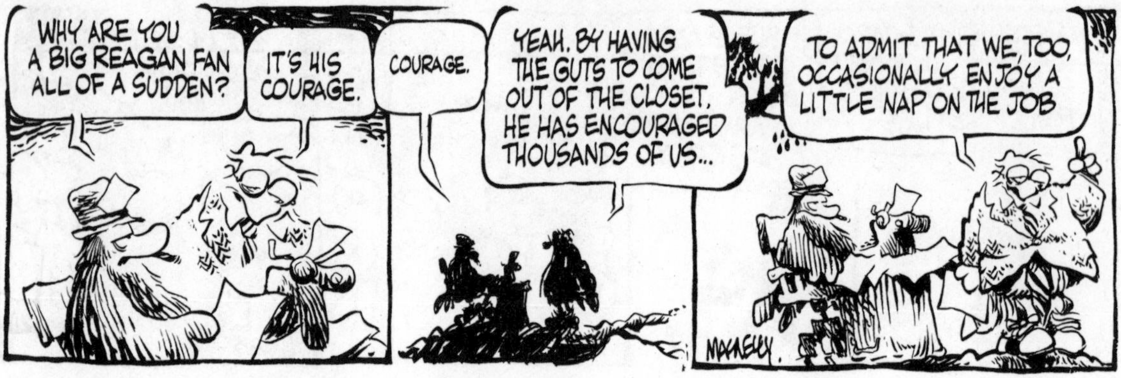
WHY ARE YOU A BIG REAGAN FAN ALL OF A SUDDEN?
IT'S HIS COURAGE.
COURAGE.
YEAH. BY HAVING THE GUTS TO COME OUT OF THE CLOSET, HE HAS ENCOURAGED THOUSANDS OF US...
TO ADMIT THAT WE, TOO, OCCASIONALLY ENJOY A LITTLE NAP ON THE JOB
MACNELLY

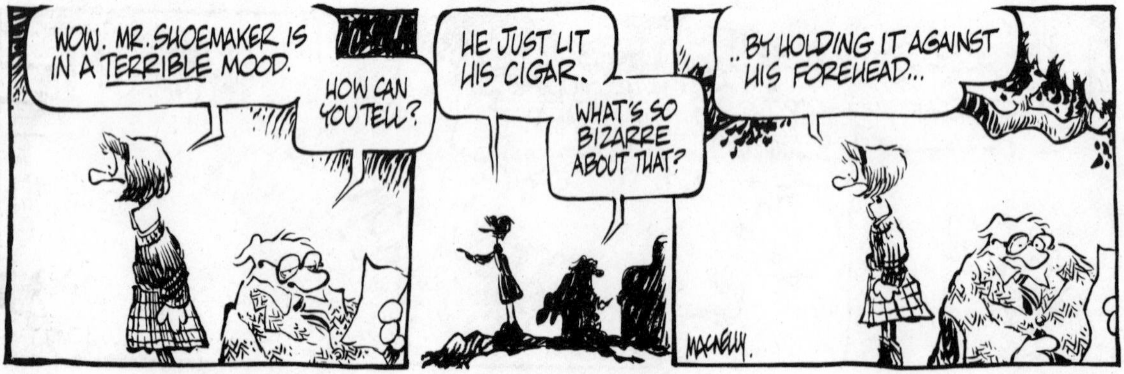
WOW. MR. SHOEMAKER IS IN A TERRIBLE MOOD.
HOW CAN YOU TELL?
HE JUST LIT HIS CIGAR.
WHAT'S SO BIZARRE ABOUT THAT?
...BY HOLDING IT AGAINST HIS FOREHEAD...
MACNELLY

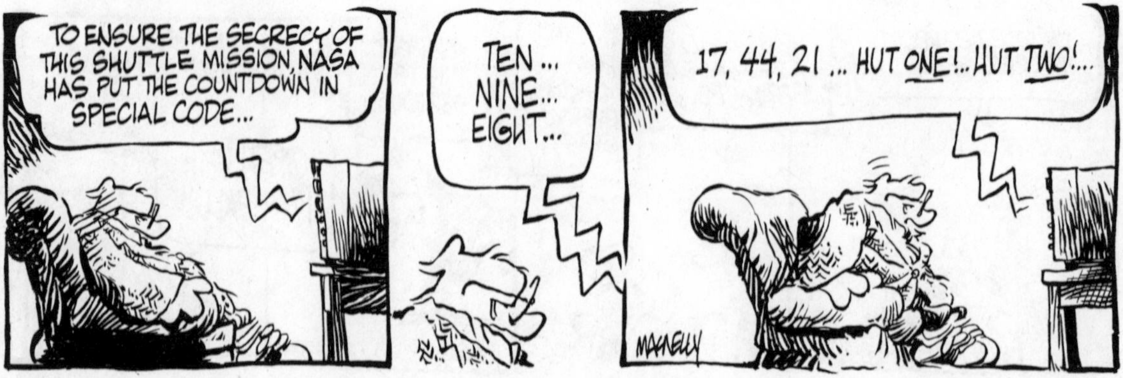
TO ENSURE THE SECRECY OF THIS SHUTTLE MISSION, NASA HAS PUT THE COUNTDOWN IN SPECIAL CODE...
TEN... NINE... EIGHT...
17, 44, 21 ... HUT ONE!.. HUT TWO!...
MACNELLY

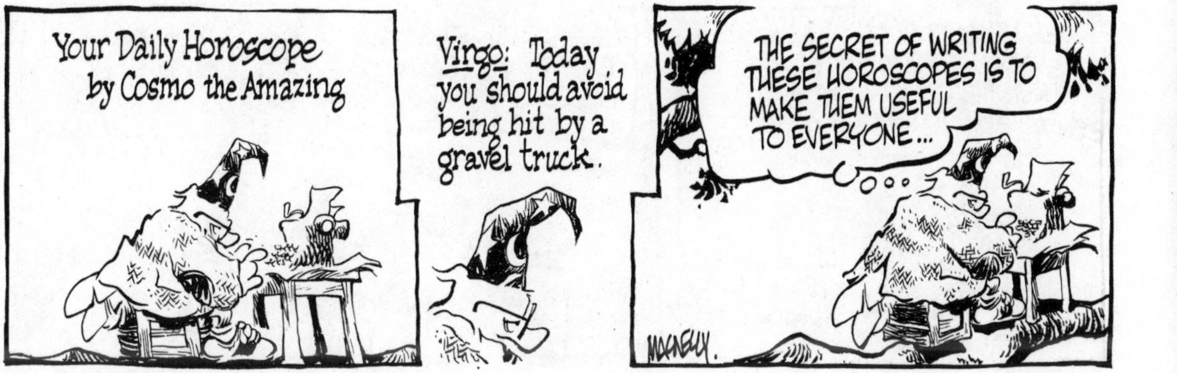
Your Daily Horoscope by Cosmo the Amazing
Vingo: Today you should avoid being hit by a gravel truck.
THE SECRET OF WRITING THESE HOROSCOPES IS TO MAKE THEM USEFUL TO EVERYONE...

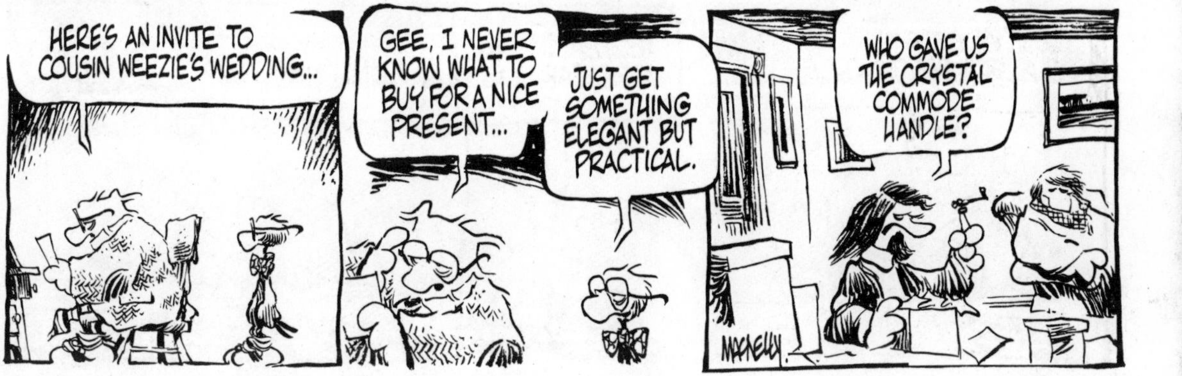
HERE'S AN INVITE TO COUSIN WEEZIE'S WEDDING...
GEE, I NEVER KNOW WHAT TO BUY FOR A NICE PRESENT...
JUST GET SOMETHING ELEGANT BUT PRACTICAL.
WHO GAVE US THE CRYSTAL COMMODE HANDLE?

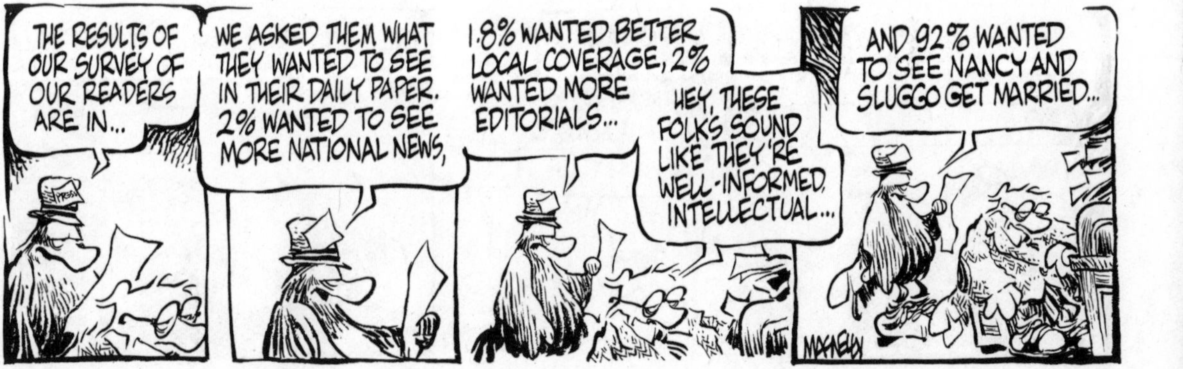
THE RESULTS OF OUR SURVEY OF OUR READERS ARE IN...
WE ASKED THEM WHAT THEY WANTED TO SEE IN THEIR DAILY PAPER. 2% WANTED TO SEE MORE NATIONAL NEWS,
1.8% WANTED BETTER LOCAL COVERAGE, 2% WANTED MORE EDITORIALS...
HEY, THESE FOLKS SOUND LIKE THEY'RE WELL-INFORMED, INTELLECTUAL...
AND 92% WANTED TO SEE NANCY AND SLUGGO GET MARRIED...
PRESS

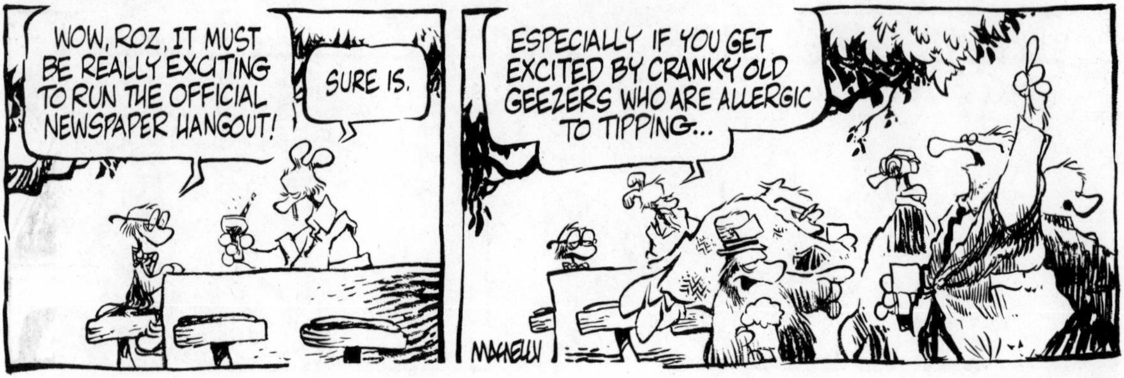
WOW, ROZ, IT MUST BE REALLY EXCITING TO RUN THE OFFICIAL NEWSPAPER HANGOUT!
SURE IS.
ESPECIALLY IF YOU GET EXCITED BY CRANKY OLD GEEZERS WHO ARE ALLERGIC TO TIPPING...
MACNELLY

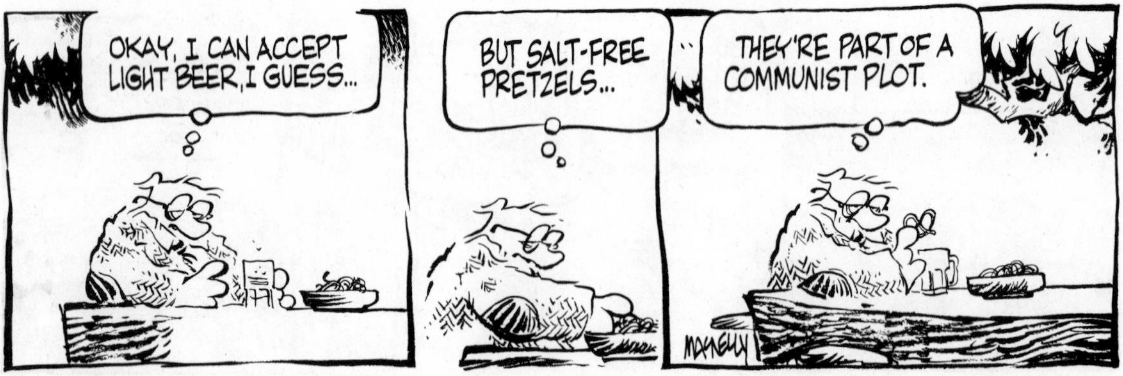
OKAY, I CAN ACCEPT LIGHT BEER, I GUESS...
BUT SALT-FREE PRETZELS...
THEY'RE PART OF A COMMUNIST PLOT.
MACNELLY

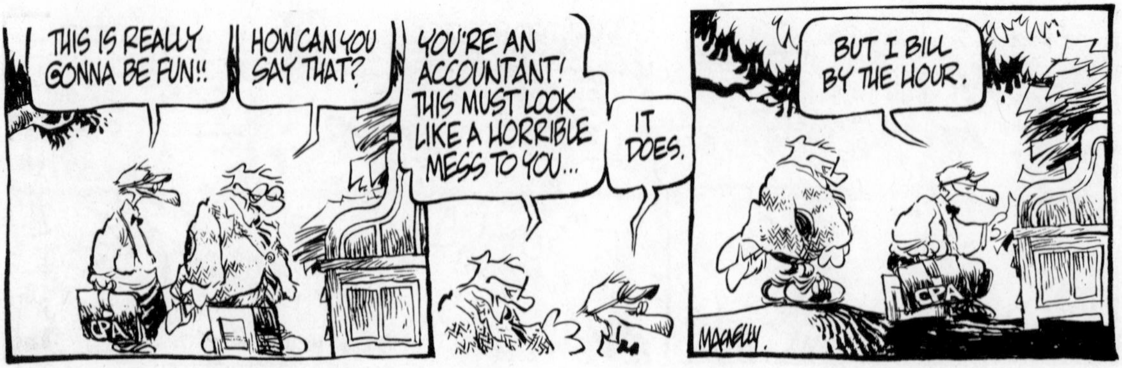
THIS IS REALLY GONNA BE FUN!!
HOW CAN YOU SAY THAT?
YOU'RE AN ACCOUNTANT! THIS MUST LOOK LIKE A HORRIBLE MESS TO YOU...
IT DOES.
BUT I BILL BY THE HOUR.
CPA
CPA
MACNELLY

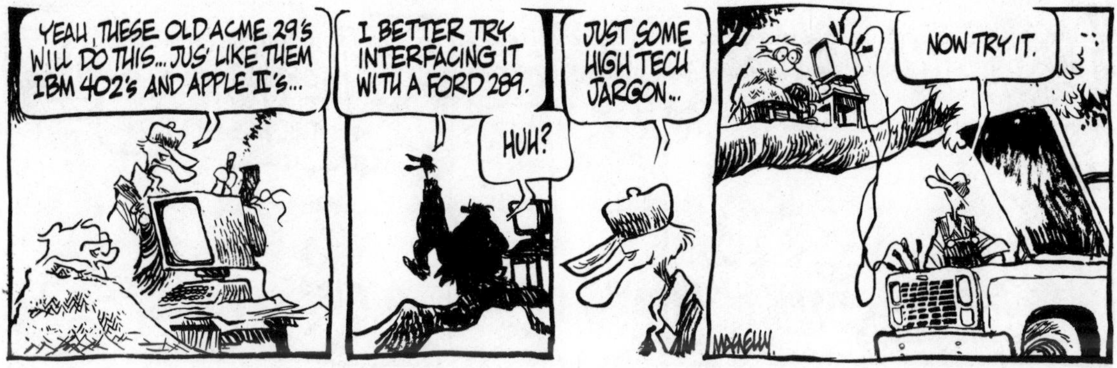
YEAH, THESE OLD ACME 29's WILL DO THIS... JUS' LIKE THEM IBM 402's AND APPLE II's...
I BETTER TRY INTERFACING IT WITH A FORD 289.
HUH?
JUST SOME HIGH TECH JARGON...
NOW TRY IT.
MACNELLY

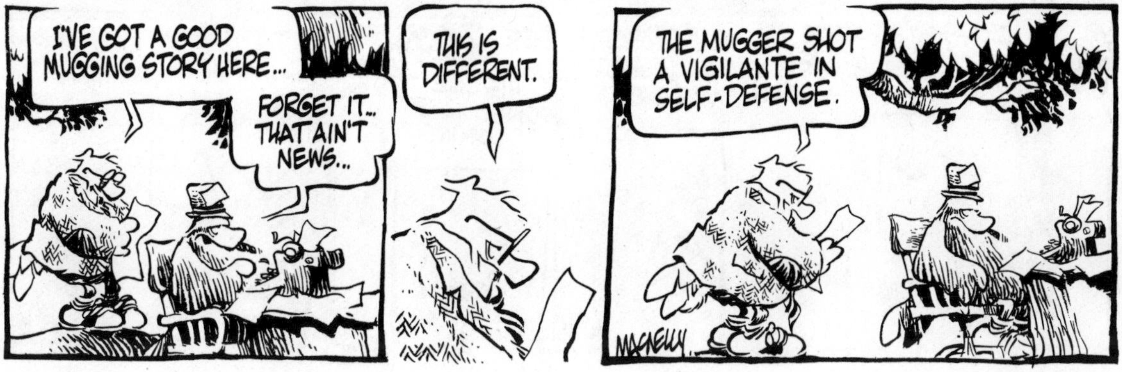
I'VE GOT A GOOD MUGGING STORY HERE...
FORGET IT... THAT AIN'T NEWS...
THIS IS DIFFERENT.
THE MUGGER SHOT A VIGILANTE IN SELF-DEFENSE.
MACNELLY

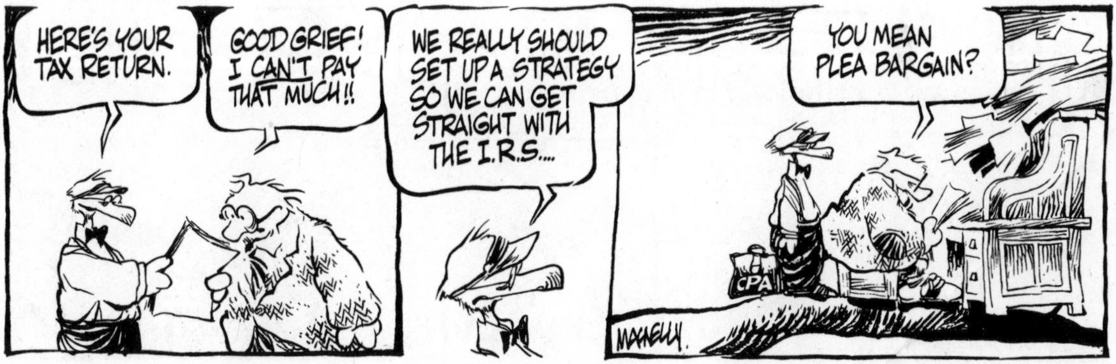
HERE'S YOUR TAX RETURN.
GOOD GRIEF! I CAN'T PAY THAT MUCH!!
WE REALLY SHOULD SET UP A STRATEGY SO WE CAN GET STRAIGHT WITH THE I.R.S....
YOU MEAN PLEA BARGAIN?
CPA
MACNELLY

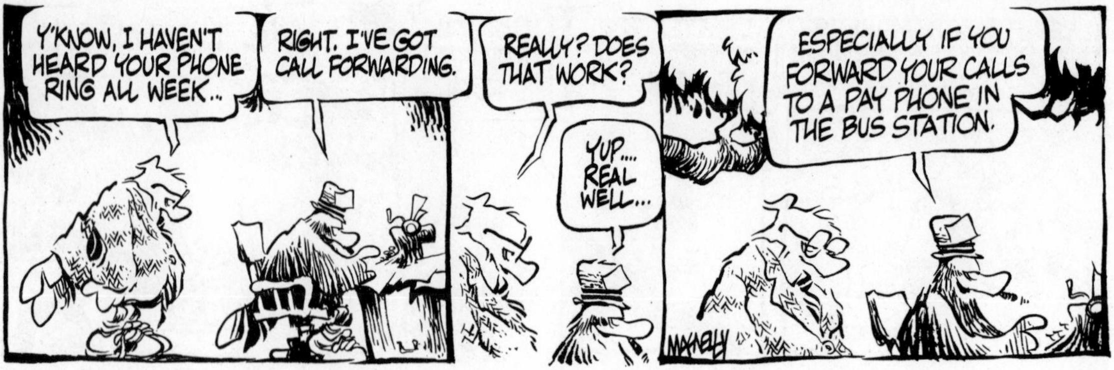
Y'KNOW, I HAVEN'T HEARD YOUR PHONE RING ALL WEEK...
RIGHT. I'VE GOT CALL FORWARDING.
REALLY? DOES THAT WORK?
YUP.... REAL WELL...
ESPECIALLY IF YOU FORWARD YOUR CALLS TO A PAY PHONE IN THE BUS STATION.

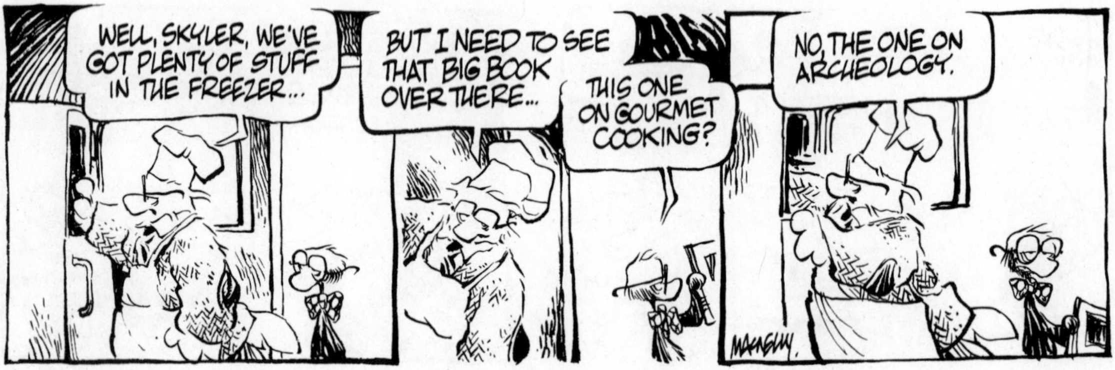
WELL, SKYLER, WE'VE GOT PLENTY OF STUFF IN THE FREEZER...
BUT I NEED TO SEE THAT BIG BOOK OVER THERE...
THIS ONE ON GOURMET COOKING?
NO, THE ONE ON ARCHEOLOGY.

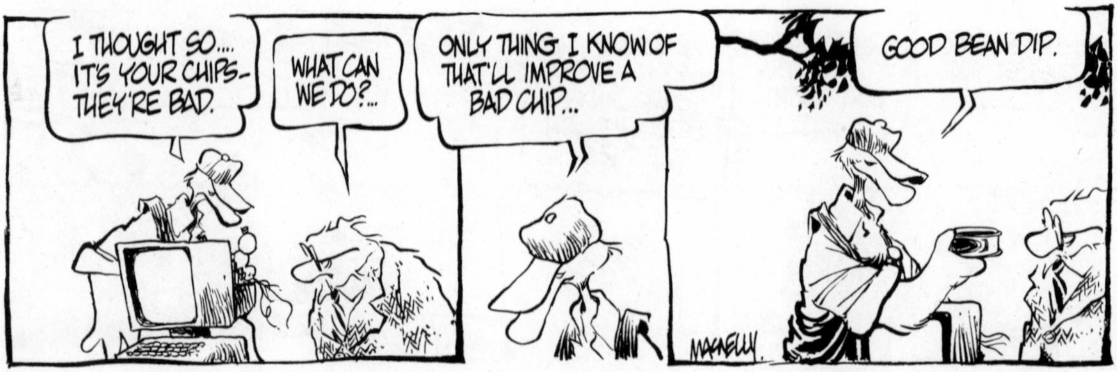
I THOUGHT SO.... IT'S YOUR CHIPS- THEY'RE BAD.
WHAT CAN WE DO?...
ONLY THING I KNOW OF THAT'LL IMPROVE A BAD CHIP...
GOOD BEAN DIP.

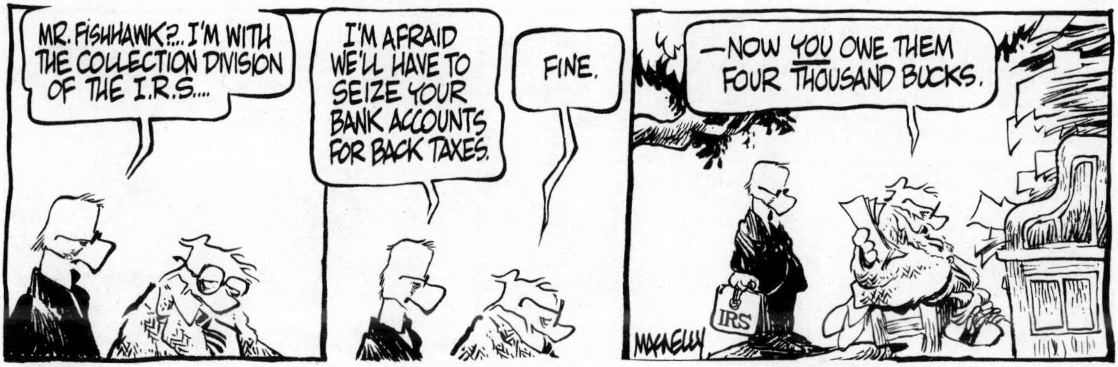
MR. FISHHAWK?... I'M WITH THE COLLECTION DIVISION OF THE I.R.S....
I'M AFRAID WE'LL HAVE TO SEIZE YOUR BANK ACCOUNTS FOR BACK TAXES.
FINE.
—NOW YOU OWE THEM FOUR THOUSAND BUCKS.
IRS
MACNELLY

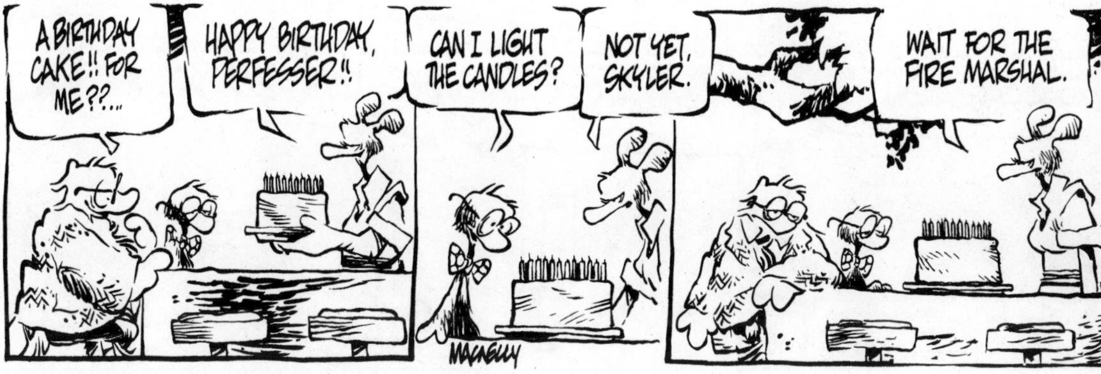
A BIRTHDAY CAKE!! FOR ME??...
HAPPY BIRTHDAY, PERFESSER!!
CAN I LIGHT THE CANDLES?
NOT YET, SKYLER.
WAIT FOR THE FIRE MARSHAL.
MACNELLY

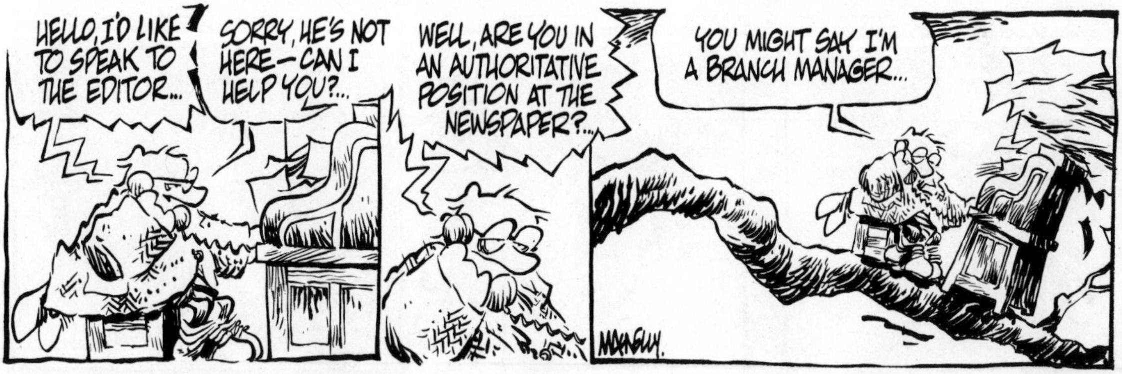
HELLO, I'D LIKE TO SPEAK TO THE EDITOR...
SORRY, HE'S NOT HERE—CAN I HELP YOU?...
WELL, ARE YOU IN AN AUTHORITATIVE POSITION AT THE NEWSPAPER?...
YOU MIGHT SAY I'M A BRANCH MANAGER...
MACNELLY.

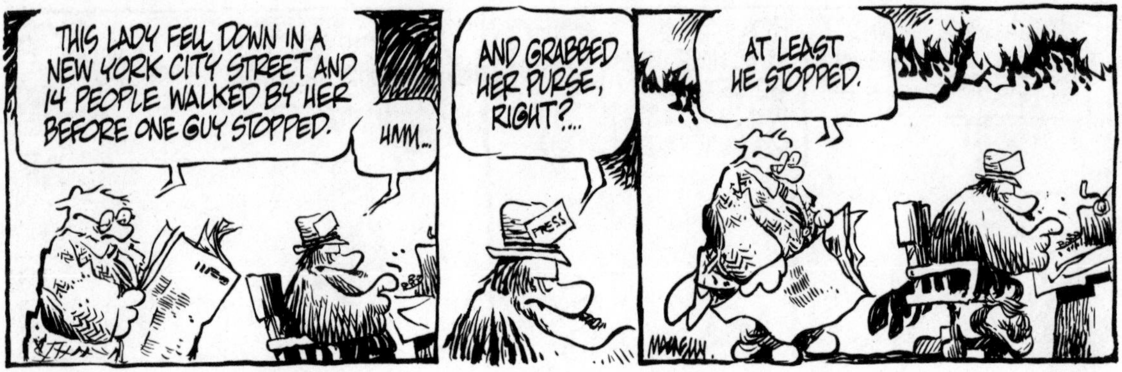
THIS LADY FELL DOWN IN A NEW YORK CITY STREET AND 14 PEOPLE WALKED BY HER BEFORE ONE GUY STOPPED.
UMM...
AND GRABBED HER PURSE, RIGHT?...
PRESS
AT LEAST HE STOPPED.

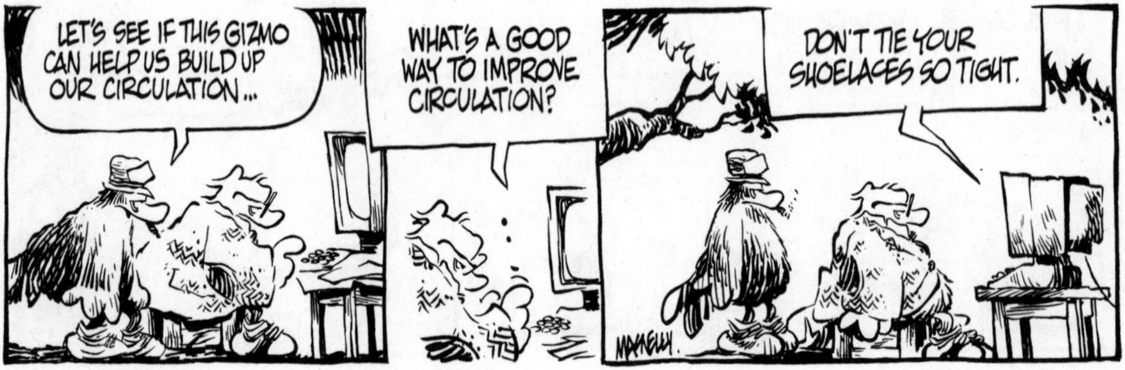
LET'S SEE IF THIS GIZMO CAN HELP US BUILD UP OUR CIRCULATION...
WHAT'S A GOOD WAY TO IMPROVE CIRCULATION?
DON'T TIE YOUR SHOELACES SO TIGHT.

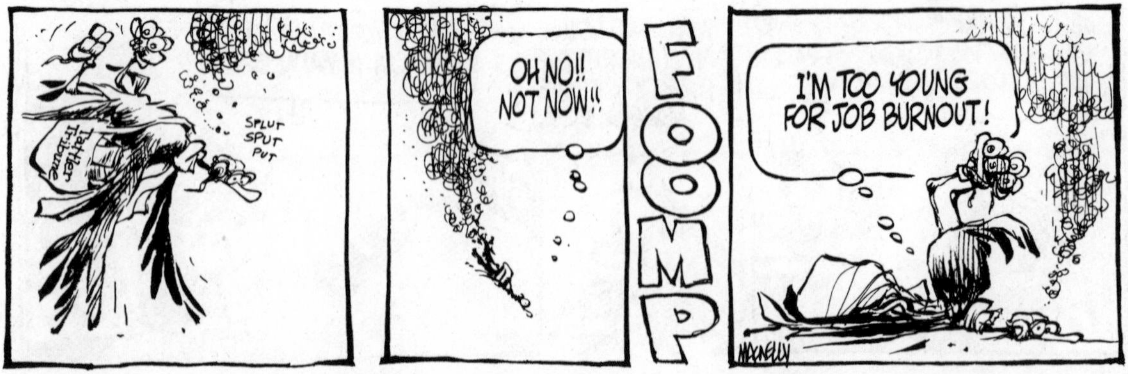
Tattler Tribune
SPLUT
SPUT
PUT
OH NO!! NOT NOW!!
FOOMP
I'M TOO YOUNG FOR JOB BURNOUT!

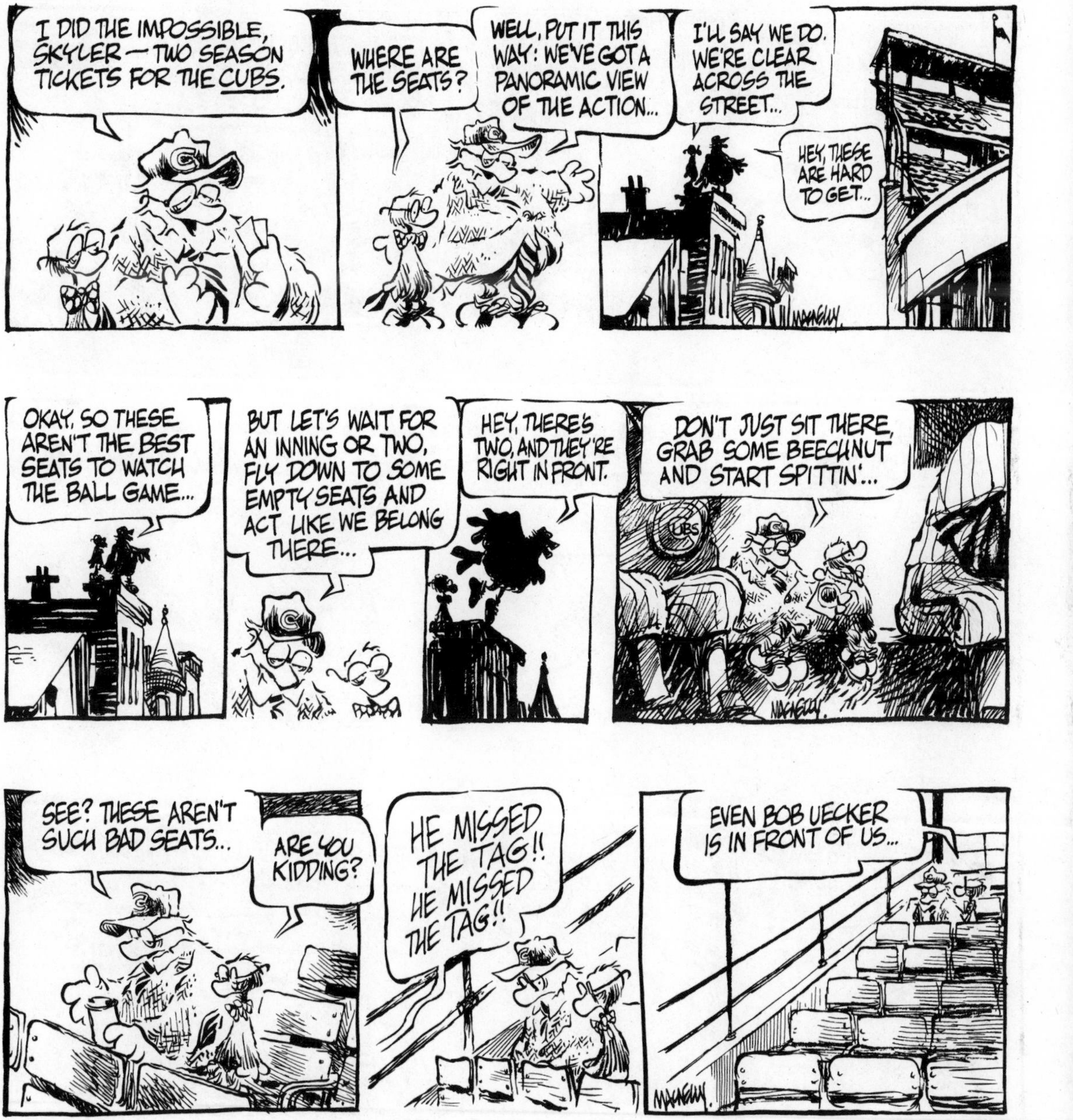
I DID THE IMPOSSIBLE, SKYLER — TWO SEASON TICKETS FOR THE CUBS.
WHERE ARE THE SEATS?
WELL, PUT IT THIS WAY: WE'VE GOT A PANORAMIC VIEW OF THE ACTION...
I'LL SAY WE DO. WE'RE CLEAR ACROSS THE STREET...
HEY, THESE ARE HARD TO GET...
MACNELLY
OKAY, SO THESE AREN'T THE BEST SEATS TO WATCH THE BALL GAME...
BUT LET'S WAIT FOR AN INNING OR TWO, FLY DOWN TO SOME EMPTY SEATS AND ACT LIKE WE BELONG THERE...
HEY, THERE'S TWO, AND THEY'RE RIGHT IN FRONT.
DON'T JUST SIT THERE, GRAB SOME BEECHNUT AND START SPITTIN'...
MACNELLY
SEE? THESE AREN'T SUCH BAD SEATS...
ARE YOU KIDDING?
HE MISSED THE TAG!! HE MISSED THE TAG!!
EVEN BOB UECKER IS IN FRONT OF US...
MACNELLY

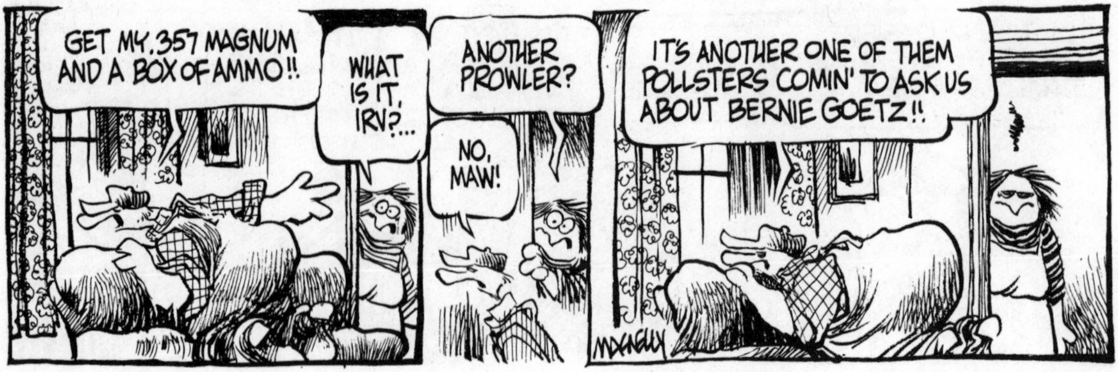
GET MY .357 MAGNUM AND A BOX OF AMMO!!
WHAT IS IT, IRV?...
ANOTHER PROWLER?
NO, MAW!
IT'S ANOTHER ONE OF THEM POLLSTERS COMIN' TO ASK US ABOUT BERNIE GOETZ!!

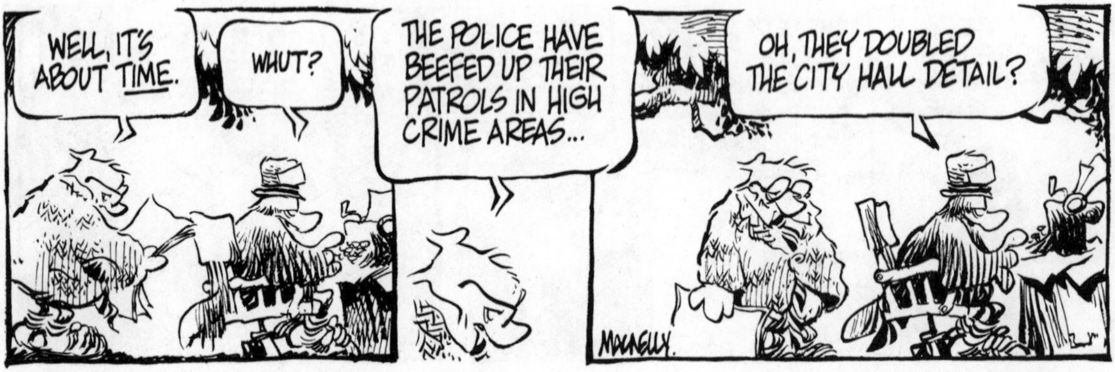
WELL, IT'S ABOUT TIME.
WHUT?
THE POLICE HAVE BEEFED UP THEIR PATROLS IN HIGH CRIME AREAS...
OH, THEY DOUBLED THE CITY HALL DETAIL?

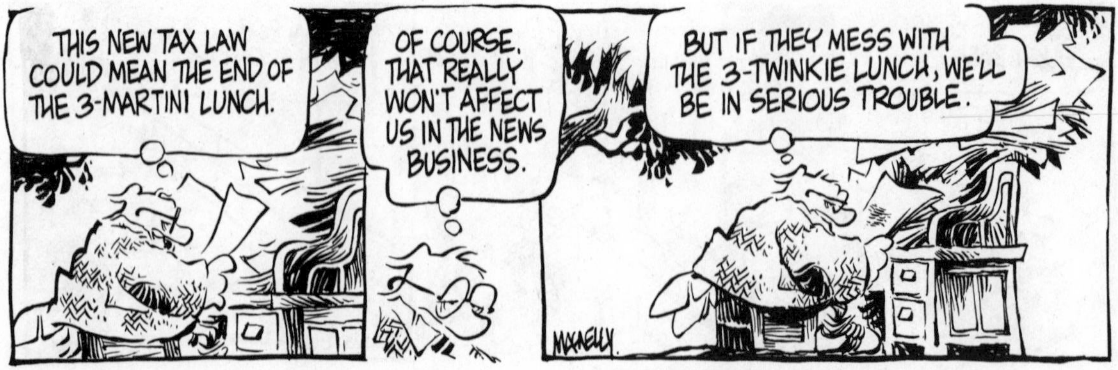
THIS NEW TAX LAW COULD MEAN THE END OF THE 3-MARTINI LUNCH.
OF COURSE, THAT REALLY WON'T AFFECT US IN THE NEWS BUSINESS.
BUT IF THEY MESS WITH THE 3-TWINKIE LUNCH, WE'LL BE IN SERIOUS TROUBLE.

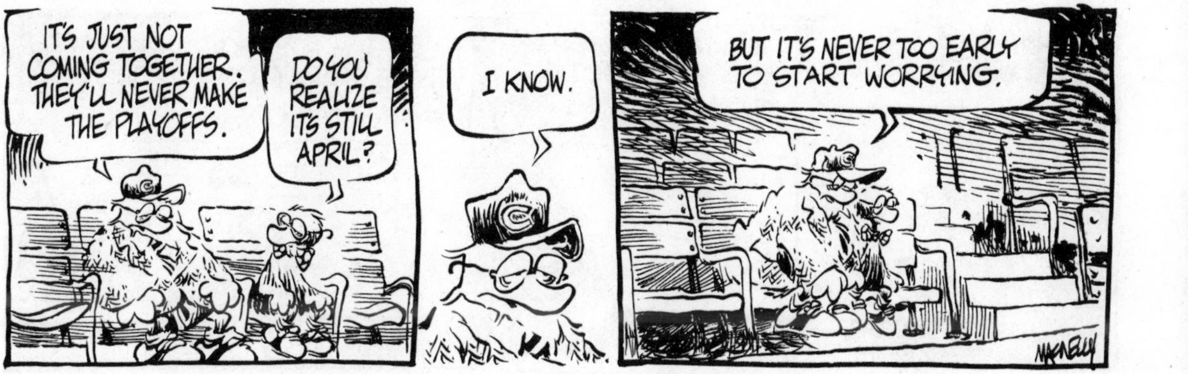
IT'S JUST NOT COMING TOGETHER. THEY'LL NEVER MAKE THE PLAYOFFS.
DO YOU REALIZE IT'S STILL APRIL?
I KNOW.
BUT IT'S NEVER TOO EARLY TO START WORRYING.
MACNELLY

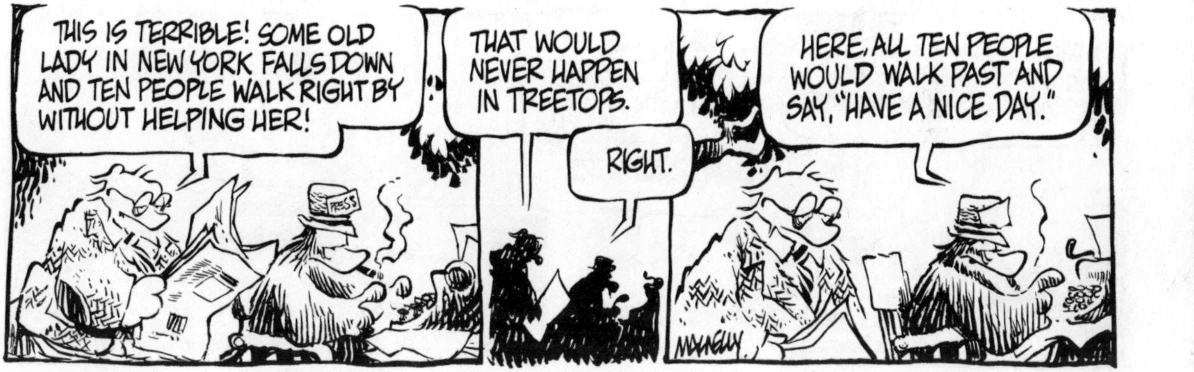
THIS IS TERRIBLE! SOME OLD LADY IN NEW YORK FALLS DOWN AND TEN PEOPLE WALK RIGHT BY WITHOUT HELPING HER!
PRESS
THAT WOULD NEVER HAPPEN IN TREETOPS.
RIGHT.
HERE, ALL TEN PEOPLE WOULD WALK PAST AND SAY, "HAVE A NICE DAY."
MACNELLY

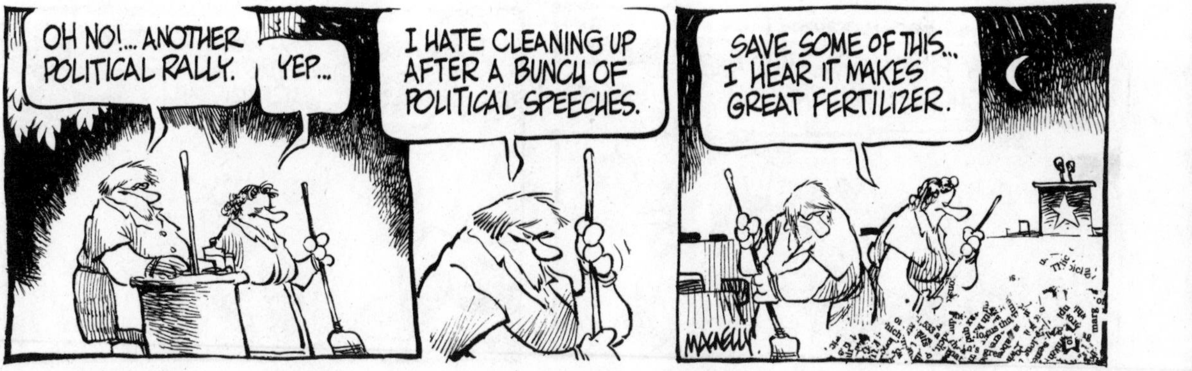
OH NO!... ANOTHER POLITICAL RALLY.
YEP...
I HATE CLEANING UP AFTER A BUNCH OF POLITICAL SPEECHES.
SAVE SOME OF THIS... I HEAR IT MAKES GREAT FERTILIZER.
MACNELLY

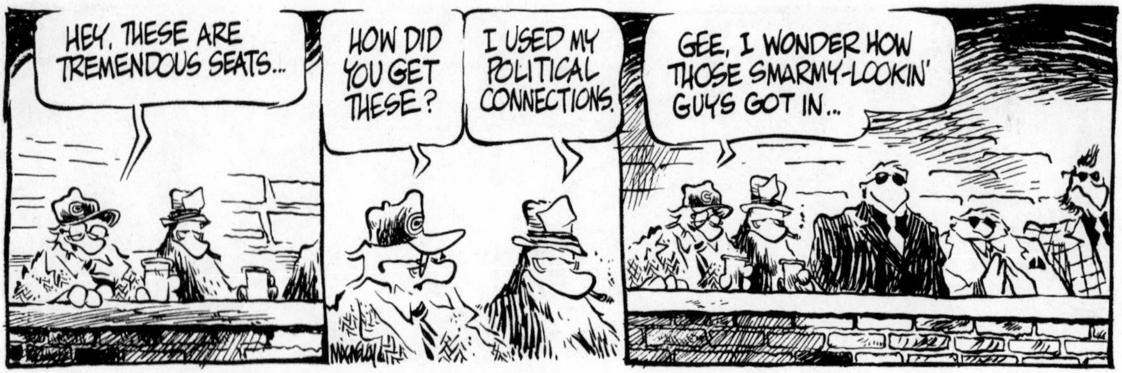
HEY, THESE ARE TREMENDOUS SEATS...
HOW DID YOU GET THESE?
I USED MY POLITICAL CONNECTIONS.
GEE, I WONDER HOW THOSE SMARMY-LOOKIN' GUYS GOT IN...
MACNELLY

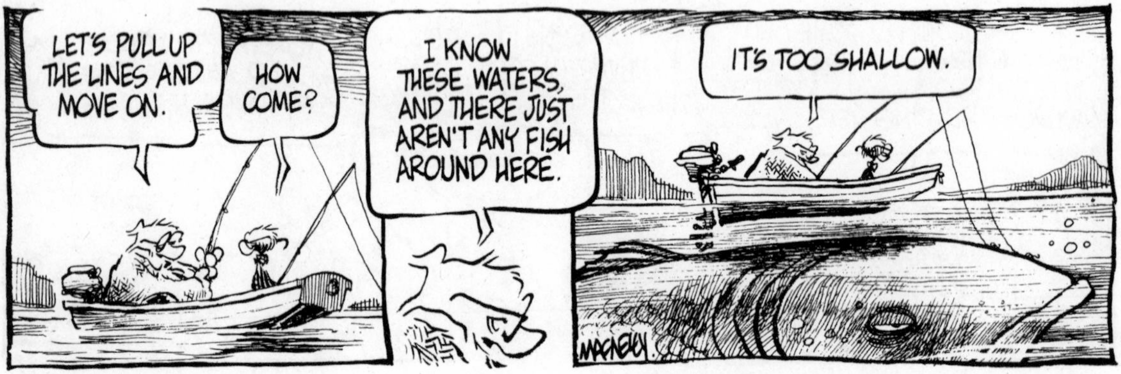
LET'S PULL UP THE LINES AND MOVE ON.
HOW COME?
I KNOW THESE WATERS, AND THERE JUST AREN'T ANY FISH AROUND HERE.
IT'S TOO SHALLOW.
MACNELLY.

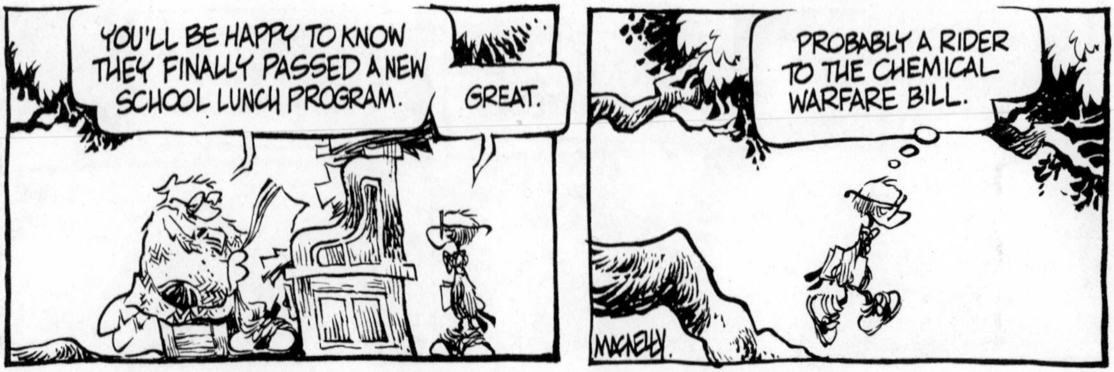
YOU'LL BE HAPPY TO KNOW THEY FINALLY PASSED A NEW SCHOOL LUNCH PROGRAM.
GREAT.
PROBABLY A RIDER TO THE CHEMICAL WARFARE BILL.
MACNELLY.

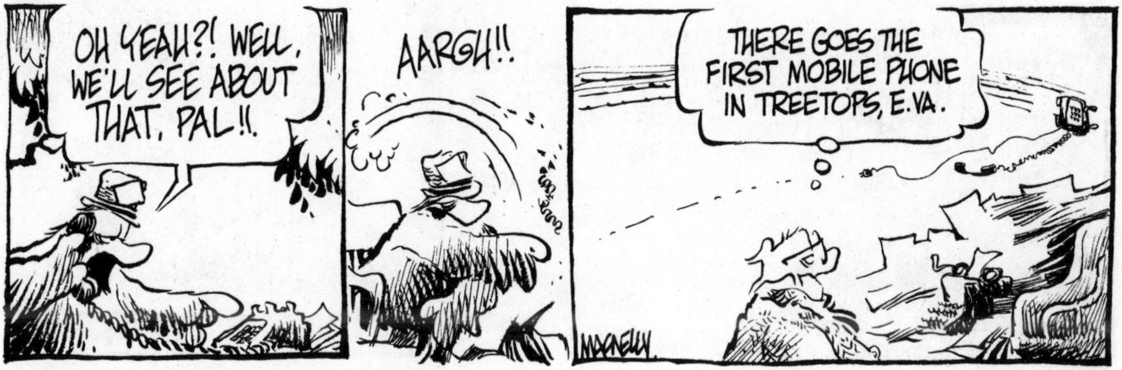
OH YEAH?! WELL, WE'LL SEE ABOUT THAT, PAL!!
AARGH!!
THERE GOES THE FIRST MOBILE PHONE IN TREETOPS, E.VA.
MACNELLY

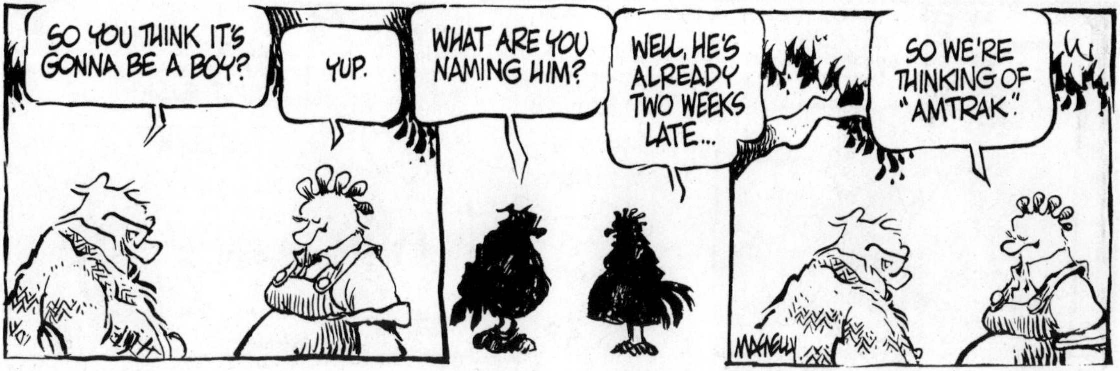
SO YOU THINK IT'S GONNA BE A BOY?
YUP.
WHAT ARE YOU NAMING HIM?
WELL, HE'S ALREADY TWO WEEKS LATE...
SO WE'RE THINKING OF "AMTRAK."
MACNELLY

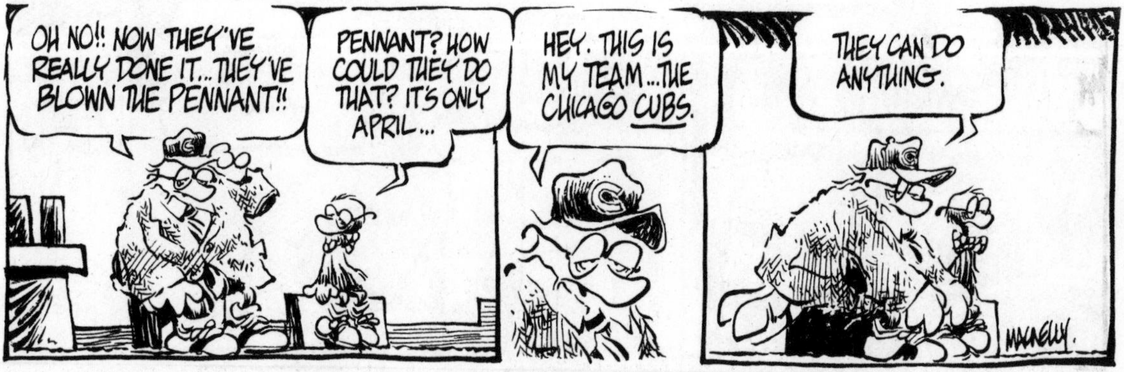
OH NO!! NOW THEY'VE REALLY DONE IT...THEY'VE BLOWN THE PENNANT!!
PENNANT? HOW COULD THEY DO THAT? IT'S ONLY APRIL...
HEY. THIS IS MY TEAM...THE CHICAGO CUBS.
THEY CAN DO ANYTHING.
MACNELLY.

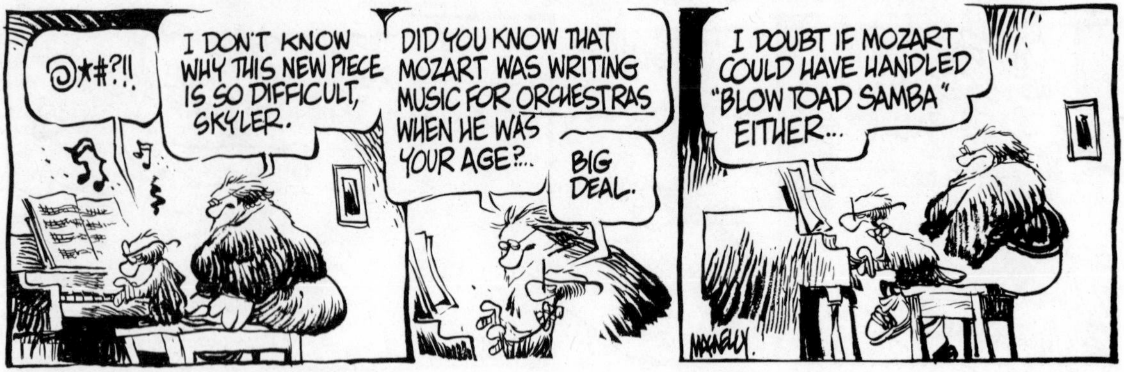
@★#?!!
I DON'T KNOW WHY THIS NEW PIECE IS SO DIFFICULT, SKYLER.
DID YOU KNOW THAT MOZART WAS WRITING MUSIC FOR ORCHESTRAS WHEN HE WAS YOUR AGE?...
BIG DEAL.
I DOUBT IF MOZART COULD HAVE HANDLED "BLOW TOAD SAMBA" EITHER...
MACNELLY.

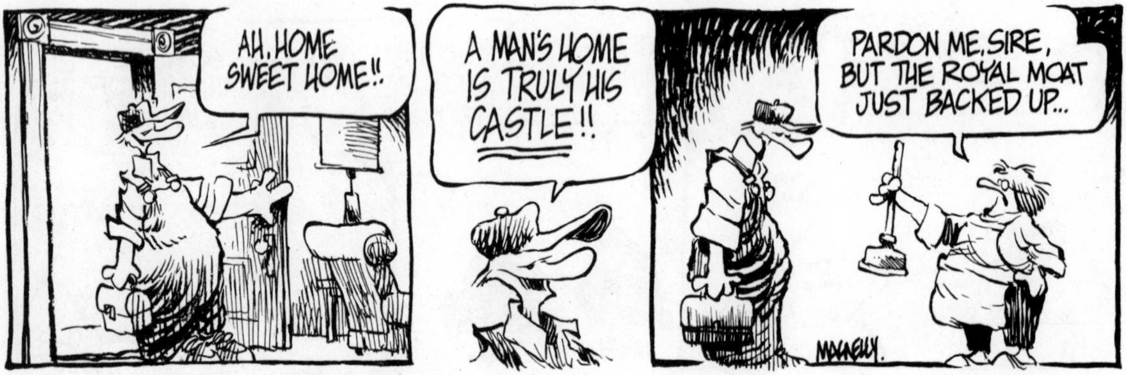
AH, HOME SWEET HOME!!
A MAN'S HOME IS TRULY HIS CASTLE!!
PARDON ME, SIRE, BUT THE ROYAL MOAT JUST BACKED UP...
MACNELLY.

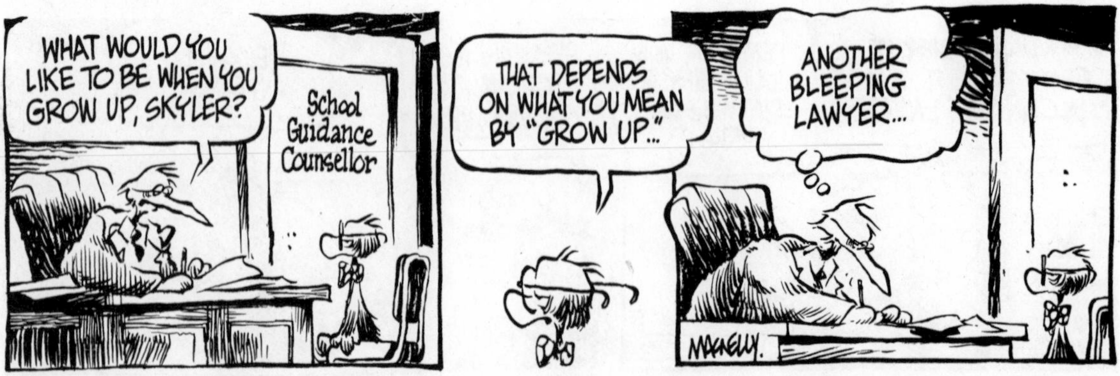
WHAT WOULD YOU LIKE TO BE WHEN YOU GROW UP, SKYLER?
School Guidance Counsellor
THAT DEPENDS ON WHAT YOU MEAN BY "GROW UP."
ANOTHER BLEEPING LAWYER...
MACNELLY.

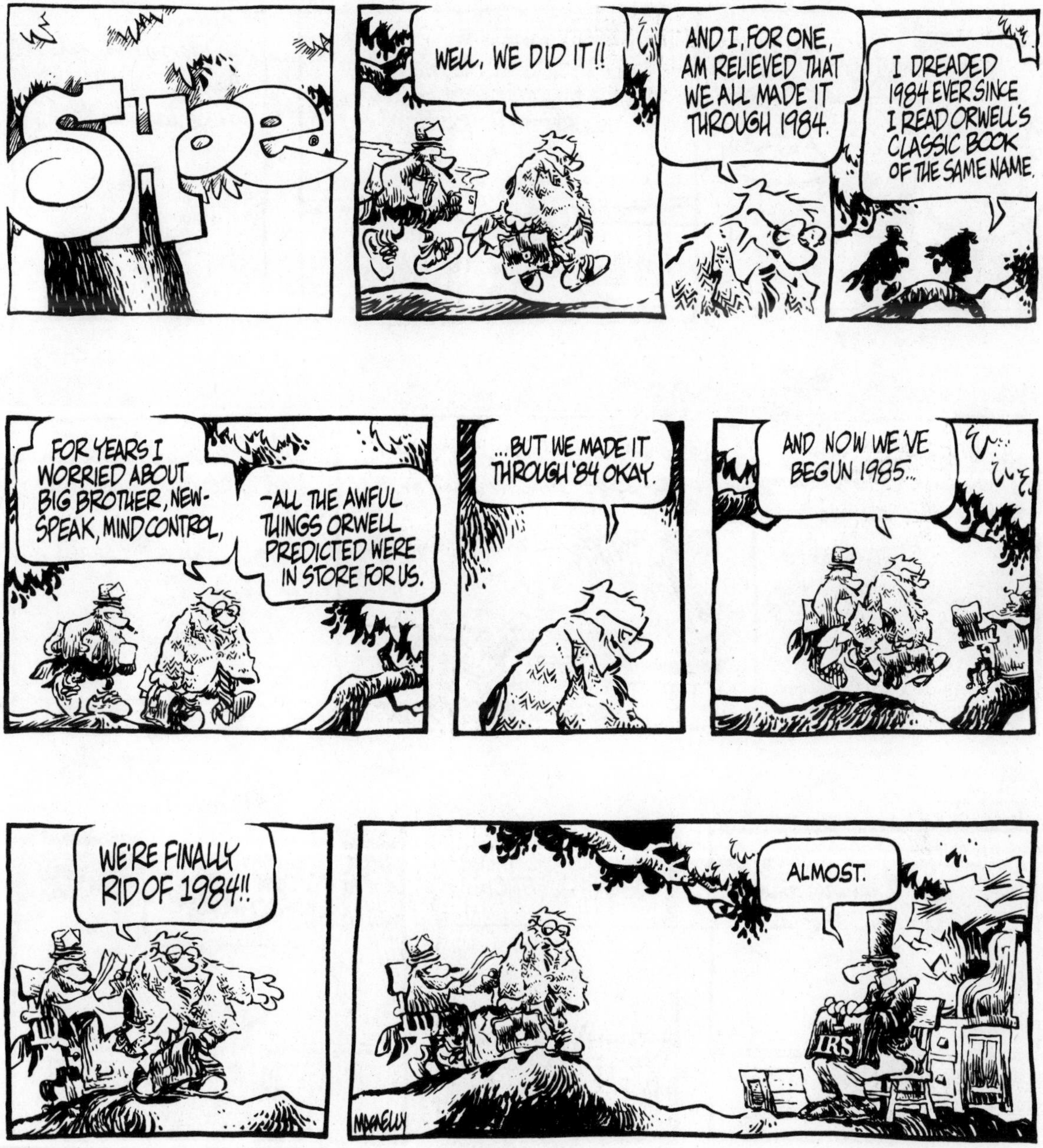

SHOE®
WELL, WE DID IT!!
AND I, FOR ONE, AM RELIEVED THAT WE ALL MADE IT THROUGH 1984.
I DREADED 1984 EVER SINCE I READ ORWELL'S CLASSIC BOOK OF THE SAME NAME.
FOR YEARS I WORRIED ABOUT BIG BROTHER, NEW-SPEAK, MIND CONTROL,
-ALL THE AWFUL THINGS ORWELL PREDICTED WERE IN STORE FOR US.
...BUT WE MADE IT THROUGH '84 OKAY.
AND NOW WE'VE BEGUN 1985...
WE'RE FINALLY RID OF 1984!!
ALMOST.
IRS
MACNELLY

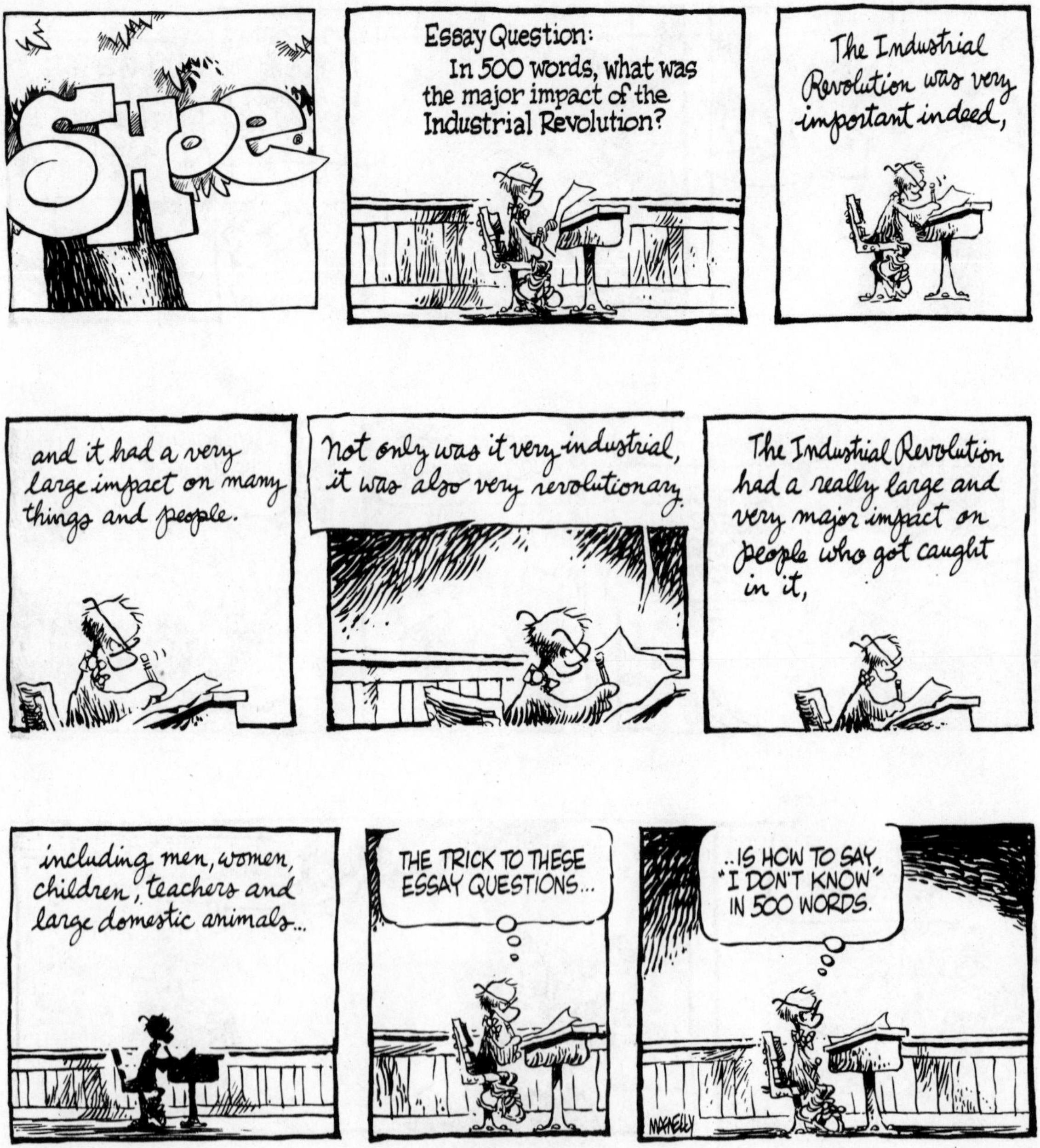
SHOE
Essay Question:
In 500 words, what was the major impact of the Industrial Revolution?
The Industrial Revolution was very important indeed,
and it had a very large impact on many things and people.
Not only was it very industrial, it was also very revolutionary.
The Industrial Revolution had a really large and very major impact on people who got caught in it,
including men, women, children, teachers and large domestic animals...
THE TRICK TO THESE ESSAY QUESTIONS...
...IS HOW TO SAY "I DON'T KNOW" IN 500 WORDS.
MACNELLY

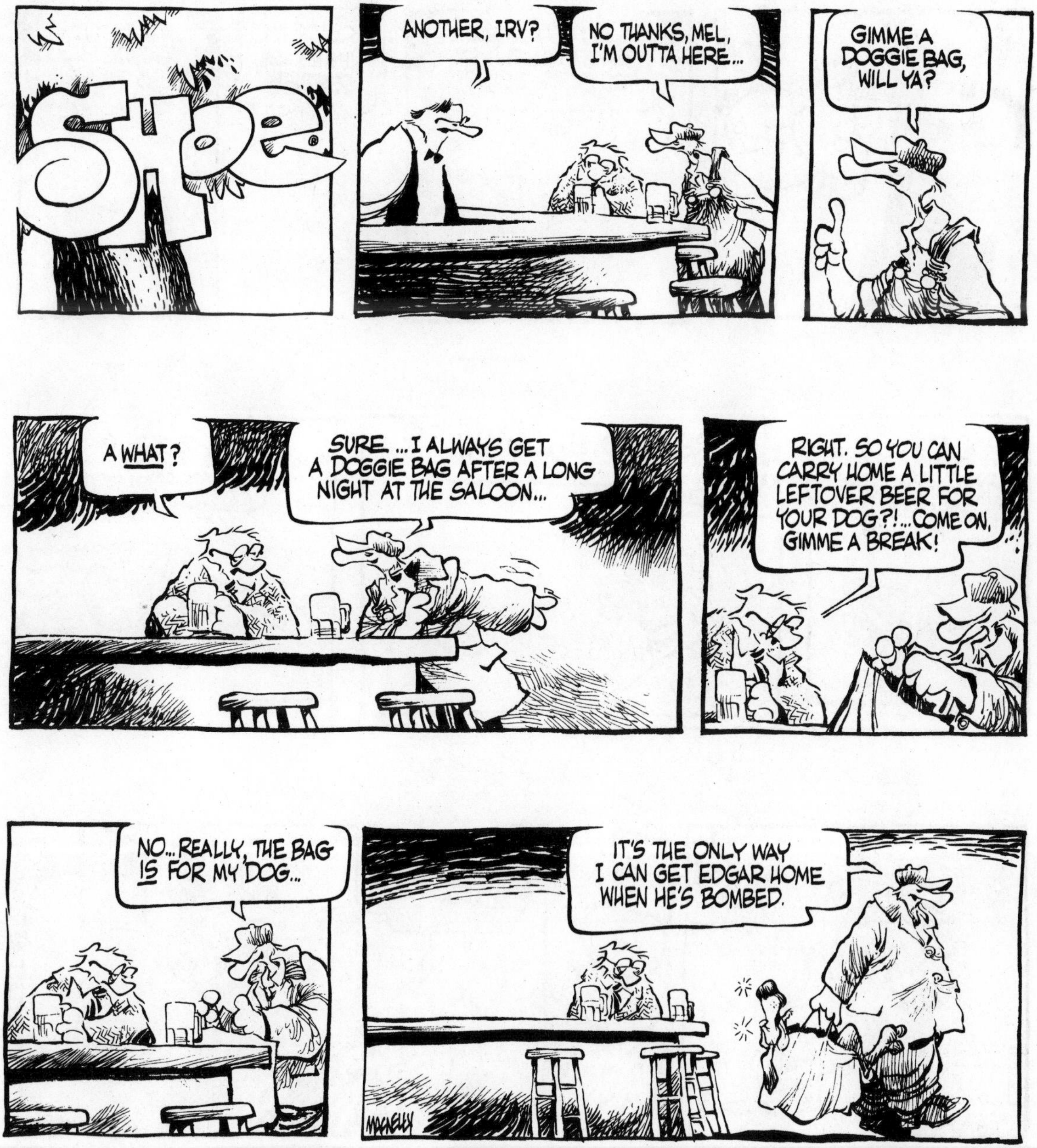
SHOE
ANOTHER, IRV?
NO THANKS, MEL, I'M OUTTA HERE...
GIMME A DOGGIE BAG, WILL YA?
A WHAT?
SURE ... I ALWAYS GET A DOGGIE BAG AFTER A LONG NIGHT AT THE SALOON...
RIGHT. SO YOU CAN CARRY HOME A LITTLE LEFTOVER BEER FOR YOUR DOG?!...COME ON, GIMME A BREAK!
NO...REALLY, THE BAG IS FOR MY DOG...
IT'S THE ONLY WAY I CAN GET EDGAR HOME WHEN HE'S BOMBED.
MACNELLY

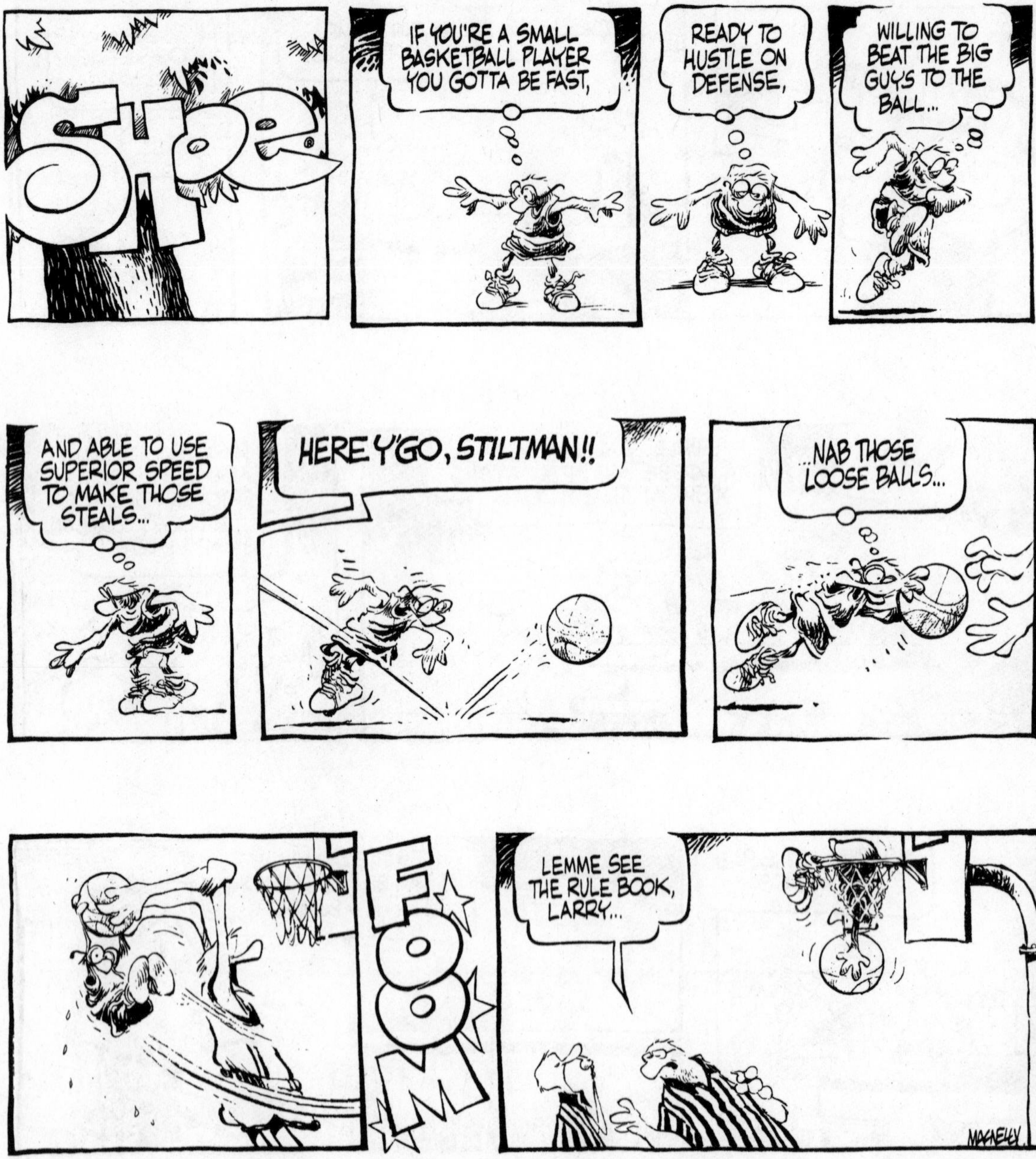
SHOE®
IF YOU'RE A SMALL BASKETBALL PLAYER YOU GOTTA BE FAST,
READY TO HUSTLE ON DEFENSE,
WILLING TO BEAT THE BIG GUYS TO THE BALL...
AND ABLE TO USE SUPERIOR SPEED TO MAKE THOSE STEALS...
HERE Y'GO, STILTMAN!!
...NAB THOSE LOOSE BALLS...
FOOM
LEMME SEE THE RULE BOOK, LARRY...
MACNELLY

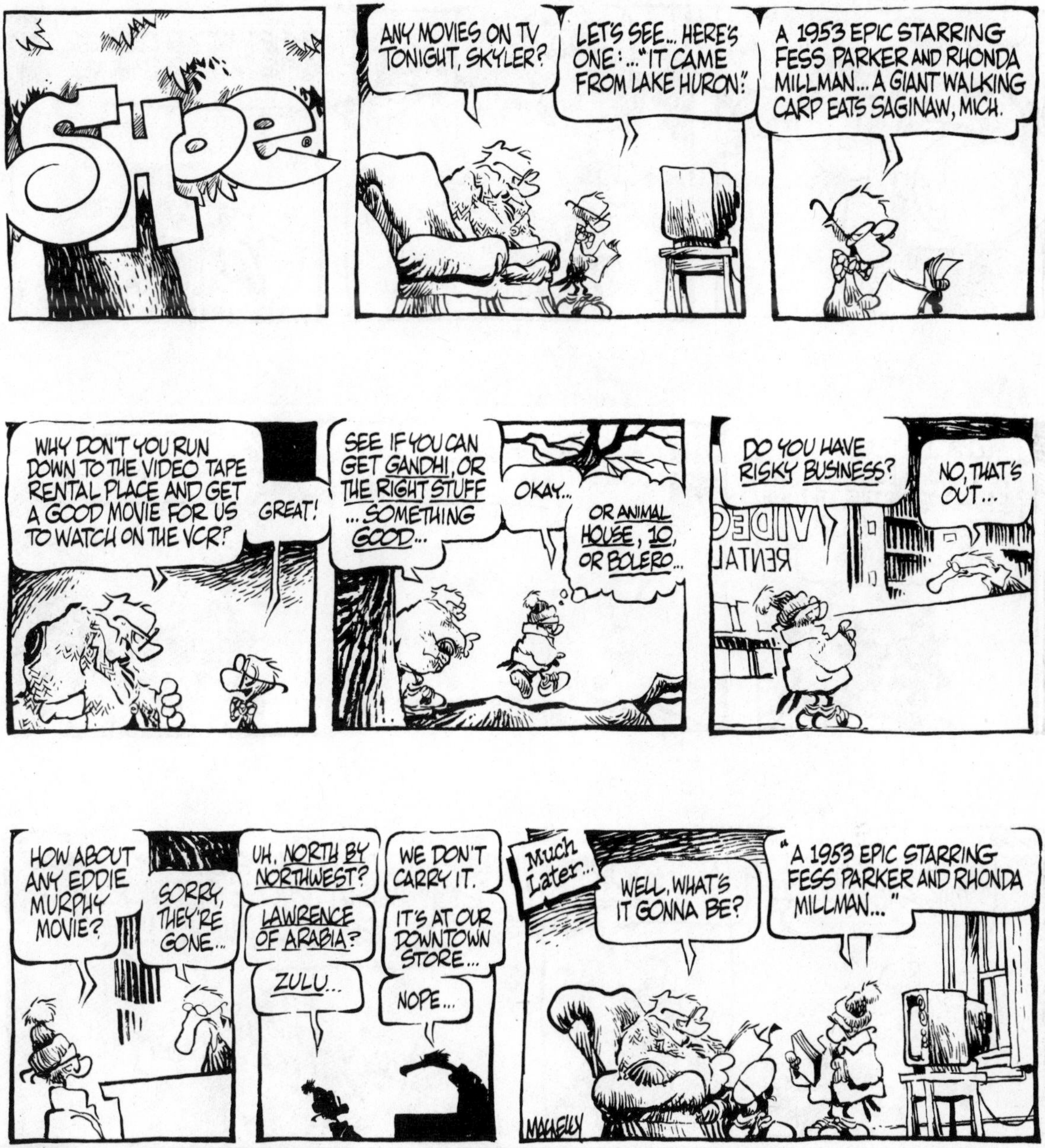
SHOE®
ANY MOVIES ON TV TONIGHT, SKYLER?
LET'S SEE... HERE'S ONE: ..."IT CAME FROM LAKE HURON."
A 1953 EPIC STARRING FESS PARKER AND RHONDA MILLMAN... A GIANT WALKING CARP EATS SAGINAW, MICH.
WHY DON'T YOU RUN DOWN TO THE VIDEO TAPE RENTAL PLACE AND GET A GOOD MOVIE FOR US TO WATCH ON THE VCR?
GREAT!
SEE IF YOU CAN GET GANDHI, OR THE RIGHT STUFF ...SOMETHING GOOD...
OKAY...
OR ANIMAL HOUSE, 10, OR BOLERO...
VIDEO RENTAL
DO YOU HAVE RISKY BUSINESS?
NO, THAT'S OUT...
HOW ABOUT ANY EDDIE MURPHY MOVIE?
SORRY, THEY'RE GONE...
UH, NORTH BY NORTHWEST?
WE DON'T CARRY IT.
LAWRENCE OF ARABIA?
IT'S AT OUR DOWNTOWN STORE...
ZULU...
NOPE...
Much Later...
WELL, WHAT'S IT GONNA BE?
"A 1953 EPIC STARRING FESS PARKER AND RHONDA MILLMAN..."
MACNELLY

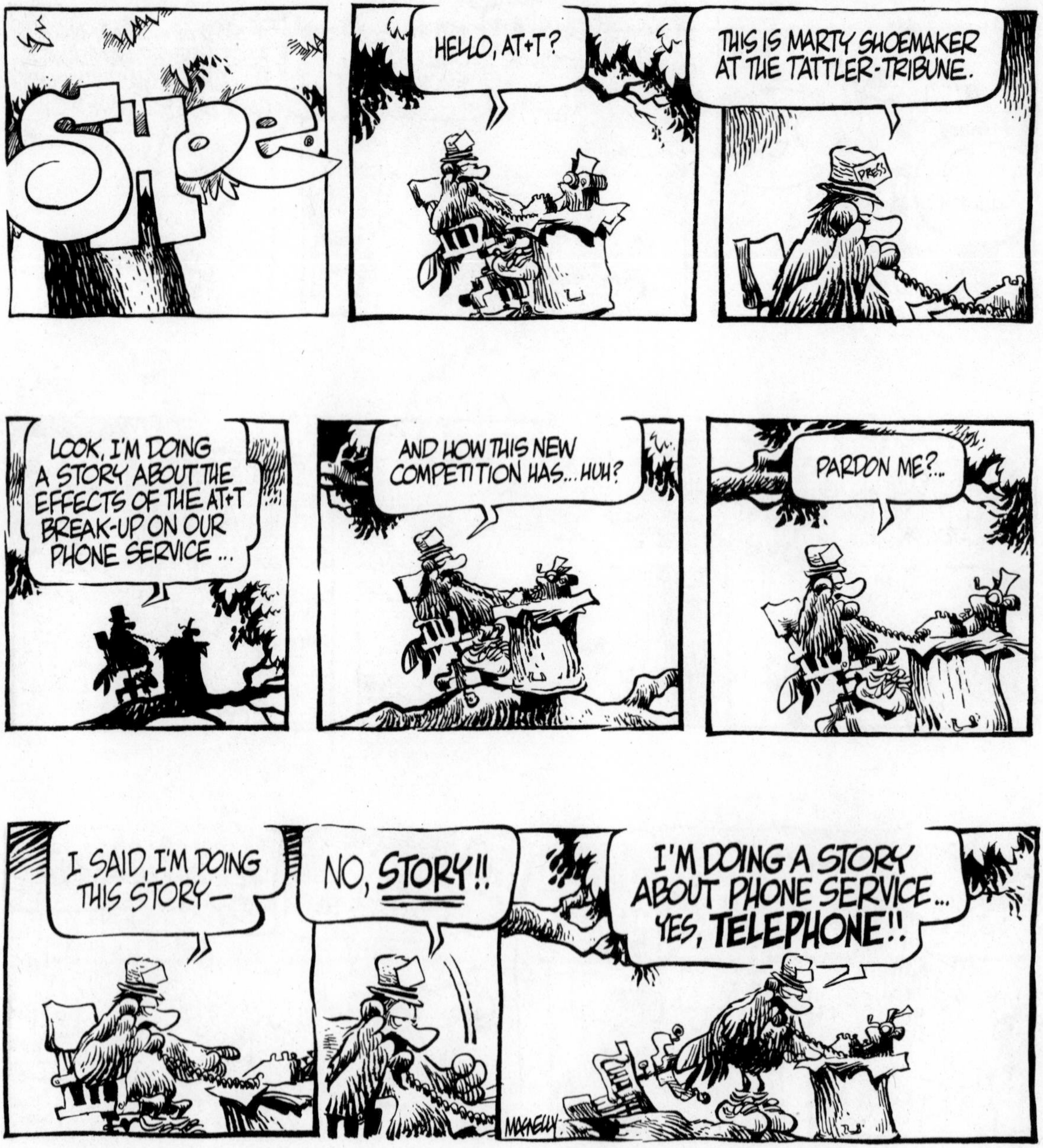
SHOE
HELLO, AT+T?
THIS IS MARTY SHOEMAKER AT THE TATTLER-TRIBUNE.
PRESS
LOOK, I'M DOING A STORY ABOUT THE EFFECTS OF THE AT+T BREAK-UP ON OUR PHONE SERVICE...
AND HOW THIS NEW COMPETITION HAS... HUH?
PARDON ME?...
I SAID, I'M DOING THIS STORY—
NO, STORY!!
I'M DOING A STORY ABOUT PHONE SERVICE... YES, TELEPHONE!!
MACNELLY

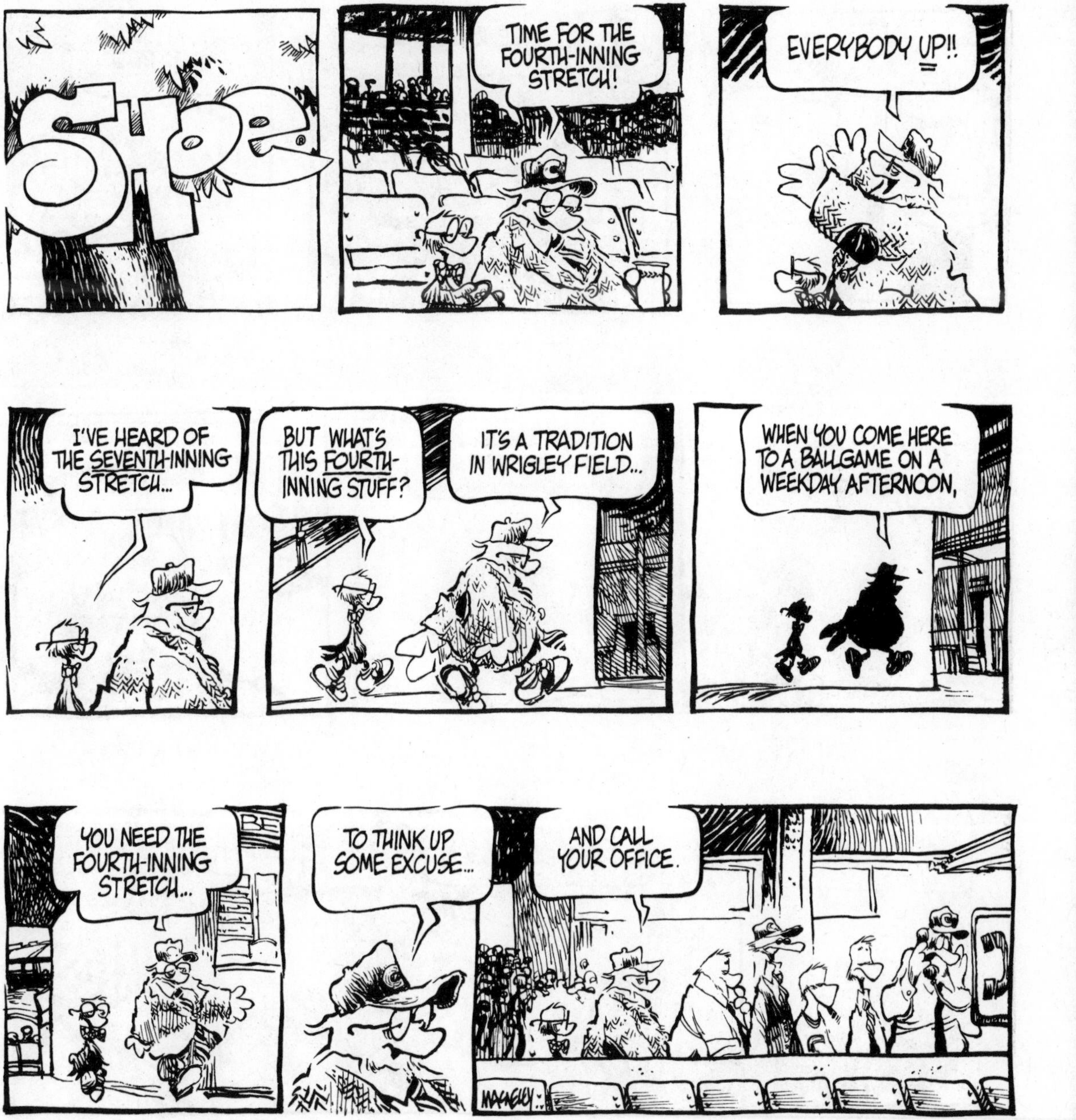
SHOE
TIME FOR THE FOURTH-INNING STRETCH!
EVERYBODY UP!!
I'VE HEARD OF THE SEVENTH-INNING STRETCH...
BUT WHAT'S THIS FOURTH-INNING STUFF?
IT'S A TRADITION IN WRIGLEY FIELD...
WHEN YOU COME HERE TO A BALLGAME ON A WEEKDAY AFTERNOON,
YOU NEED THE FOURTH-INNING STRETCH...
TO THINK UP SOME EXCUSE...
AND CALL YOUR OFFICE.

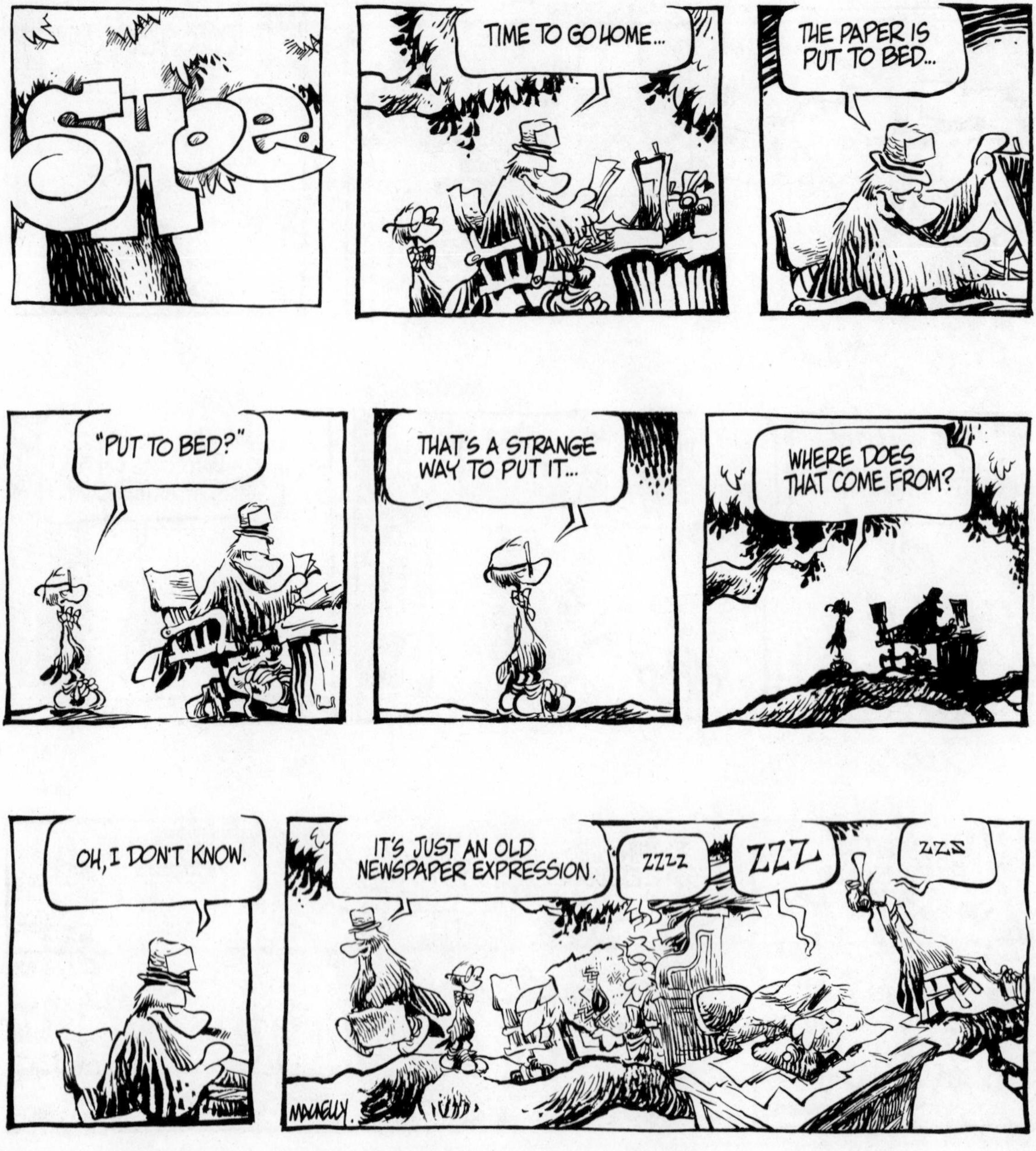
SHOE®
TIME TO GO HOME...
THE PAPER IS PUT TO BED...
"PUT TO BED?"
THAT'S A STRANGE WAY TO PUT IT...
WHERE DOES THAT COME FROM?
OH, I DON'T KNOW.
IT'S JUST AN OLD NEWSPAPER EXPRESSION.
ZZZZ
ZZZ
ZZZ
MACNELLY

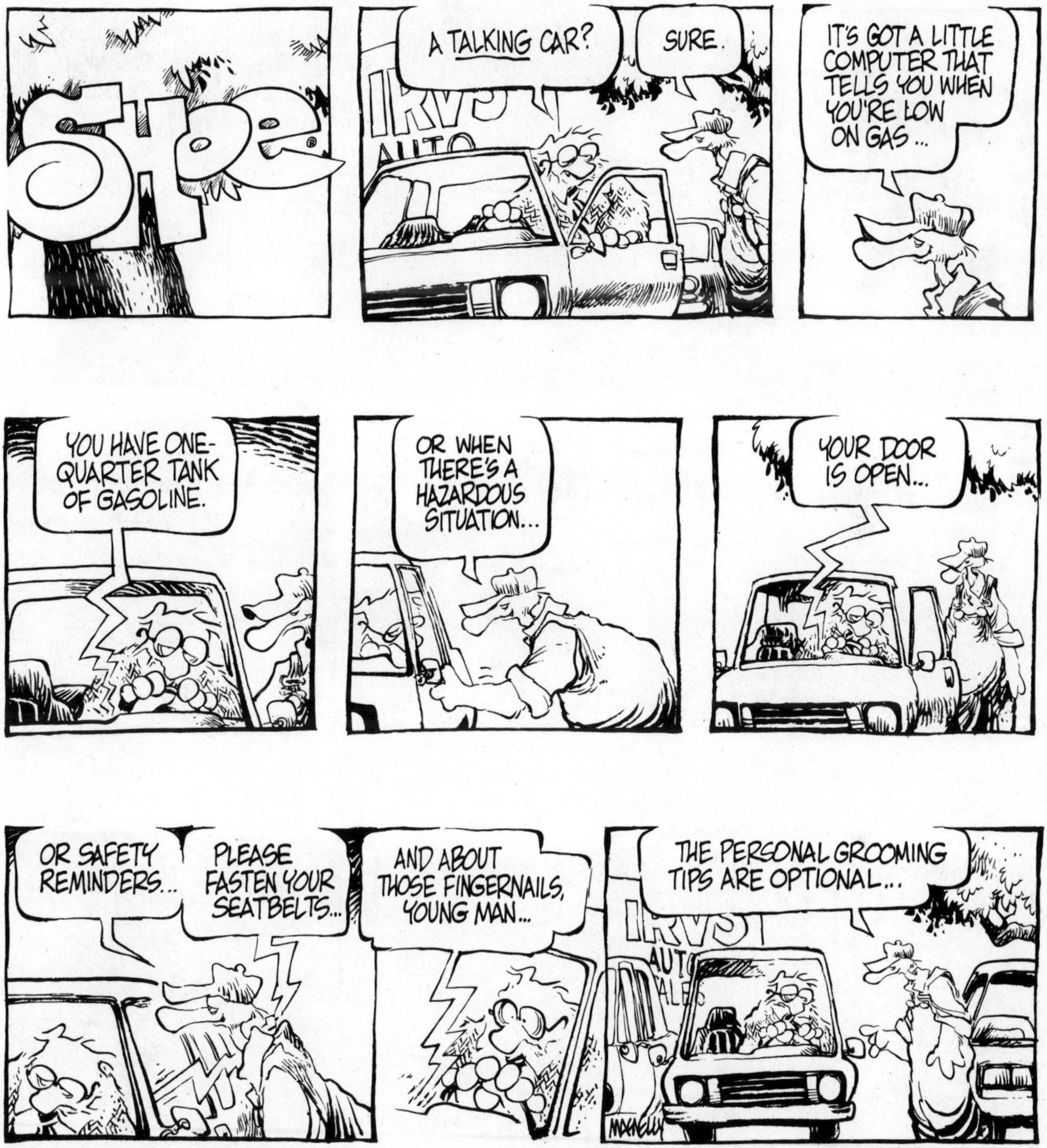
SHOE
A TALKING CAR?
SURE.
IRV'S AUTO
IT'S GOT A LITTLE COMPUTER THAT TELLS YOU WHEN YOU'RE LOW ON GAS...
YOU HAVE ONE-QUARTER TANK OF GASOLINE.
OR WHEN THERE'S A HAZARDOUS SITUATION...
YOUR DOOR IS OPEN...
OR SAFETY REMINDERS...
PLEASE FASTEN YOUR SEATBELTS...
AND ABOUT THOSE FINGERNAILS, YOUNG MAN...
THE PERSONAL GROOMING TIPS ARE OPTIONAL...
MACNELLY

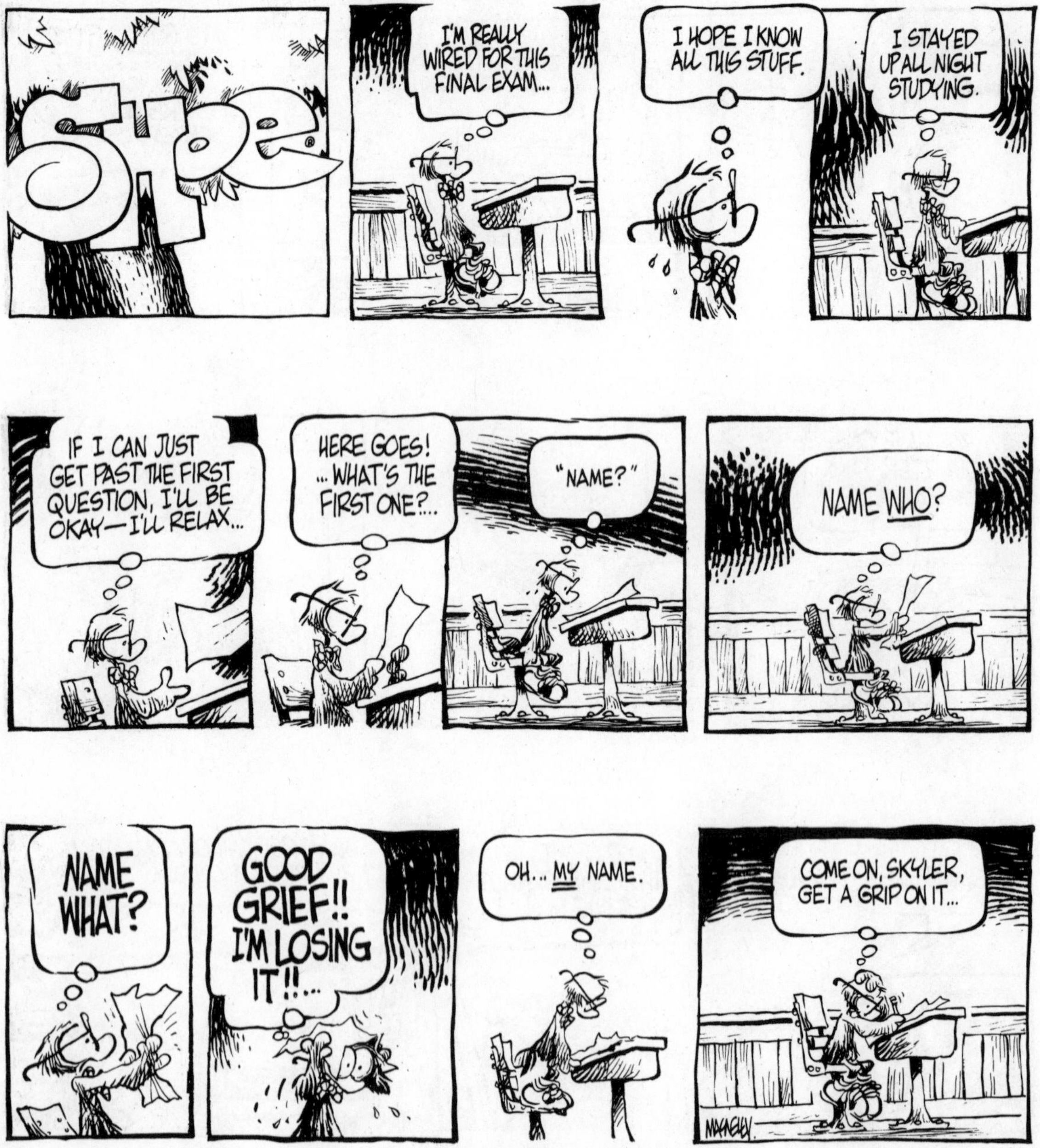
SHOE
I'M REALLY WIRED FOR THIS FINAL EXAM...
I HOPE I KNOW ALL THIS STUFF.
I STAYED UP ALL NIGHT STUDYING.
IF I CAN JUST GET PAST THE FIRST QUESTION, I'LL BE OKAY—I'LL RELAX...
HERE GOES! ...WHAT'S THE FIRST ONE?...
"NAME?"
NAME WHO?
NAME WHAT?
GOOD GRIEF!! I'M LOSING IT!!...
OH... MY NAME.
COME ON, SKYLER, GET A GRIP ON IT...
MACNELLY

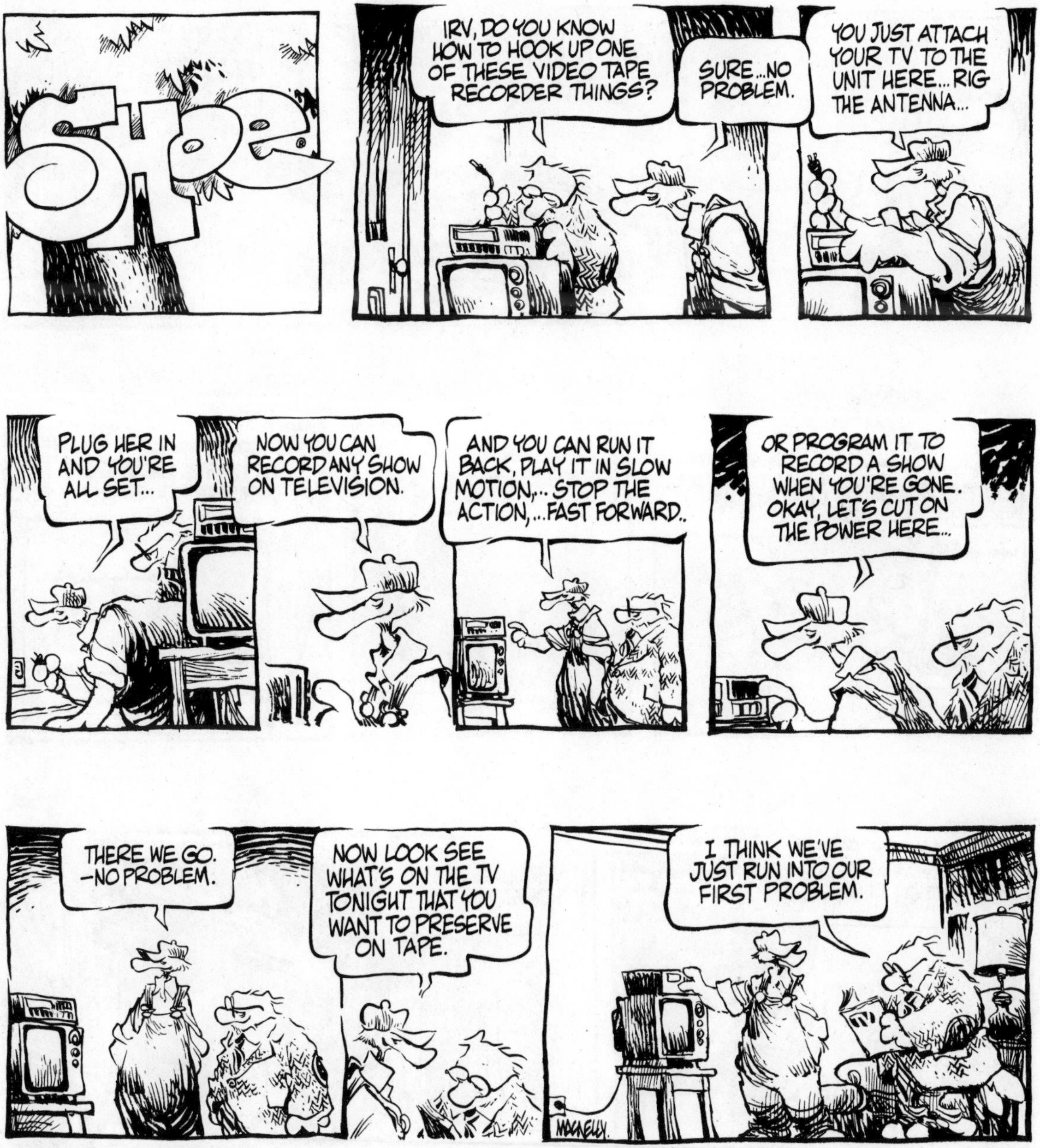
SHOE
IRV, DO YOU KNOW HOW TO HOOK UP ONE OF THESE VIDEO TAPE RECORDER THINGS?
SURE...NO PROBLEM.
YOU JUST ATTACH YOUR TV TO THE UNIT HERE...RIG THE ANTENNA...
PLUG HER IN AND YOU'RE ALL SET...
NOW YOU CAN RECORD ANY SHOW ON TELEVISION.
AND YOU CAN RUN IT BACK, PLAY IT IN SLOW MOTION,... STOP THE ACTION,...FAST FORWARD..
OR PROGRAM IT TO RECORD A SHOW WHEN YOU'RE GONE. OKAY, LET'S CUT ON THE POWER HERE...
THERE WE GO. -NO PROBLEM.
NOW LOOK SEE WHAT'S ON THE TV TONIGHT THAT YOU WANT TO PRESERVE ON TAPE.
I THINK WE'VE JUST RUN INTO OUR FIRST PROBLEM.
MACNELLY

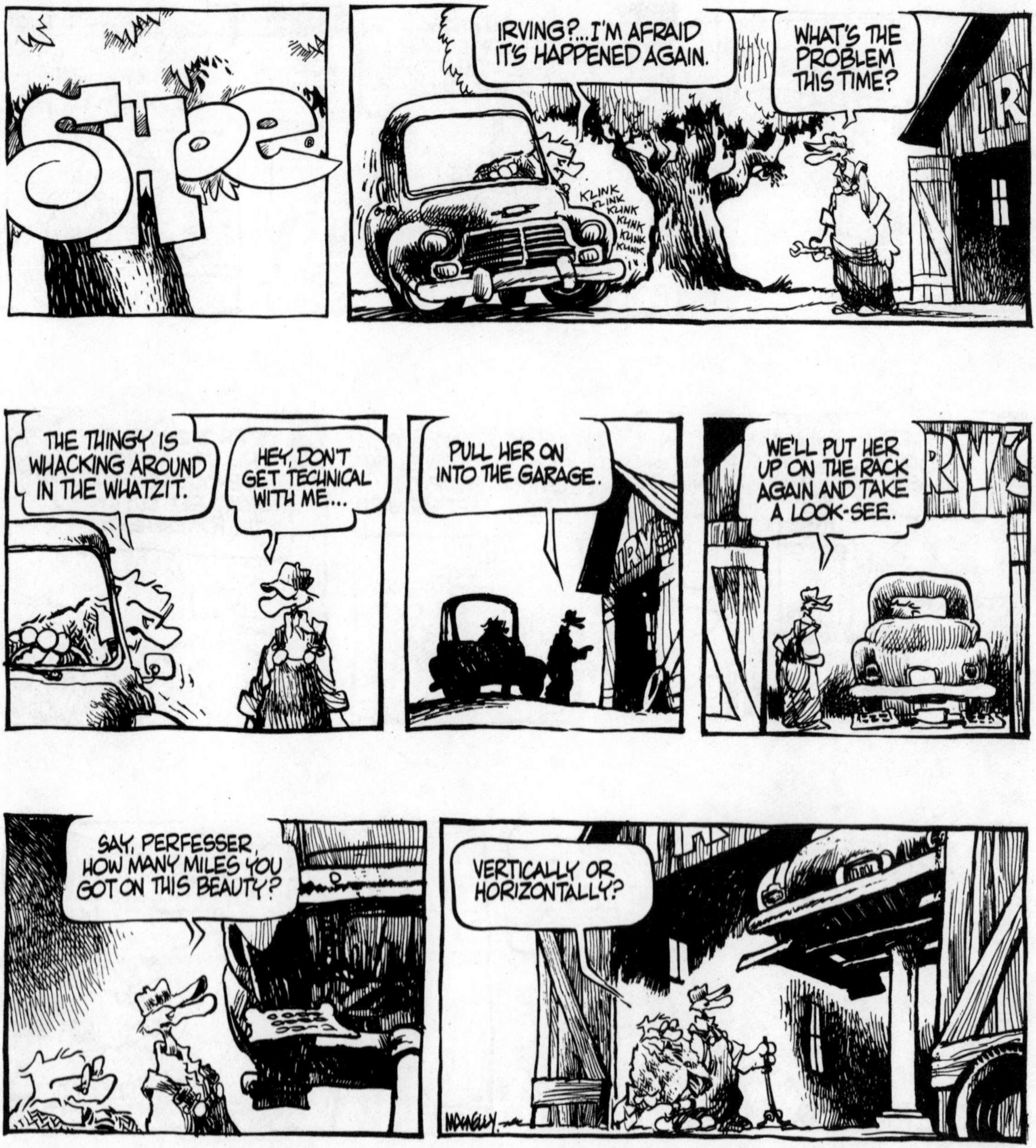SHOE®
IRVING?...I'M AFRAID IT'S HAPPENED AGAIN.
KLINK KLINK KLINK KLINK KLINK KLINK
WHAT'S THE PROBLEM THIS TIME?
THE THINGY IS WHACKING AROUND IN THE WHATZIT.
HEY, DON'T GET TECHNICAL WITH ME...
PULL HER ON INTO THE GARAGE.
WE'LL PUT HER UP ON THE RACK AGAIN AND TAKE A LOOK-SEE.
SAY, PERFESSER, HOW MANY MILES YOU GOT ON THIS BEAUTY?
VERTICALLY OR HORIZONTALLY?
MACNELLY

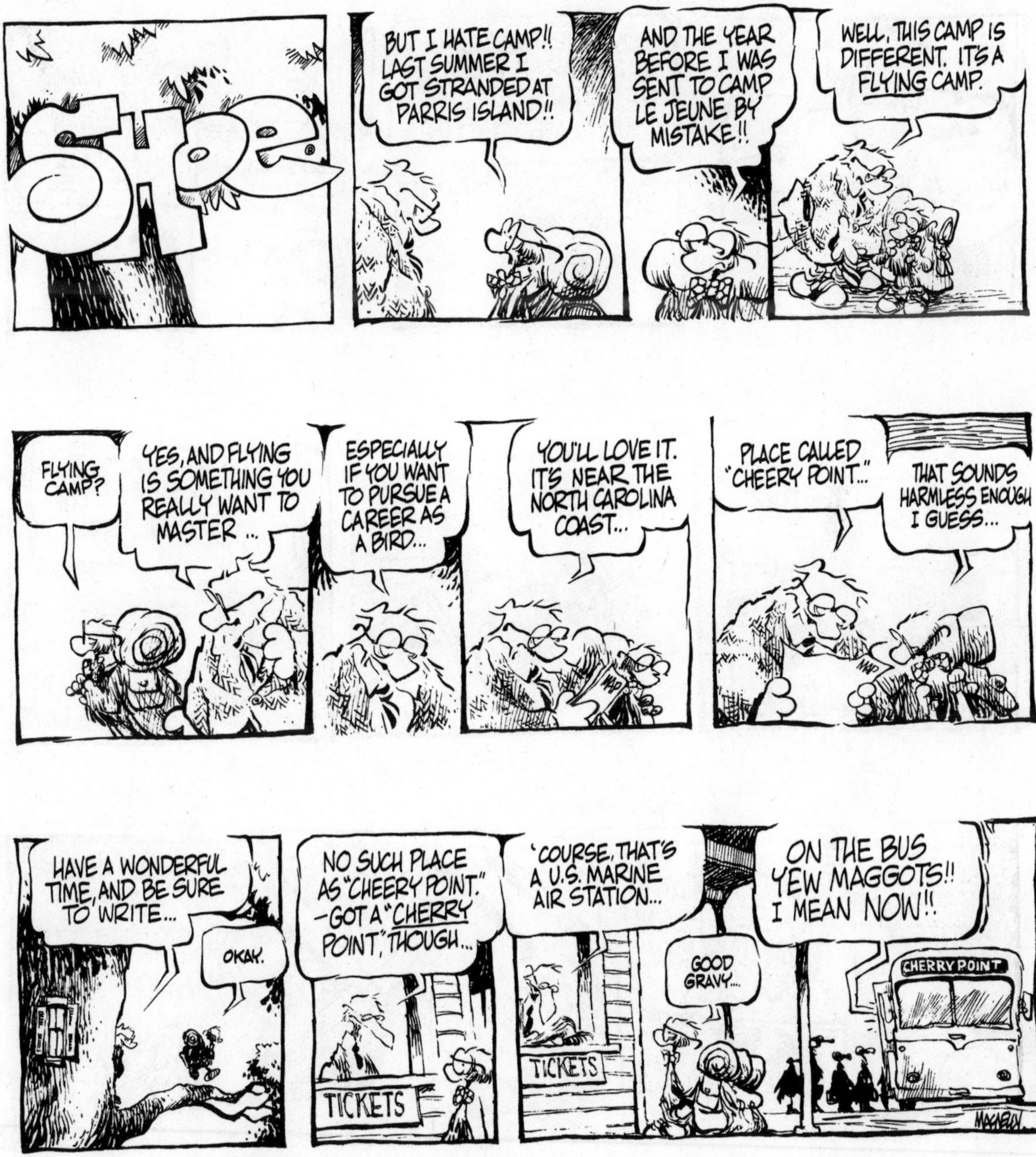

SHOE®
BUT I HATE CAMP!! LAST SUMMER I GOT STRANDED AT PARRIS ISLAND!!
AND THE YEAR BEFORE I WAS SENT TO CAMP LE JEUNE BY MISTAKE!!
WELL, THIS CAMP IS DIFFERENT. IT'S A FLYING CAMP.
FLYING CAMP?
YES, AND FLYING IS SOMETHING YOU REALLY WANT TO MASTER ...
ESPECIALLY IF YOU WANT TO PURSUE A CAREER AS A BIRD...
YOU'LL LOVE IT. IT'S NEAR THE NORTH CAROLINA COAST...
MAP
PLACE CALLED "CHEERY POINT..."
THAT SOUNDS HARMLESS ENOUGH I GUESS...
HAVE A WONDERFUL TIME, AND BE SURE TO WRITE...
OKAY.
NO SUCH PLACE AS "CHEERY POINT." -GOT A "CHERRY POINT," THOUGH...
TICKETS
'COURSE, THAT'S A U.S. MARINE AIR STATION...
TICKETS
GOOD GRAVY...
ON THE BUS YEW MAGGOTS!! I MEAN NOW!!
CHERRY POINT
MACNELLY

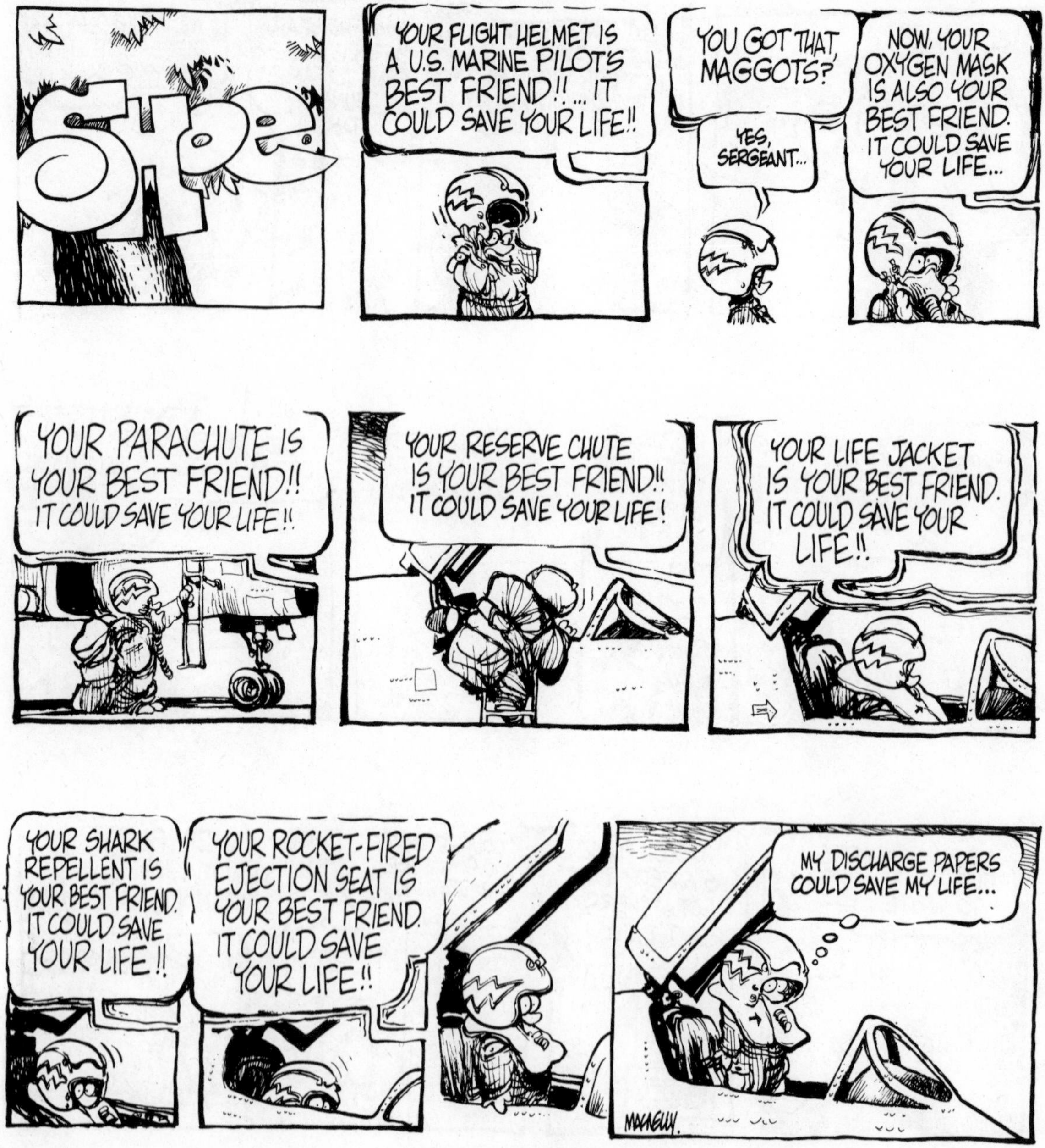
SHOE®
YOUR FLIGHT HELMET IS A U.S. MARINE PILOT'S BEST FRIEND!! ... IT COULD SAVE YOUR LIFE!!
YOU GOT THAT, MAGGOTS?
YES, SERGEANT...
NOW, YOUR OXYGEN MASK IS ALSO YOUR BEST FRIEND. IT COULD SAVE YOUR LIFE...
YOUR PARACHUTE IS YOUR BEST FRIEND!! IT COULD SAVE YOUR LIFE!!
YOUR RESERVE CHUTE IS YOUR BEST FRIEND!! IT COULD SAVE YOUR LIFE!
YOUR LIFE JACKET IS YOUR BEST FRIEND. IT COULD SAVE YOUR LIFE!!
YOUR SHARK REPELLENT IS YOUR BEST FRIEND. IT COULD SAVE YOUR LIFE!!
YOUR ROCKET-FIRED EJECTION SEAT IS YOUR BEST FRIEND. IT COULD SAVE YOUR LIFE!!
MY DISCHARGE PAPERS COULD SAVE MY LIFE...
MACNELLY.

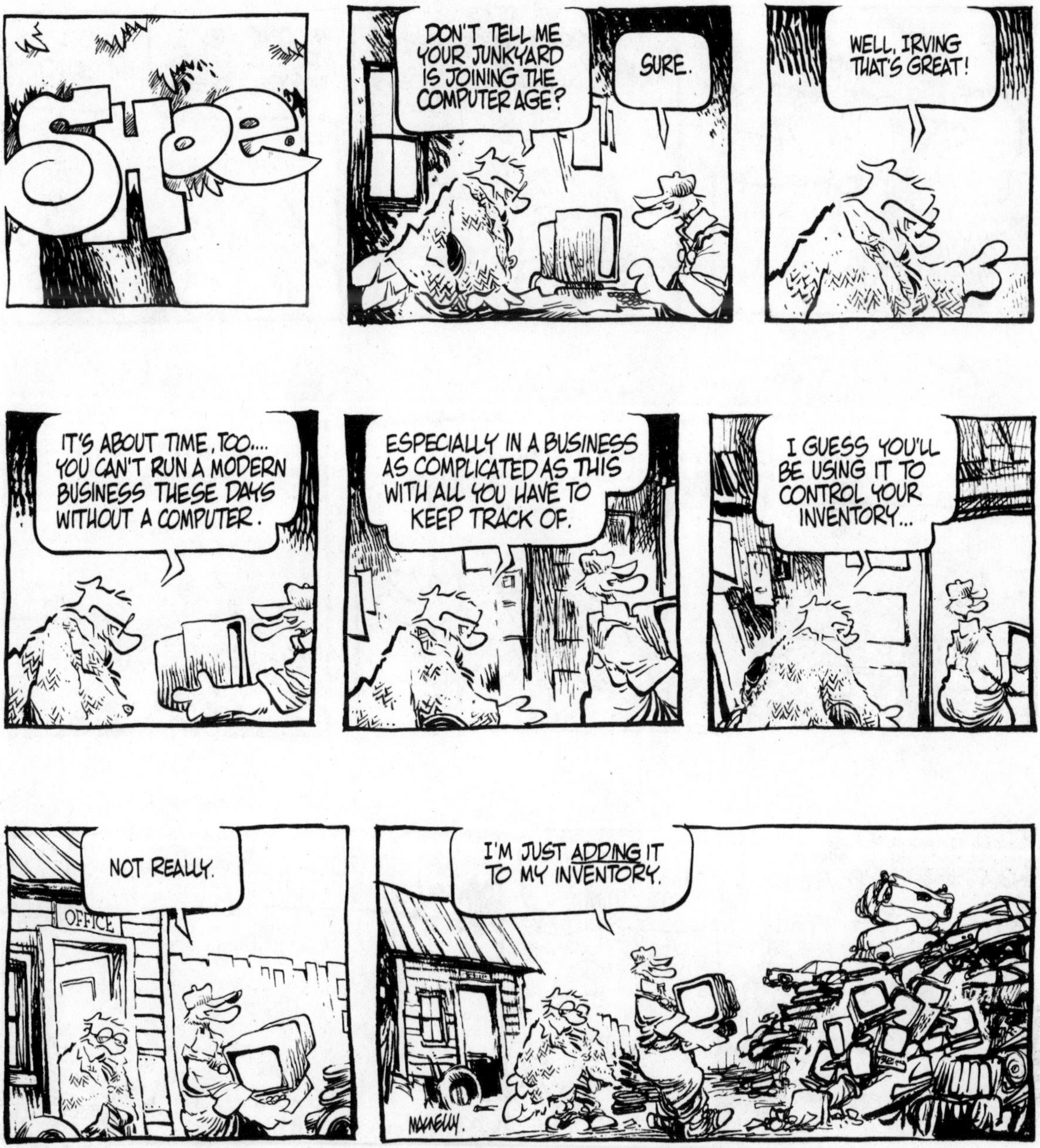
SHOE
DON'T TELL ME YOUR JUNKYARD IS JOINING THE COMPUTER AGE?
SURE.
WELL, IRVING THAT'S GREAT!
IT'S ABOUT TIME, TOO.... YOU CAN'T RUN A MODERN BUSINESS THESE DAYS WITHOUT A COMPUTER.
ESPECIALLY IN A BUSINESS AS COMPLICATED AS THIS WITH ALL YOU HAVE TO KEEP TRACK OF.
I GUESS YOU'LL BE USING IT TO CONTROL YOUR INVENTORY...
NOT REALLY.
OFFICE
I'M JUST ADDING IT TO MY INVENTORY.
MACNELLY

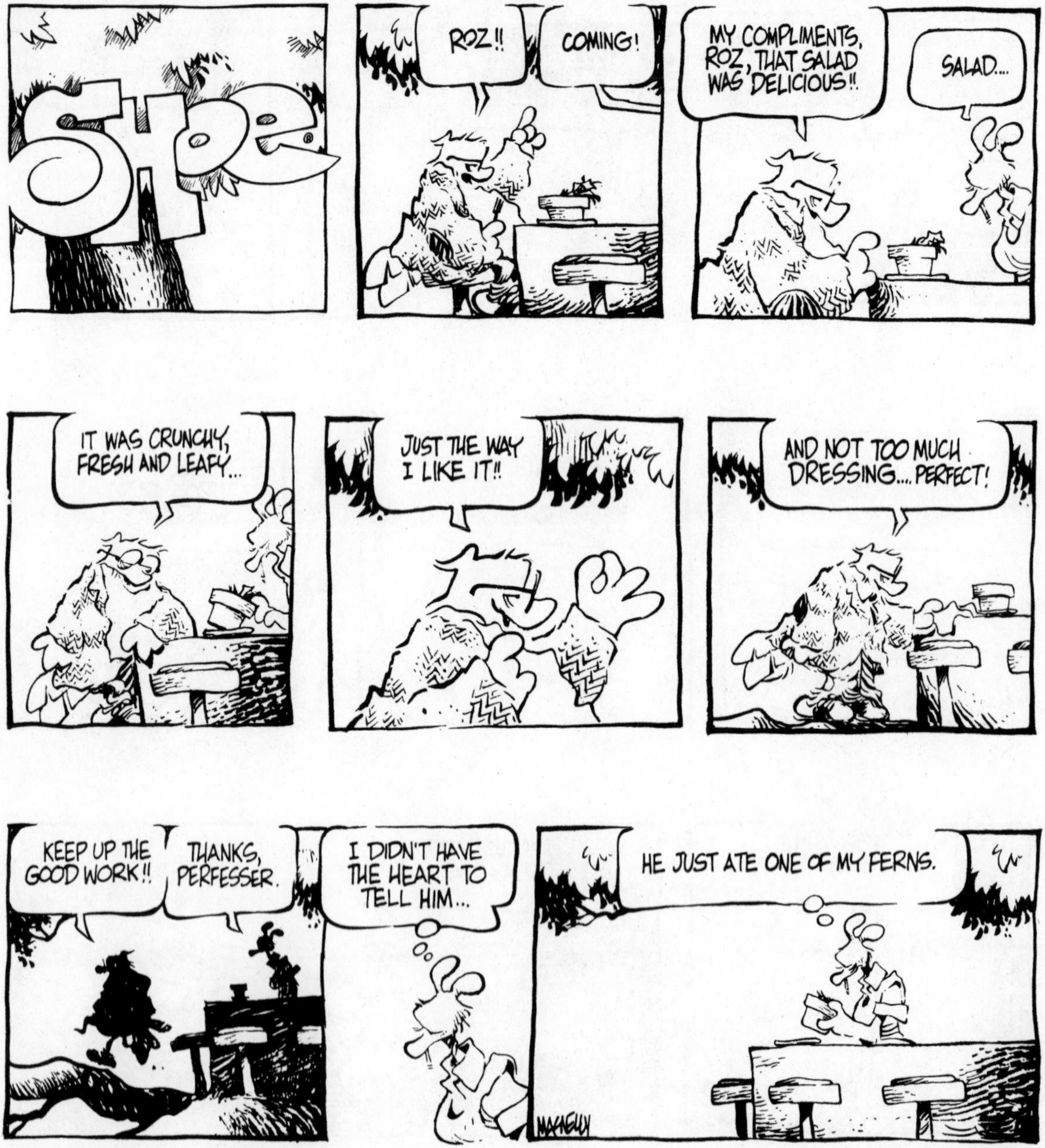
SHOE®
ROZ!!
COMING!
MY COMPLIMENTS, ROZ, THAT SALAD WAS DELICIOUS!!
SALAD....
IT WAS CRUNCHY, FRESH AND LEAFY...
JUST THE WAY I LIKE IT!!
AND NOT TOO MUCH DRESSING.... PERFECT!
KEEP UP THE GOOD WORK!!
THANKS, PERFESSER.
I DIDN'T HAVE THE HEART TO TELL HIM...
HE JUST ATE ONE OF MY FERNS.
MACNELLY

two

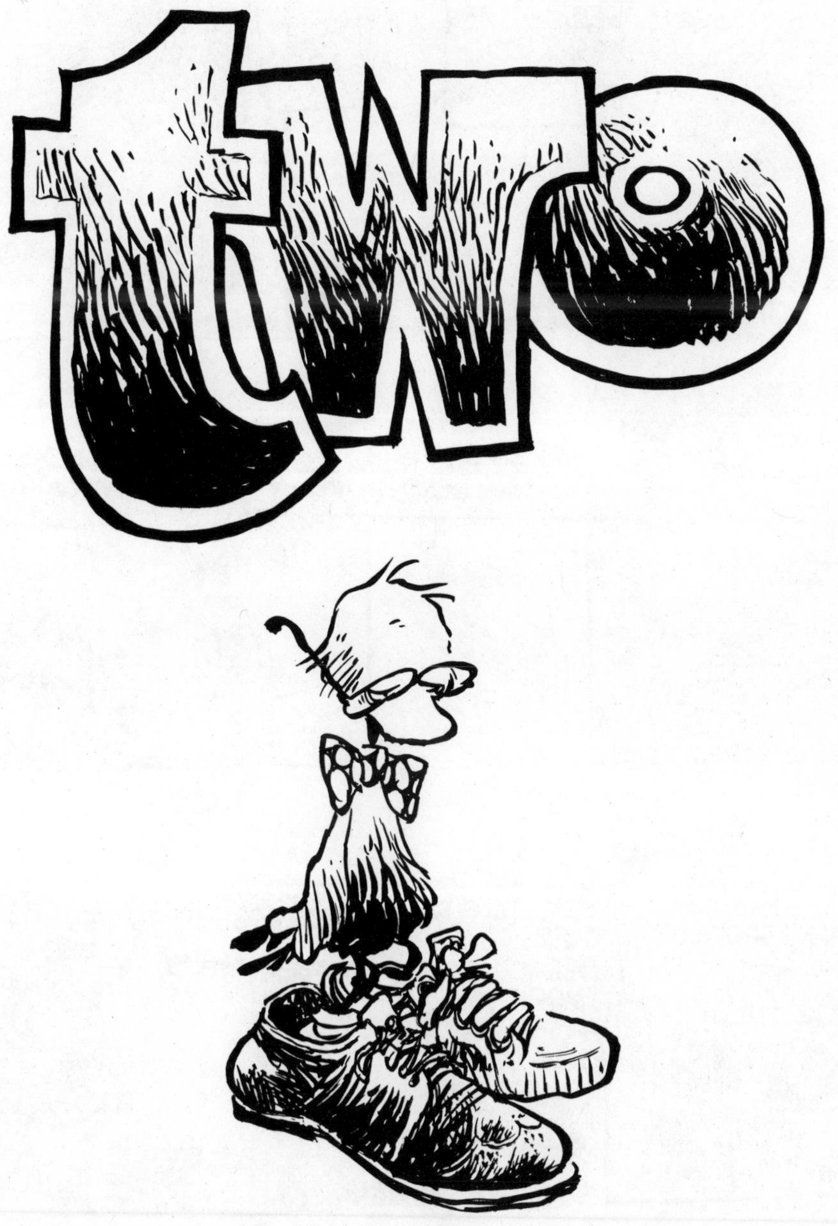

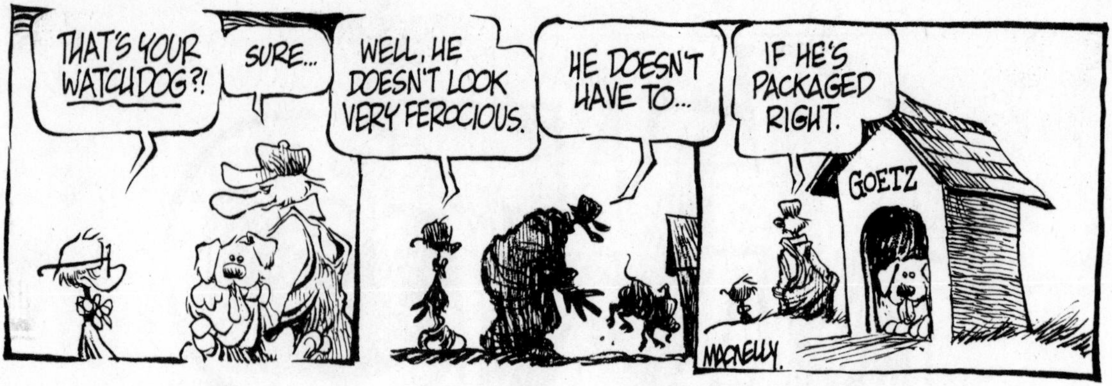
THAT'S YOUR WATCHDOG?!
SURE...
WELL, HE DOESN'T LOOK VERY FEROCIOUS.
HE DOESN'T HAVE TO...
IF HE'S PACKAGED RIGHT.
GOETZ
MACNELLY.

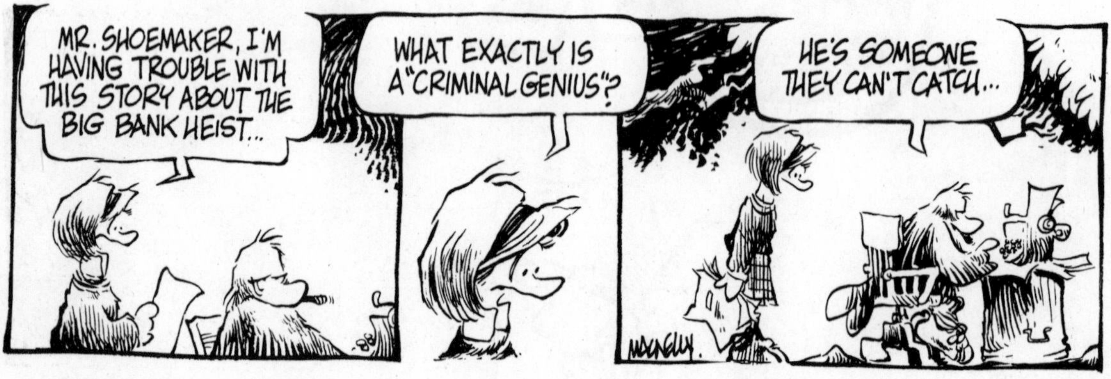
MR. SHOEMAKER, I'M HAVING TROUBLE WITH THIS STORY ABOUT THE BIG BANK HEIST...
WHAT EXACTLY IS A "CRIMINAL GENIUS"?
HE'S SOMEONE THEY CAN'T CATCH...
MACNELLY.

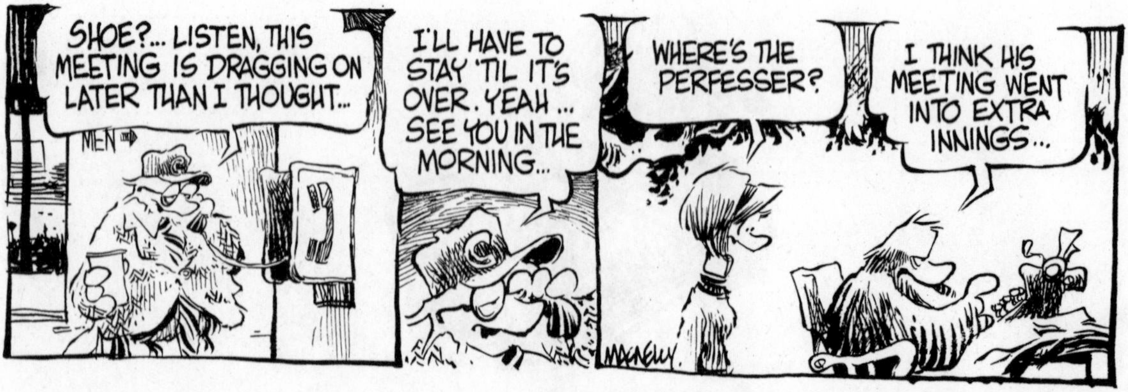
SHOE?... LISTEN, THIS MEETING IS DRAGGING ON LATER THAN I THOUGHT...
MEN
I'LL HAVE TO STAY 'TIL IT'S OVER. YEAH ... SEE YOU IN THE MORNING...
WHERE'S THE PERFESSER?
I THINK HIS MEETING WENT INTO EXTRA INNINGS...
MACNELLY.

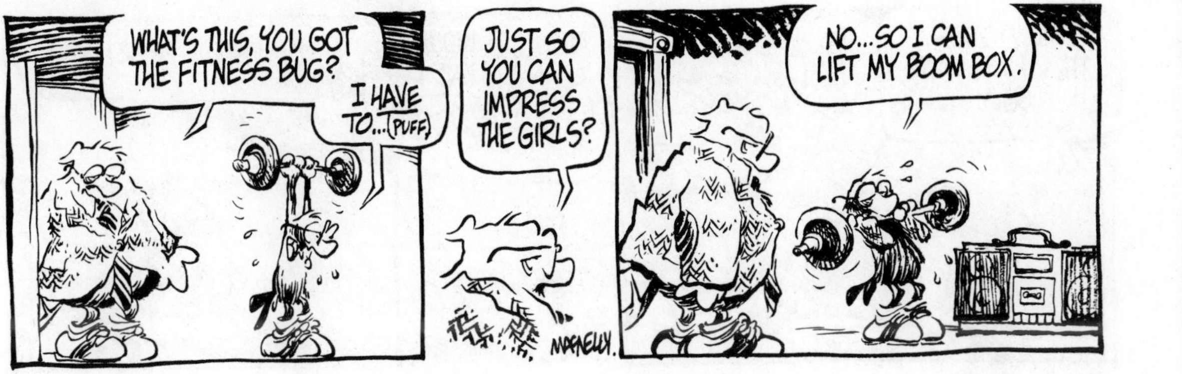
WHAT'S THIS, YOU GOT THE FITNESS BUG?
I HAVE TO...(PUFF)
JUST SO YOU CAN IMPRESS THE GIRLS?
NO...SO I CAN LIFT MY BOOM BOX.
MACNELLY.

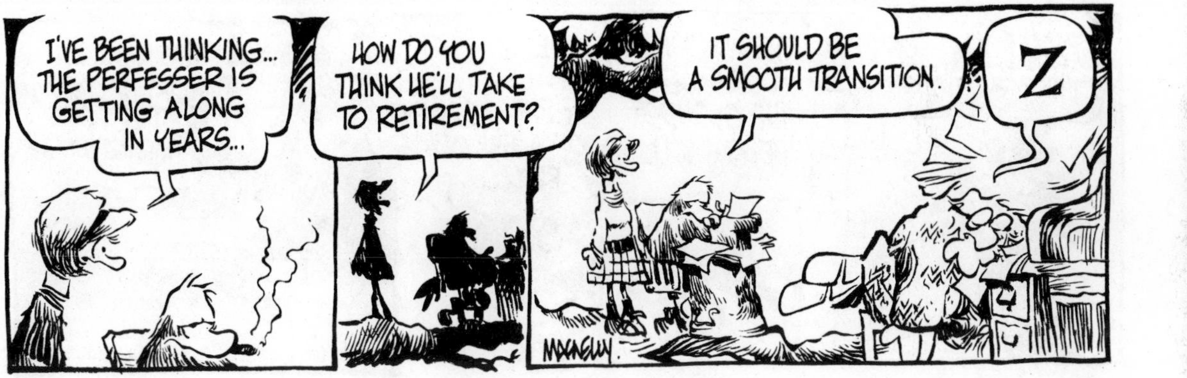
I'VE BEEN THINKING... THE PERFESSER IS GETTING ALONG IN YEARS...
HOW DO YOU THINK HE'LL TAKE TO RETIREMENT?
IT SHOULD BE A SMOOTH TRANSITION.
Z
MACNELLY.

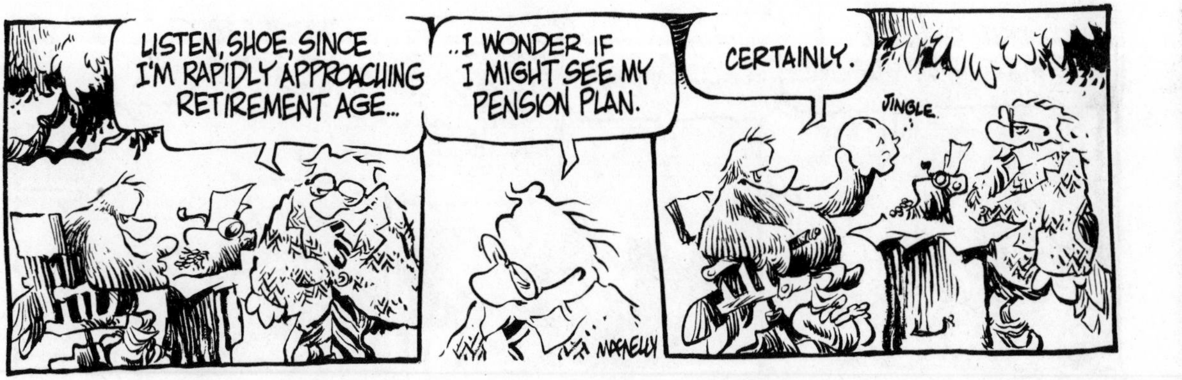
LISTEN, SHOE, SINCE I'M RAPIDLY APPROACHING RETIREMENT AGE...
..I WONDER IF I MIGHT SEE MY PENSION PLAN.
CERTAINLY.
JINGLE
MACNELLY

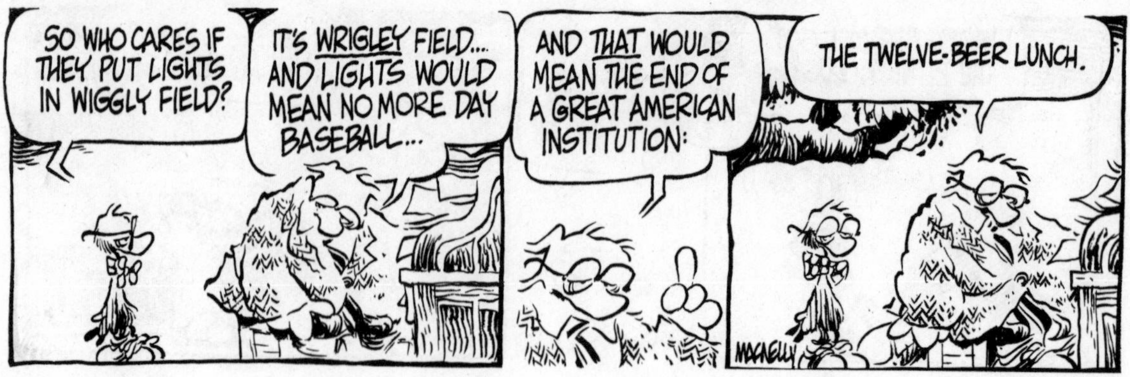
SO WHO CARES IF THEY PUT LIGHTS IN WIGGLY FIELD?
IT'S WRIGLEY FIELD... AND LIGHTS WOULD MEAN NO MORE DAY BASEBALL...
AND THAT WOULD MEAN THE END OF A GREAT AMERICAN INSTITUTION:
THE TWELVE-BEER LUNCH.

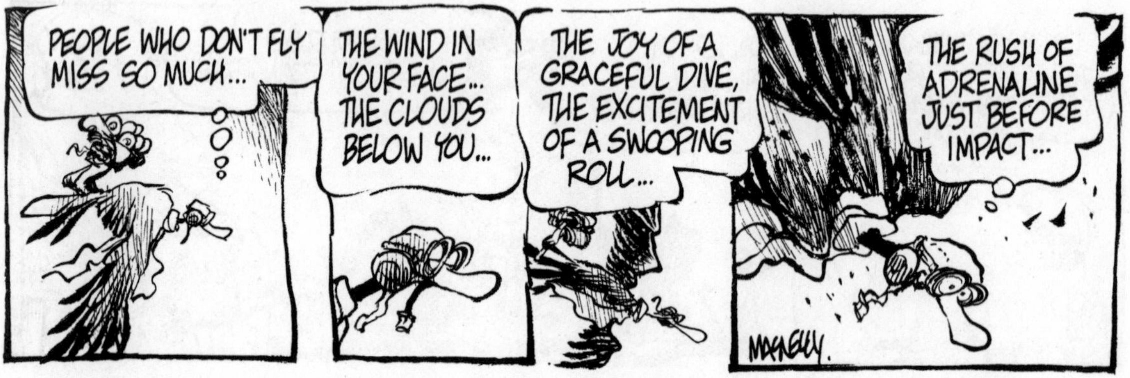
PEOPLE WHO DON'T FLY MISS SO MUCH...
THE WIND IN YOUR FACE... THE CLOUDS BELOW YOU...
THE JOY OF A GRACEFUL DIVE, THE EXCITEMENT OF A SWOOPING ROLL...
THE RUSH OF ADRENALINE JUST BEFORE IMPACT...

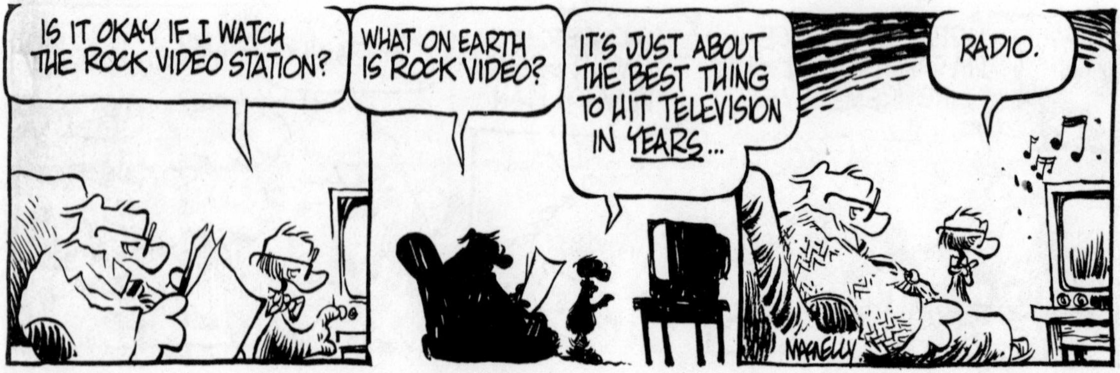
IS IT OKAY IF I WATCH THE ROCK VIDEO STATION?
WHAT ON EARTH IS ROCK VIDEO?
IT'S JUST ABOUT THE BEST THING TO HIT TELEVISION IN YEARS...
RADIO.

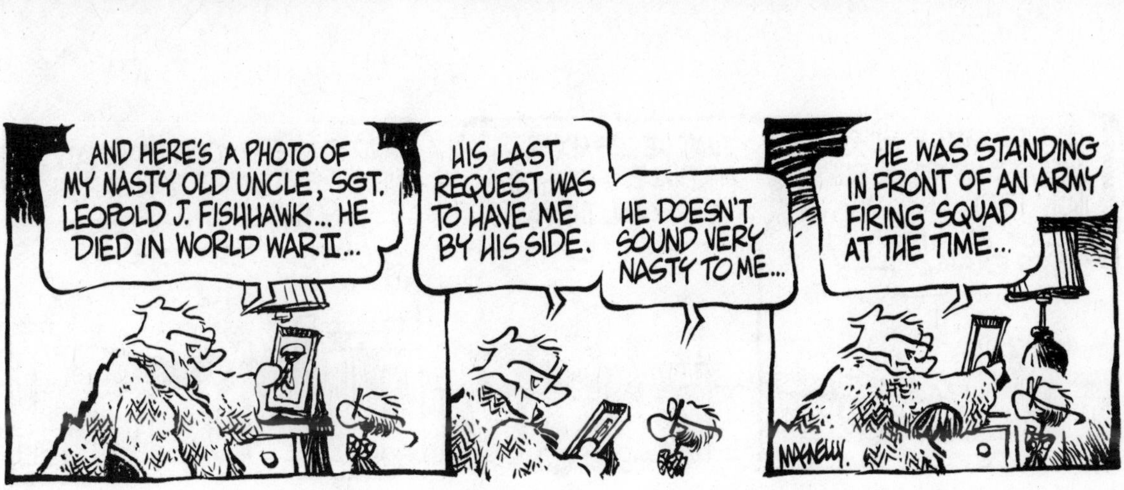
AND HERE'S A PHOTO OF MY NASTY OLD UNCLE, SGT. LEOPOLD J. FISHHAWK... HE DIED IN WORLD WAR II...
HIS LAST REQUEST WAS TO HAVE ME BY HIS SIDE.
HE DOESN'T SOUND VERY NASTY TO ME...
HE WAS STANDING IN FRONT OF AN ARMY FIRING SQUAD AT THE TIME...
MACNELLY

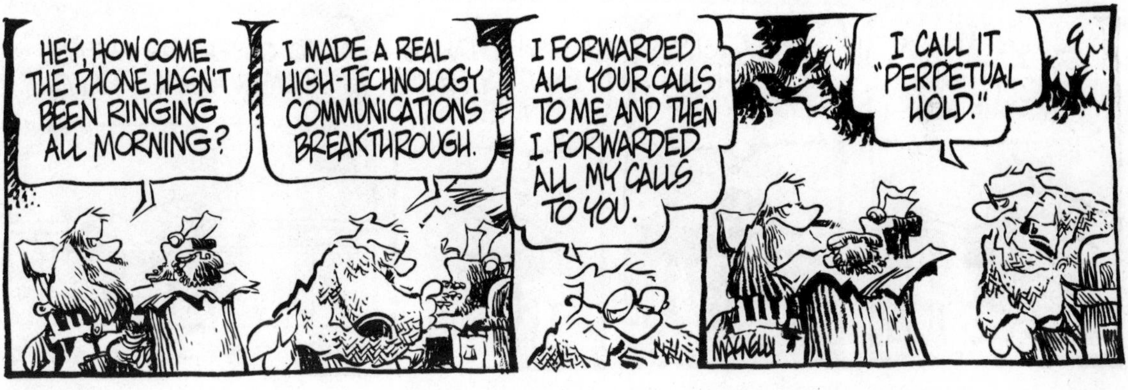
HEY, HOW COME THE PHONE HASN'T BEEN RINGING ALL MORNING?
I MADE A REAL HIGH-TECHNOLOGY COMMUNICATIONS BREAKTHROUGH.
I FORWARDED ALL YOUR CALLS TO ME AND THEN I FORWARDED ALL MY CALLS TO YOU.
I CALL IT "PERPETUAL HOLD."
MACNELLY

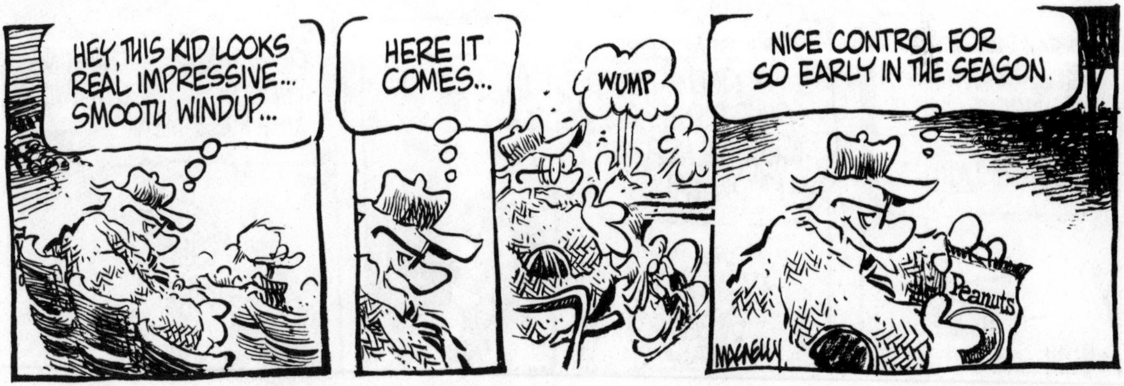
HEY, THIS KID LOOKS REAL IMPRESSIVE... SMOOTH WINDUP...
HERE IT COMES...
WUMP
NICE CONTROL FOR SO EARLY IN THE SEASON.
Peanuts
MACNELLY

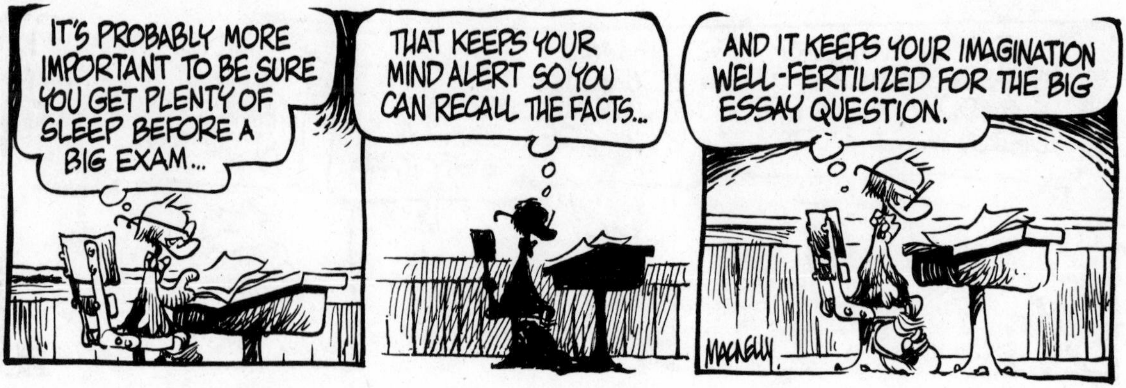
IT'S PROBABLY MORE IMPORTANT TO BE SURE YOU GET PLENTY OF SLEEP BEFORE A BIG EXAM...
THAT KEEPS YOUR MIND ALERT SO YOU CAN RECALL THE FACTS...
AND IT KEEPS YOUR IMAGINATION WELL-FERTILIZED FOR THE BIG ESSAY QUESTION.
MACNELLY.

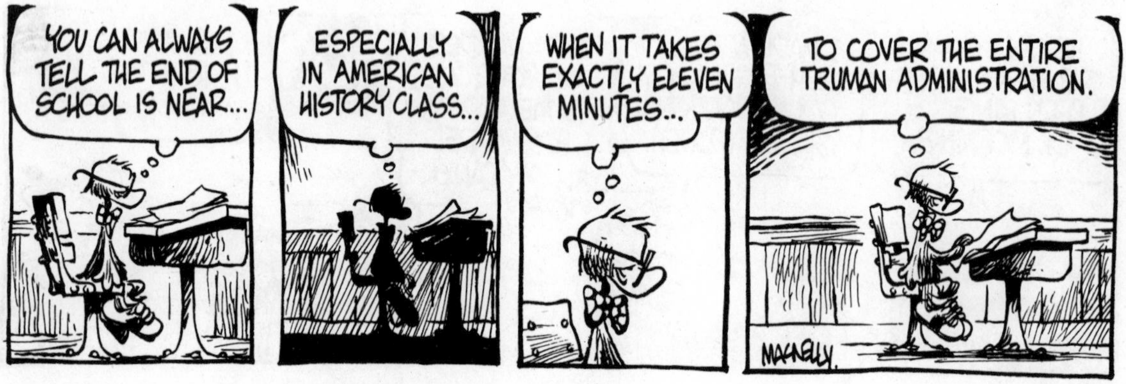
YOU CAN ALWAYS TELL THE END OF SCHOOL IS NEAR...
ESPECIALLY IN AMERICAN HISTORY CLASS...
WHEN IT TAKES EXACTLY ELEVEN MINUTES...
TO COVER THE ENTIRE TRUMAN ADMINISTRATION.
MACNELLY.

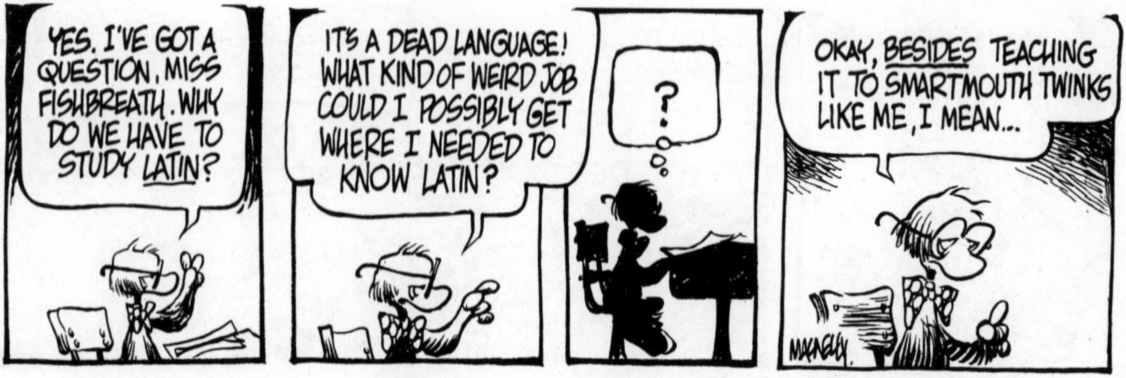
YES. I'VE GOT A QUESTION, MISS FISHBREATH. WHY DO WE HAVE TO STUDY LATIN?
IT'S A DEAD LANGUAGE! WHAT KIND OF WEIRD JOB COULD I POSSIBLY GET WHERE I NEEDED TO KNOW LATIN?
?
OKAY, BESIDES TEACHING IT TO SMARTMOUTH TWINKS LIKE ME, I MEAN...
MACNELLY.

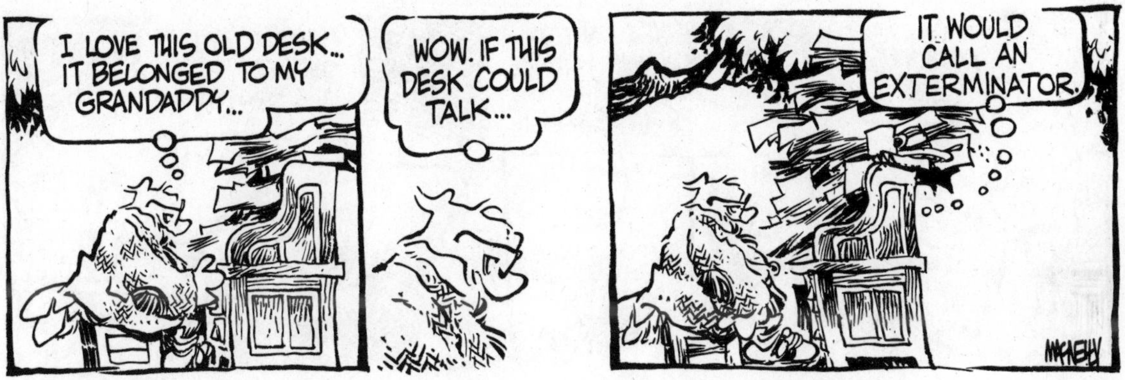
I LOVE THIS OLD DESK... IT BELONGED TO MY GRANDADDY...
WOW. IF THIS DESK COULD TALK...
IT WOULD CALL AN EXTERMINATOR.
MACNELLY

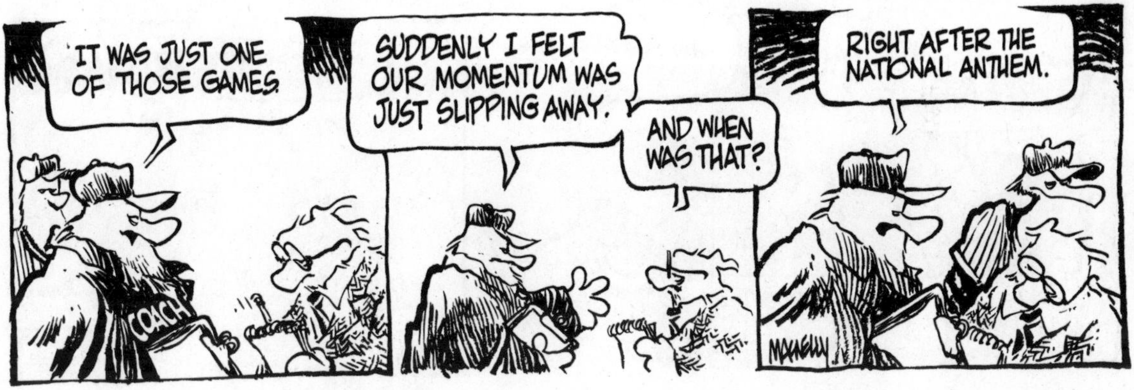
IT WAS JUST ONE OF THOSE GAMES.
COACH
SUDDENLY I FELT OUR MOMENTUM WAS JUST SLIPPING AWAY.
AND WHEN WAS THAT?
RIGHT AFTER THE NATIONAL ANTHEM.
MACNELLY

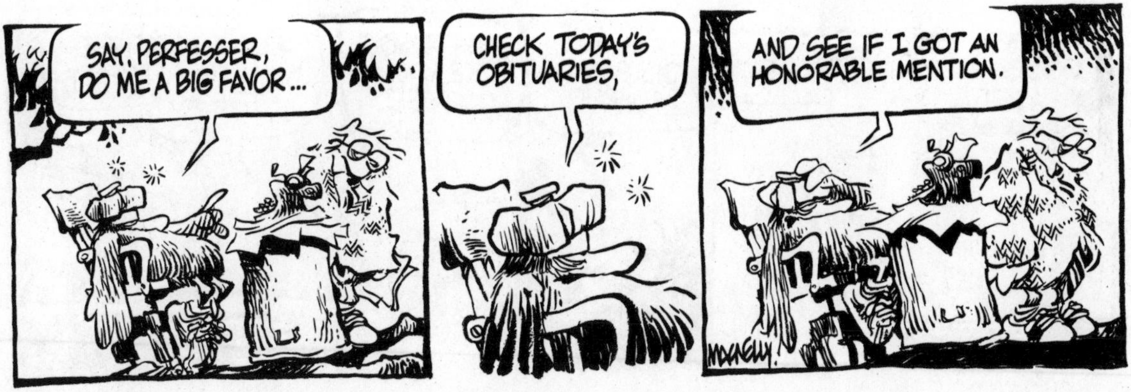
SAY, PERFESSER, DO ME A BIG FAVOR...
CHECK TODAY'S OBITUARIES,
AND SEE IF I GOT AN HONORABLE MENTION.
MACNELLY

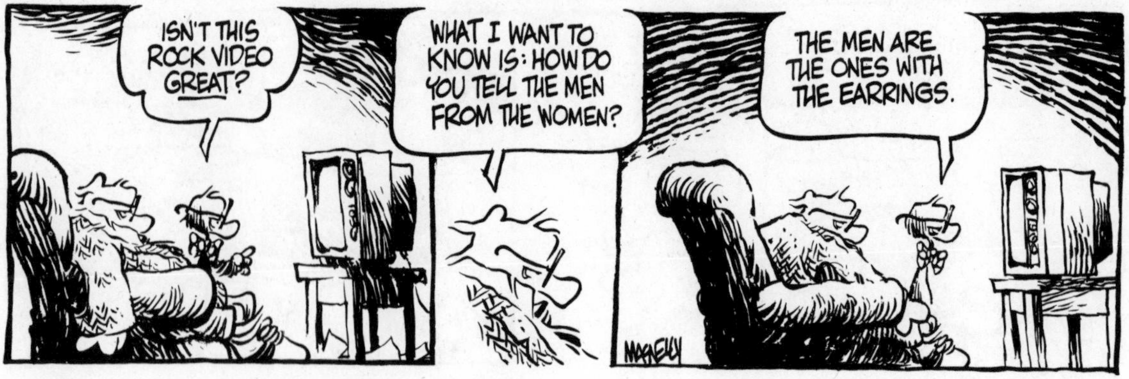
ISN'T THIS ROCK VIDEO GREAT?
WHAT I WANT TO KNOW IS: HOW DO YOU TELL THE MEN FROM THE WOMEN?
THE MEN ARE THE ONES WITH THE EARRINGS.
MACNELLY

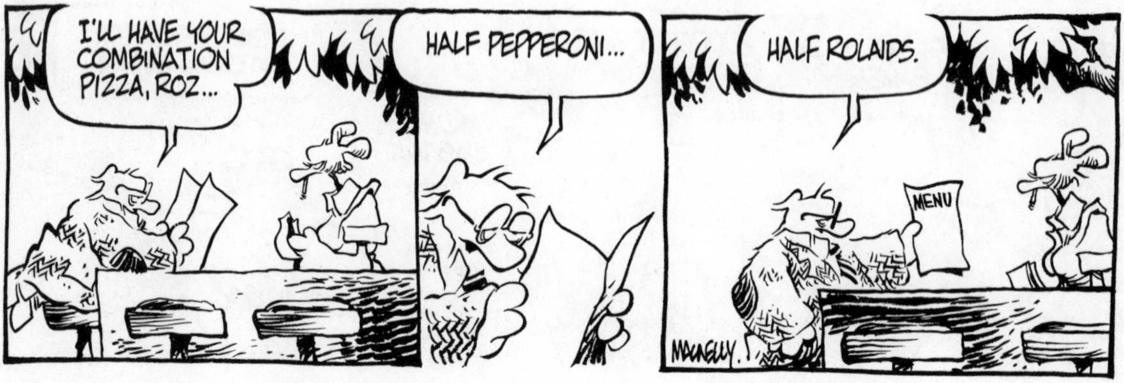
I'LL HAVE YOUR COMBINATION PIZZA, ROZ...
HALF PEPPERONI...
HALF ROLAIDS.
MENU
MACNELLY

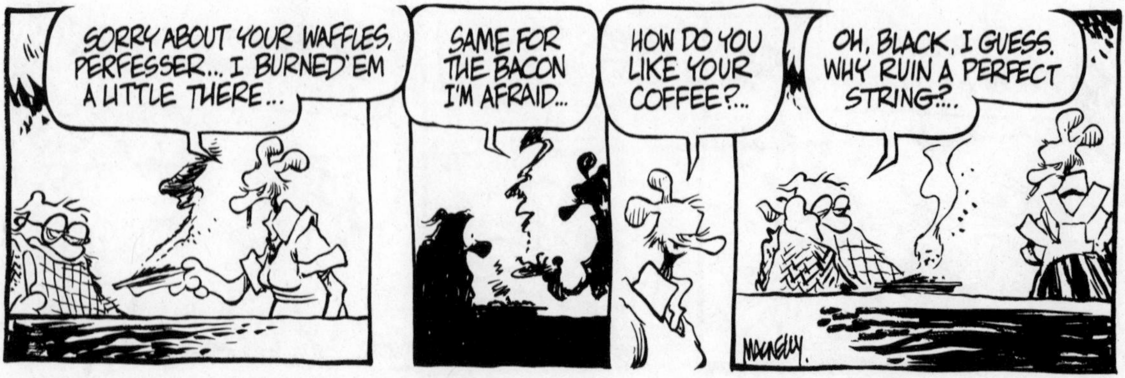
SORRY ABOUT YOUR WAFFLES, PERFESSER... I BURNED'EM A LITTLE THERE...
SAME FOR THE BACON I'M AFRAID...
HOW DO YOU LIKE YOUR COFFEE?...
OH, BLACK, I GUESS. WHY RUIN A PERFECT STRING?...
MACNELLY

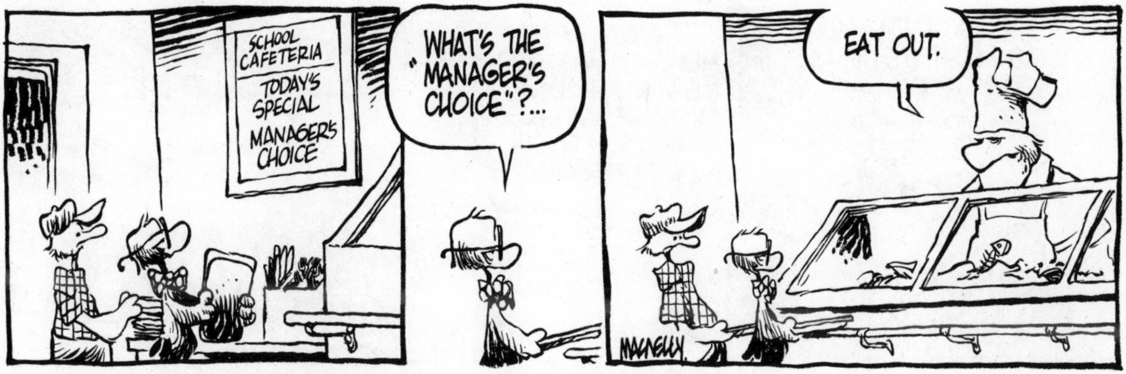
SCHOOL CAFETERIA
TODAY'S SPECIAL
MANAGER'S CHOICE
WHAT'S THE "MANAGER'S CHOICE"?...
EAT OUT.

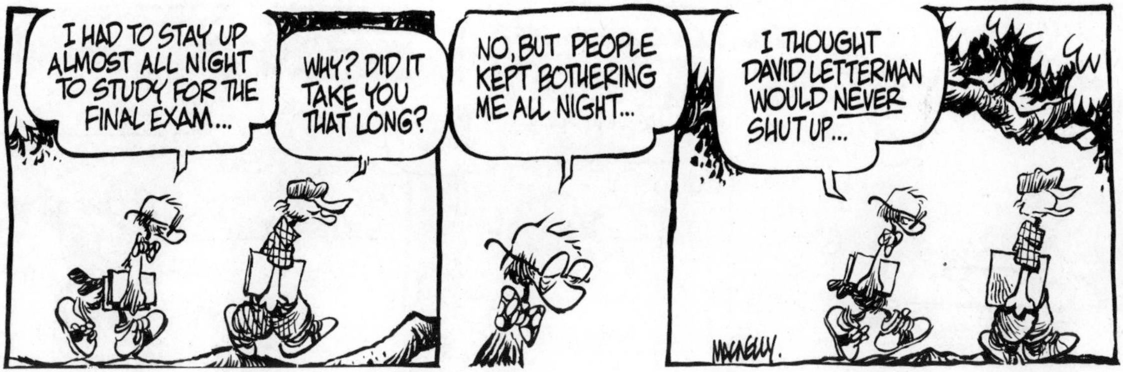
I HAD TO STAY UP ALMOST ALL NIGHT TO STUDY FOR THE FINAL EXAM...
WHY? DID IT TAKE YOU THAT LONG?
NO, BUT PEOPLE KEPT BOTHERING ME ALL NIGHT...
I THOUGHT DAVID LETTERMAN WOULD NEVER SHUT UP...

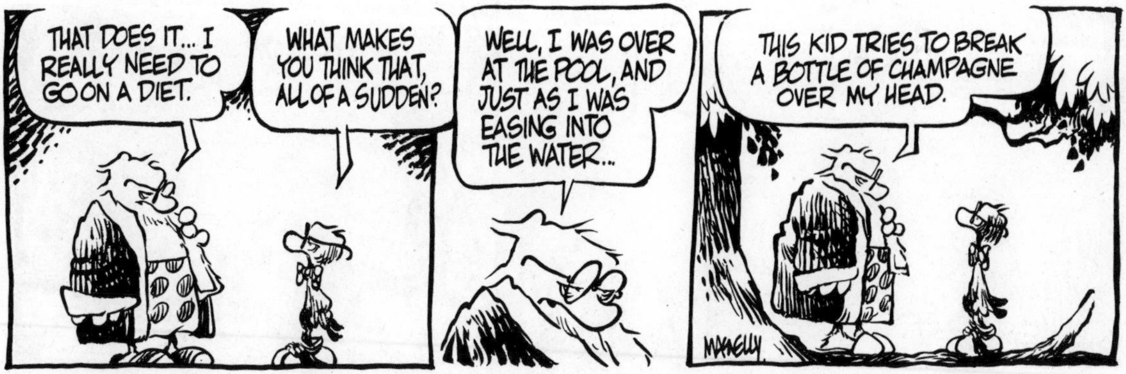
THAT DOES IT... I REALLY NEED TO GO ON A DIET.
WHAT MAKES YOU THINK THAT, ALL OF A SUDDEN?
WELL, I WAS OVER AT THE POOL, AND JUST AS I WAS EASING INTO THE WATER...
THIS KID TRIES TO BREAK A BOTTLE OF CHAMPAGNE OVER MY HEAD.

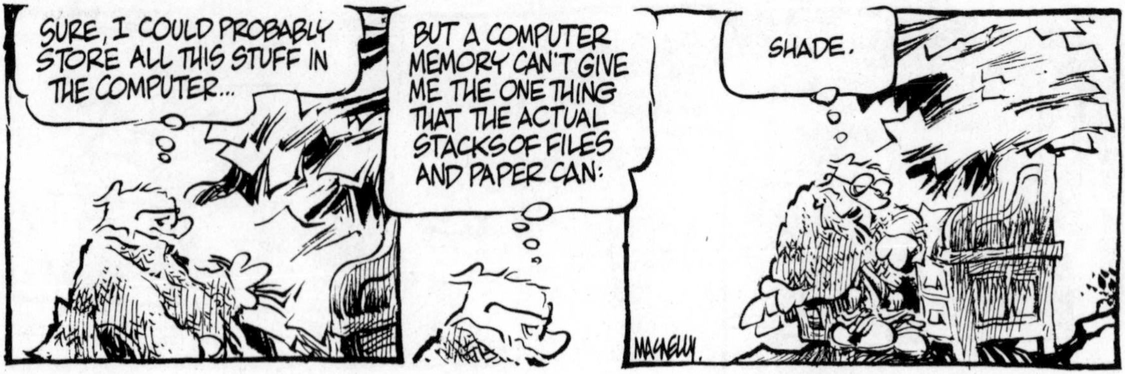
SURE, I COULD PROBABLY STORE ALL THIS STUFF IN THE COMPUTER...
BUT A COMPUTER MEMORY CAN'T GIVE ME THE ONE THING THAT THE ACTUAL STACKS OF FILES AND PAPER CAN:
SHADE.
MAGNELLY.

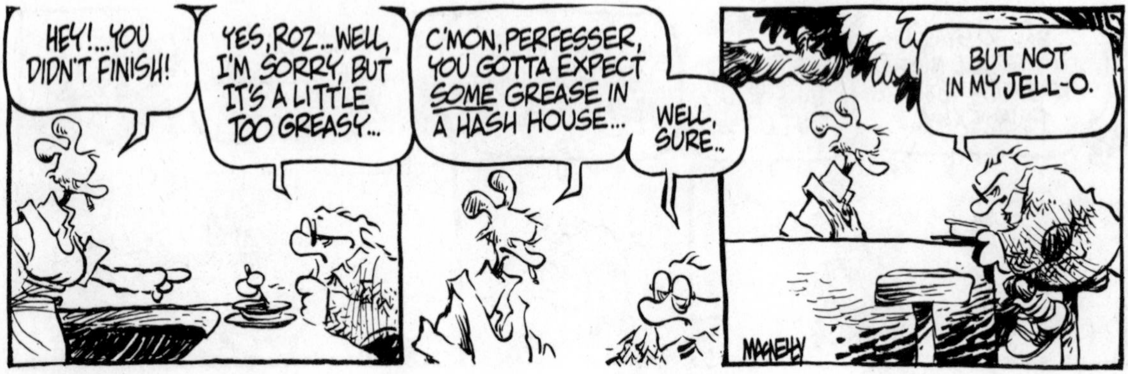
HEY!...YOU DIDN'T FINISH!
YES, ROZ...WELL, I'M SORRY, BUT IT'S A LITTLE TOO GREASY...
C'MON, PERFESSER, YOU GOTTA EXPECT SOME GREASE IN A HASH HOUSE...
WELL, SURE..
BUT NOT IN MY JELL-O.
MAGNELLY

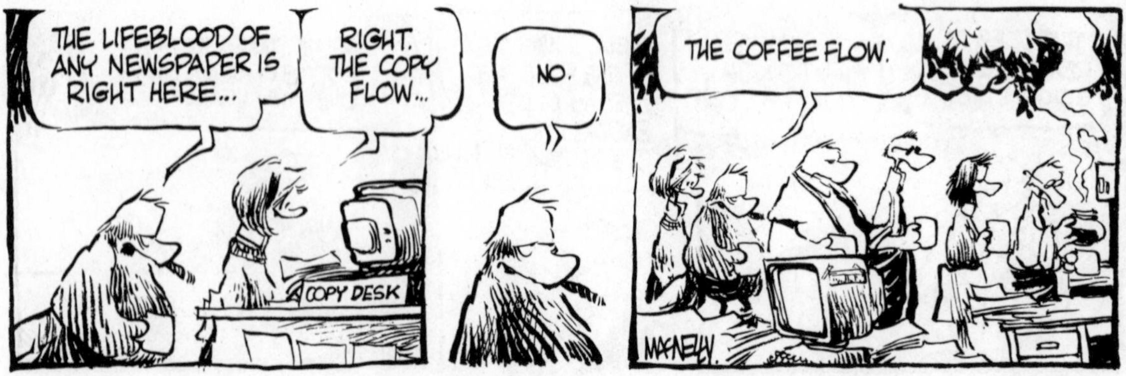
THE LIFEBLOOD OF ANY NEWSPAPER IS RIGHT HERE...
RIGHT. THE COPY FLOW...
COPY DESK
NO.
THE COFFEE FLOW.
MAGNELLY.

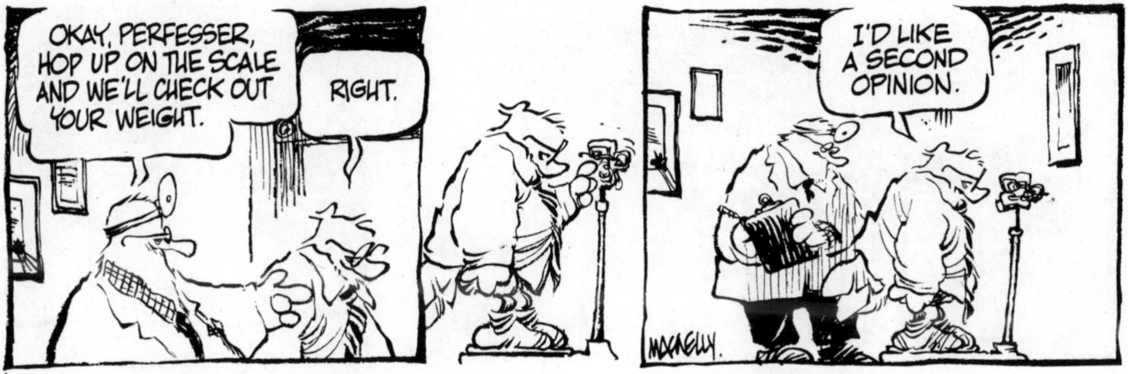

OKAY, PERFESSER, HOP UP ON THE SCALE AND WE'LL CHECK OUT YOUR WEIGHT.
RIGHT.
I'D LIKE A SECOND OPINION.
MACNELLY.

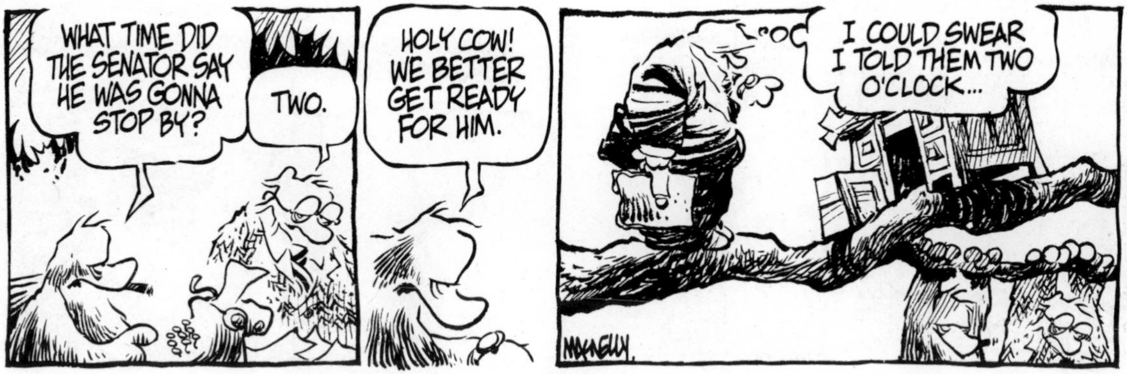

WHAT TIME DID THE SENATOR SAY HE WAS GONNA STOP BY?
TWO.
HOLY COW! WE BETTER GET READY FOR HIM.
I COULD SWEAR I TOLD THEM TWO O'CLOCK...
MACNELLY.

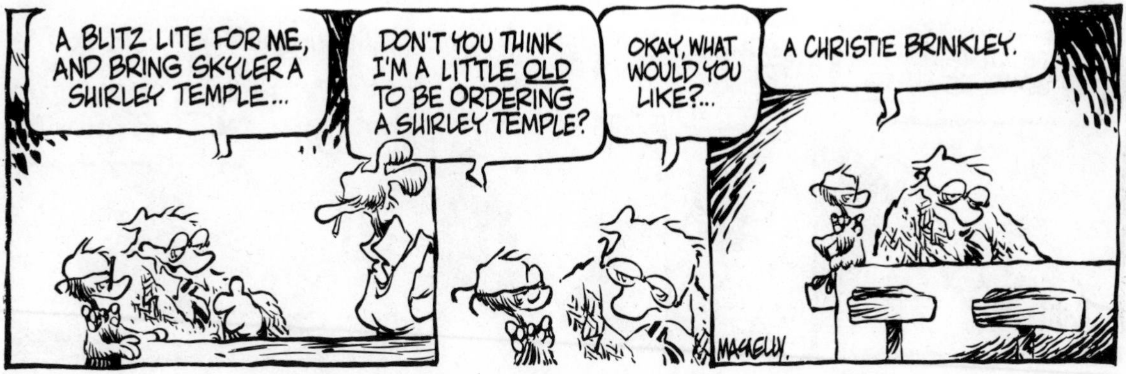

A BLITZ LITE FOR ME, AND BRING SKYLER A SHIRLEY TEMPLE...
DON'T YOU THINK I'M A LITTLE OLD TO BE ORDERING A SHIRLEY TEMPLE?
OKAY, WHAT WOULD YOU LIKE?...
A CHRISTIE BRINKLEY.
MACNELLY.

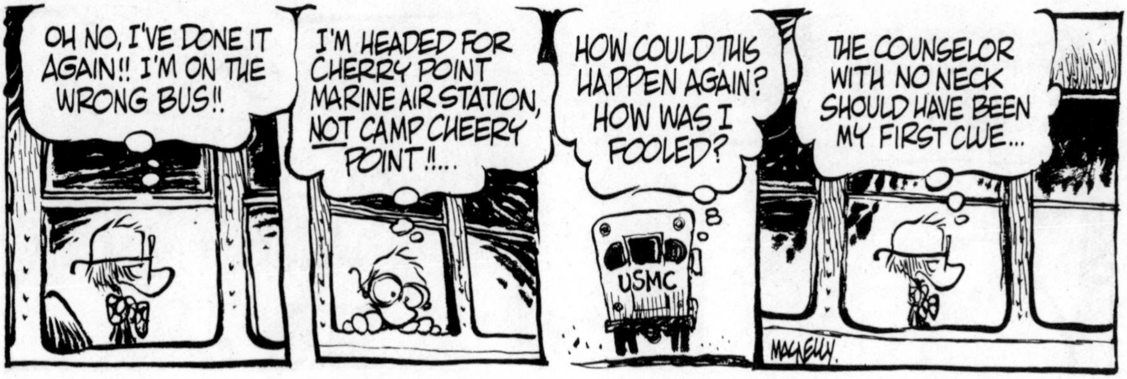
OH NO, I'VE DONE IT AGAIN!! I'M ON THE WRONG BUS!!
I'M HEADED FOR CHERRY POINT MARINE AIR STATION, NOT CAMP CHEERY POINT!!...
HOW COULD THIS HAPPEN AGAIN? HOW WAS I FOOLED?
USMC
THE COUNSELOR WITH NO NECK SHOULD HAVE BEEN MY FIRST CLUE...
MACNELLY.

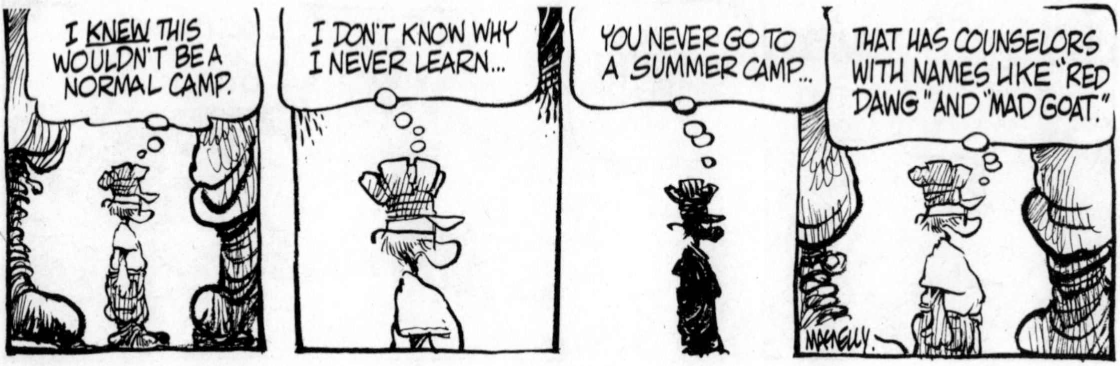
I KNEW THIS WOULDN'T BE A NORMAL CAMP.
I DON'T KNOW WHY I NEVER LEARN...
YOU NEVER GO TO A SUMMER CAMP...
THAT HAS COUNSELORS WITH NAMES LIKE "RED DAWG" AND "MAD GOAT."
MACNELLY.

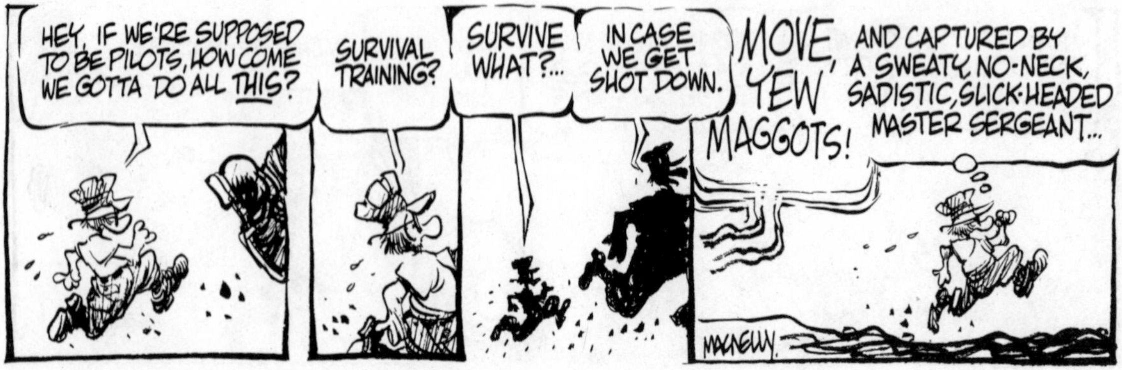
HEY, IF WE'RE SUPPOSED TO BE PILOTS, HOW COME WE GOTTA DO ALL THIS?
SURVIVAL TRAINING?
SURVIVE WHAT?...
IN CASE WE GET SHOT DOWN.
MOVE, YEW MAGGOTS!
AND CAPTURED BY A SWEATY, NO-NECK, SADISTIC, SLICK-HEADED MASTER SERGEANT...
MACNELLY.

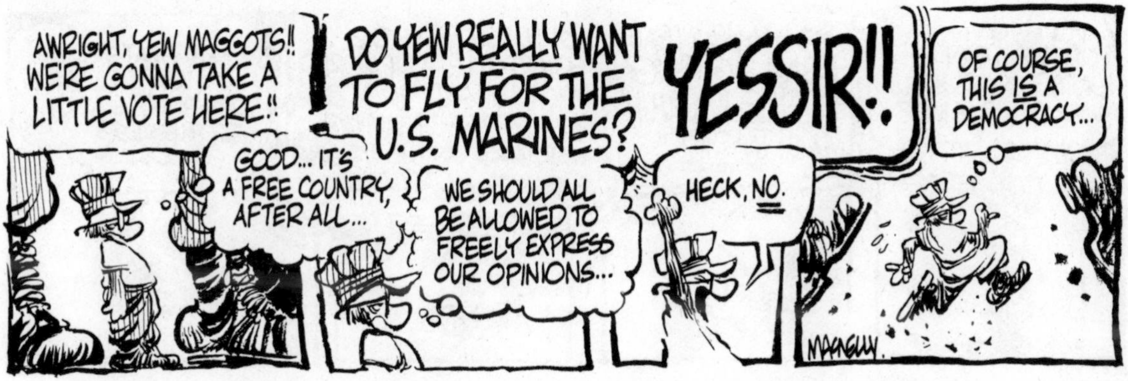
AWRIGHT, YEW MAGGOTS!! WE'RE GONNA TAKE A LITTLE VOTE HERE!!
GOOD... IT'S A FREE COUNTRY, AFTER ALL...
DO YEW REALLY WANT TO FLY FOR THE U.S. MARINES?
WE SHOULD ALL BE ALLOWED TO FREELY EXPRESS OUR OPINIONS...
YESSIR!!
HECK, NO.
OF COURSE, THIS IS A DEMOCRACY...
MACNELLY

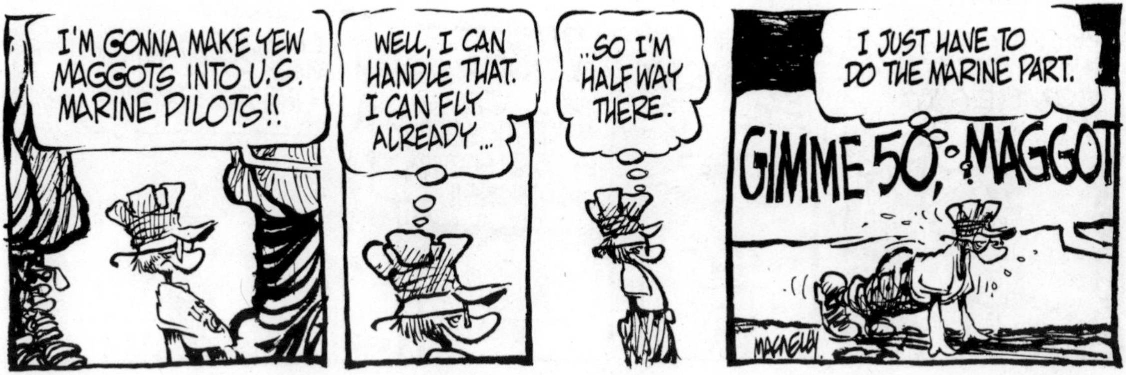
I'M GONNA MAKE YEW MAGGOTS INTO U.S. MARINE PILOTS!!
WELL, I CAN HANDLE THAT. I CAN FLY ALREADY...
...SO I'M HALFWAY THERE.
I JUST HAVE TO DO THE MARINE PART.
GIMME 50, MAGGOT
MACNELLY

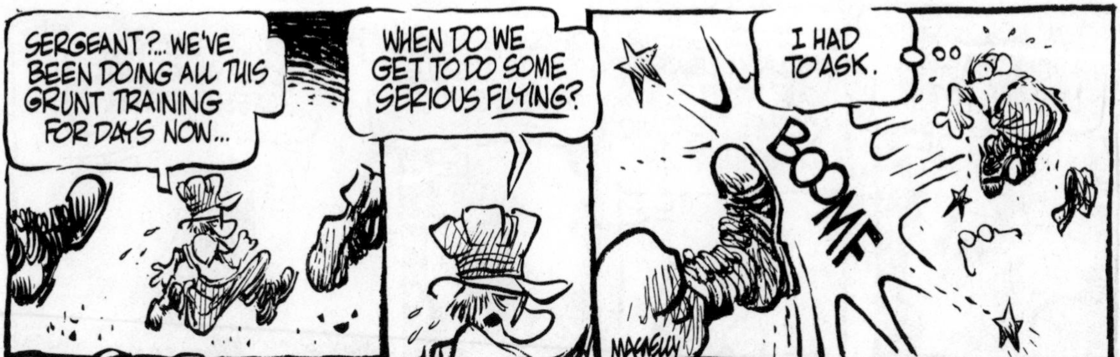
SERGEANT?... WE'VE BEEN DOING ALL THIS GRUNT TRAINING FOR DAYS NOW...
WHEN DO WE GET TO DO SOME SERIOUS FLYING?
BOOMF
I HAD TO ASK.
MACNELLY

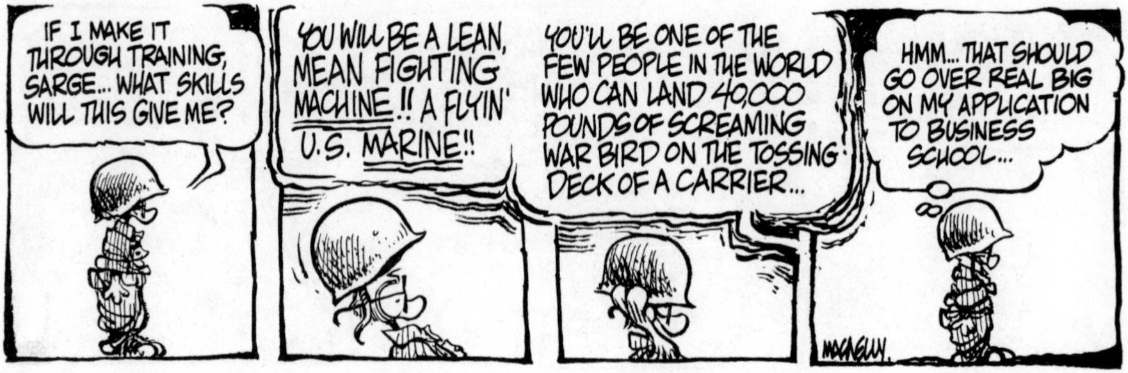
IF I MAKE IT THROUGH TRAINING, SARGE... WHAT SKILLS WILL THIS GIVE ME?
YOU WILL BE A LEAN, MEAN FIGHTING MACHINE!! A FLYIN' U.S. MARINE!!
YOU'LL BE ONE OF THE FEW PEOPLE IN THE WORLD WHO CAN LAND 40,000 POUNDS OF SCREAMING WAR BIRD ON THE TOSSING DECK OF A CARRIER...
HMM... THAT SHOULD GO OVER REAL BIG ON MY APPLICATION TO BUSINESS SCHOOL...
MACNELLY.

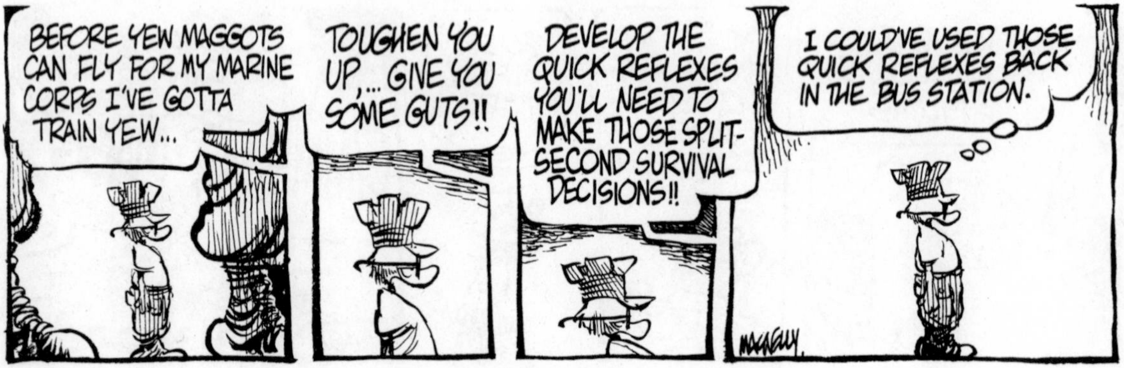
BEFORE YEW MAGGOTS CAN FLY FOR MY MARINE CORPS I'VE GOTTA TRAIN YEW...
TOUGHEN YOU UP,... GIVE YOU SOME GUTS!!
DEVELOP THE QUICK REFLEXES YOU'LL NEED TO MAKE THOSE SPLIT-SECOND SURVIVAL DECISIONS!!
I COULD'VE USED THOSE QUICK REFLEXES BACK IN THE BUS STATION.
MACNELLY.

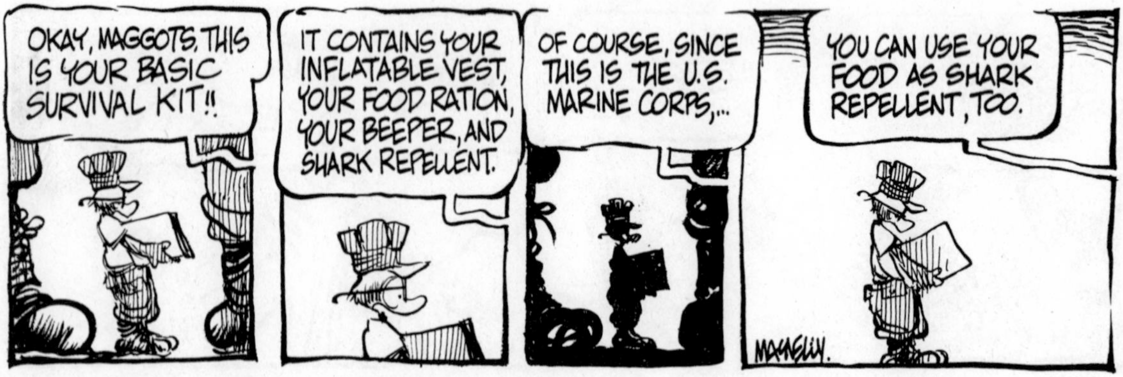
OKAY, MAGGOTS, THIS IS YOUR BASIC SURVIVAL KIT!!
IT CONTAINS YOUR INFLATABLE VEST, YOUR FOOD RATION, YOUR BEEPER, AND SHARK REPELLENT.
OF COURSE, SINCE THIS IS THE U.S. MARINE CORPS,...
YOU CAN USE YOUR FOOD AS SHARK REPELLENT, TOO.
MACNELLY.

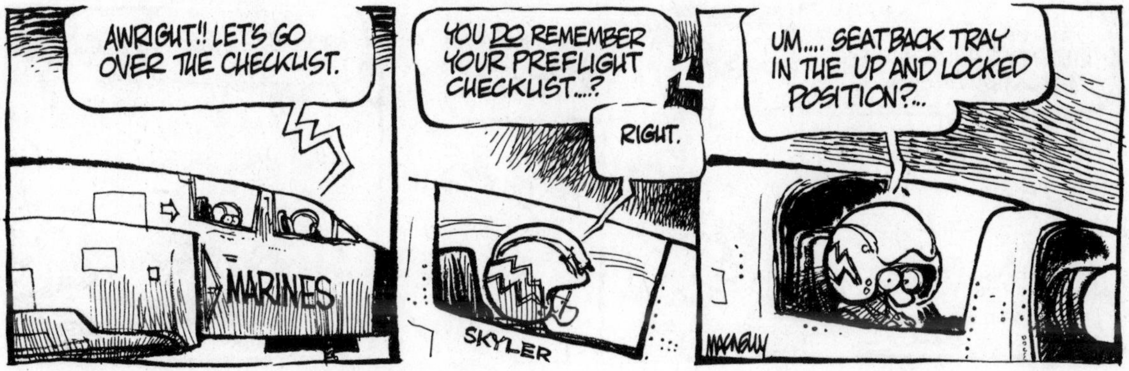
AWRIGHT!! LET'S GO OVER THE CHECKLIST.
MARINES
YOU DO REMEMBER YOUR PREFLIGHT CHECKLIST....?
RIGHT.
SKYLER
UM.... SEATBACK TRAY IN THE UP AND LOCKED POSITION?...
MACNELLY

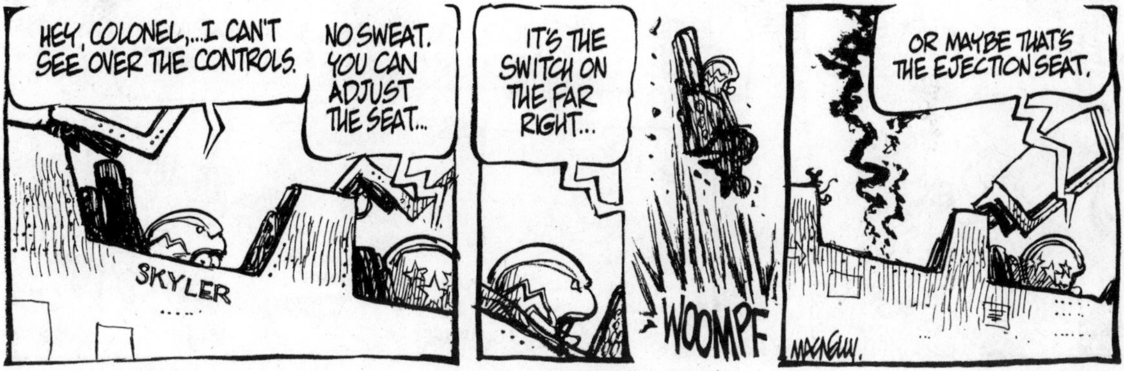
HEY, COLONEL,...I CAN'T SEE OVER THE CONTROLS.
NO SWEAT. YOU CAN ADJUST THE SEAT...
SKYLER
IT'S THE SWITCH ON THE FAR RIGHT...
WOOMPF
OR MAYBE THAT'S THE EJECTION SEAT.
MACNELLY.

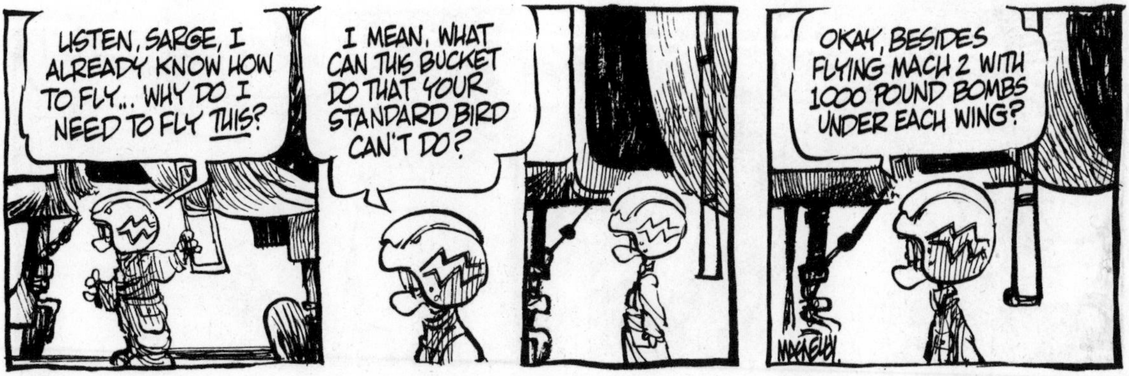
LISTEN, SARGE, I ALREADY KNOW HOW TO FLY... WHY DO I NEED TO FLY THIS?
I MEAN, WHAT CAN THIS BUCKET DO THAT YOUR STANDARD BIRD CAN'T DO?
OKAY, BESIDES FLYING MACH 2 WITH 1000 POUND BOMBS UNDER EACH WING?
MACNELLY.

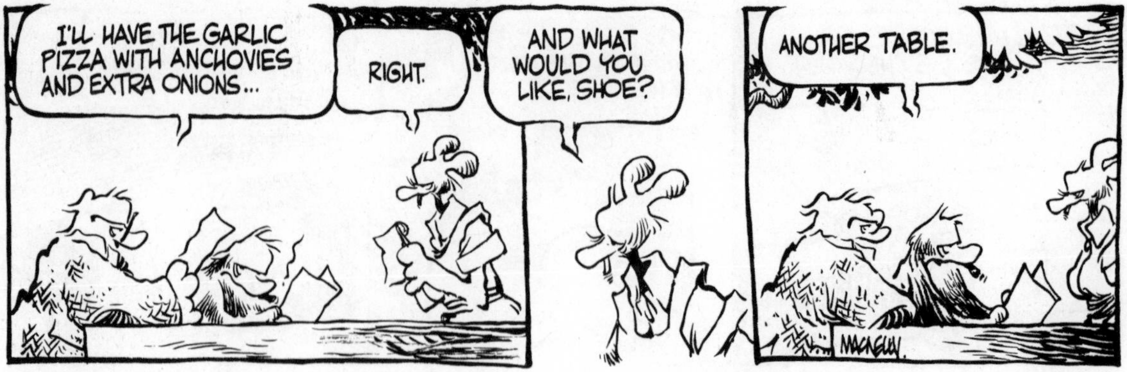
I'LL HAVE THE GARLIC PIZZA WITH ANCHOVIES AND EXTRA ONIONS...
RIGHT.
AND WHAT WOULD YOU LIKE, SHOE?
ANOTHER TABLE.
MACNELLY

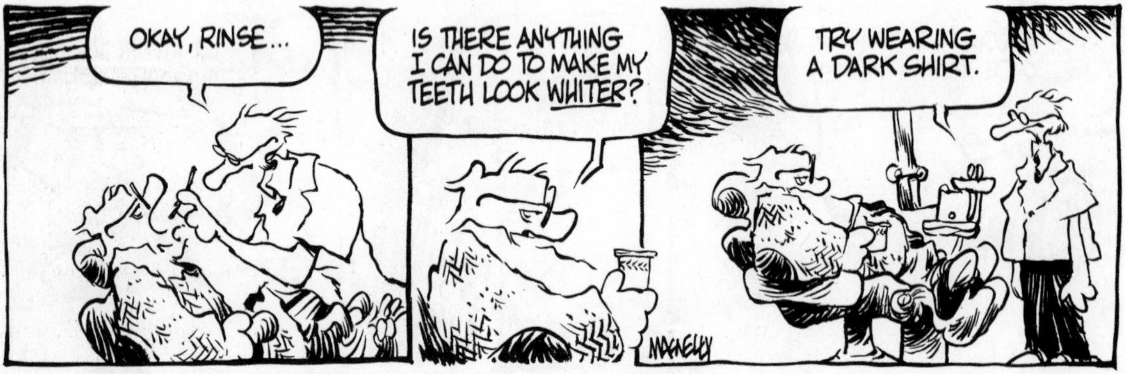
OKAY, RINSE...
IS THERE ANYTHING I CAN DO TO MAKE MY TEETH LOOK WHITER?
TRY WEARING A DARK SHIRT.
MACNELLY

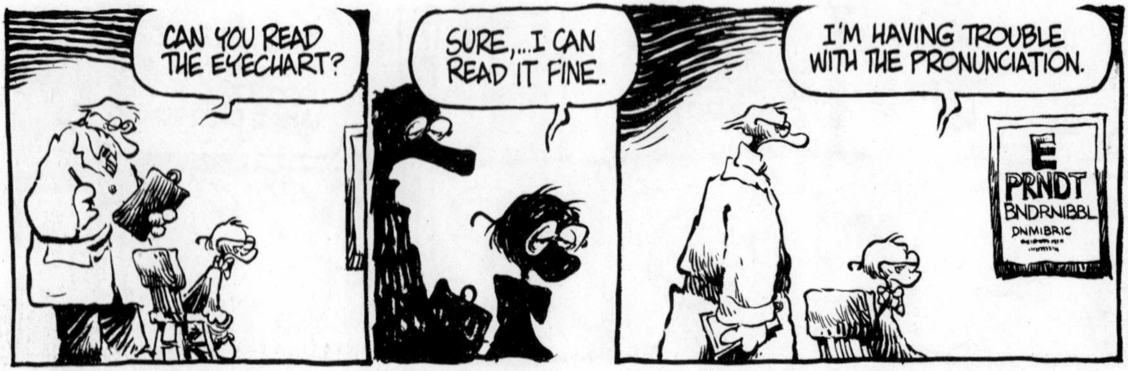
CAN YOU READ THE EYECHART?
SURE,...I CAN READ IT FINE.
I'M HAVING TROUBLE WITH THE PRONUNCIATION.
E
PRNDT
BNDRNIBBL
DNMIBRIC

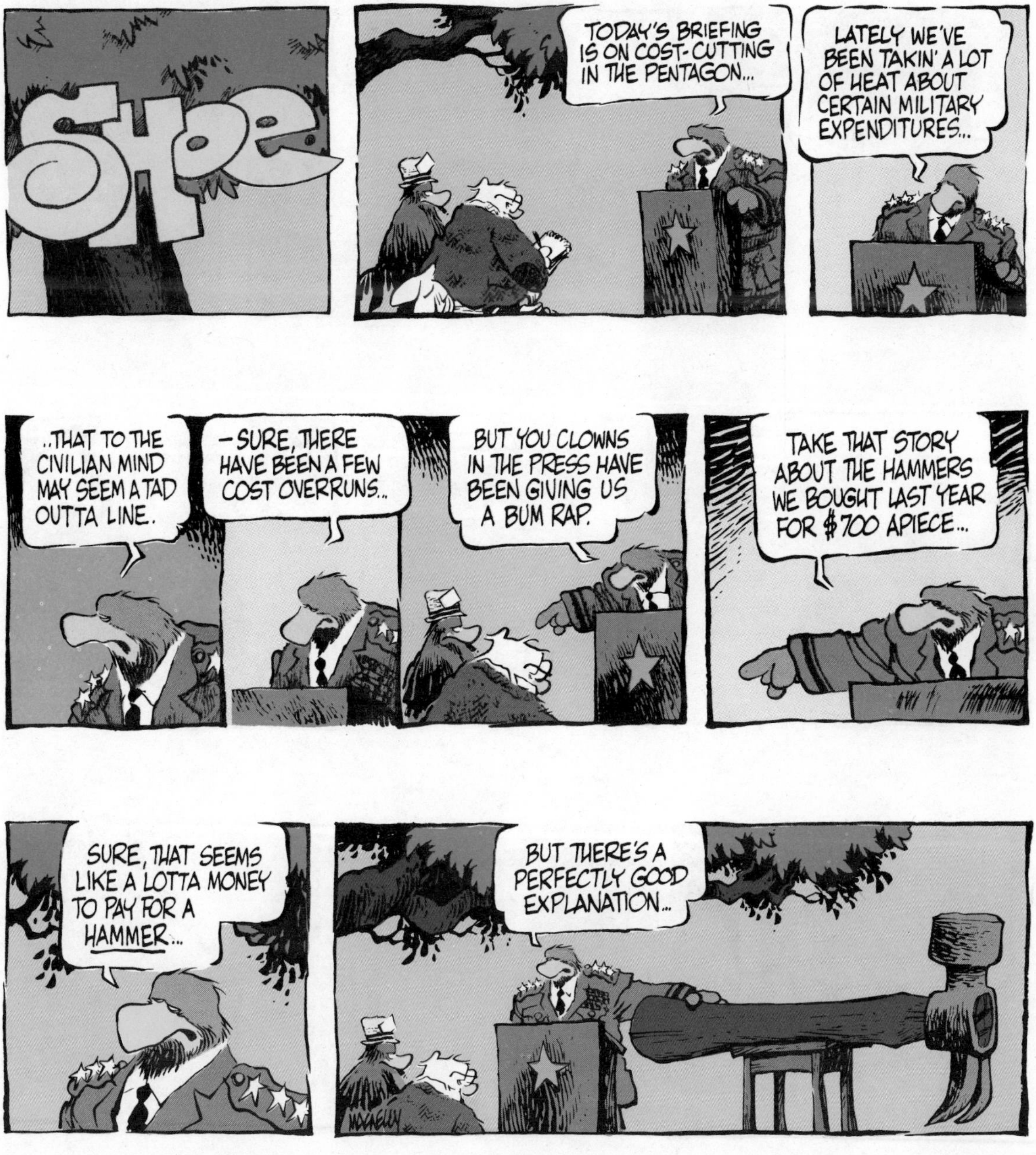
SHOE
TODAY'S BRIEFING IS ON COST-CUTTING IN THE PENTAGON...
LATELY WE'VE BEEN TAKIN' A LOT OF HEAT ABOUT CERTAIN MILITARY EXPENDITURES...
..THAT TO THE CIVILIAN MIND MAY SEEM A TAD OUTTA LINE.
-SURE, THERE HAVE BEEN A FEW COST OVERRUNS..
BUT YOU CLOWNS IN THE PRESS HAVE BEEN GIVING US A BUM RAP.
TAKE THAT STORY ABOUT THE HAMMERS WE BOUGHT LAST YEAR FOR $700 APIECE...
SURE, THAT SEEMS LIKE A LOTTA MONEY TO PAY FOR A HAMMER...
BUT THERE'S A PERFECTLY GOOD EXPLANATION...
MACNELLY

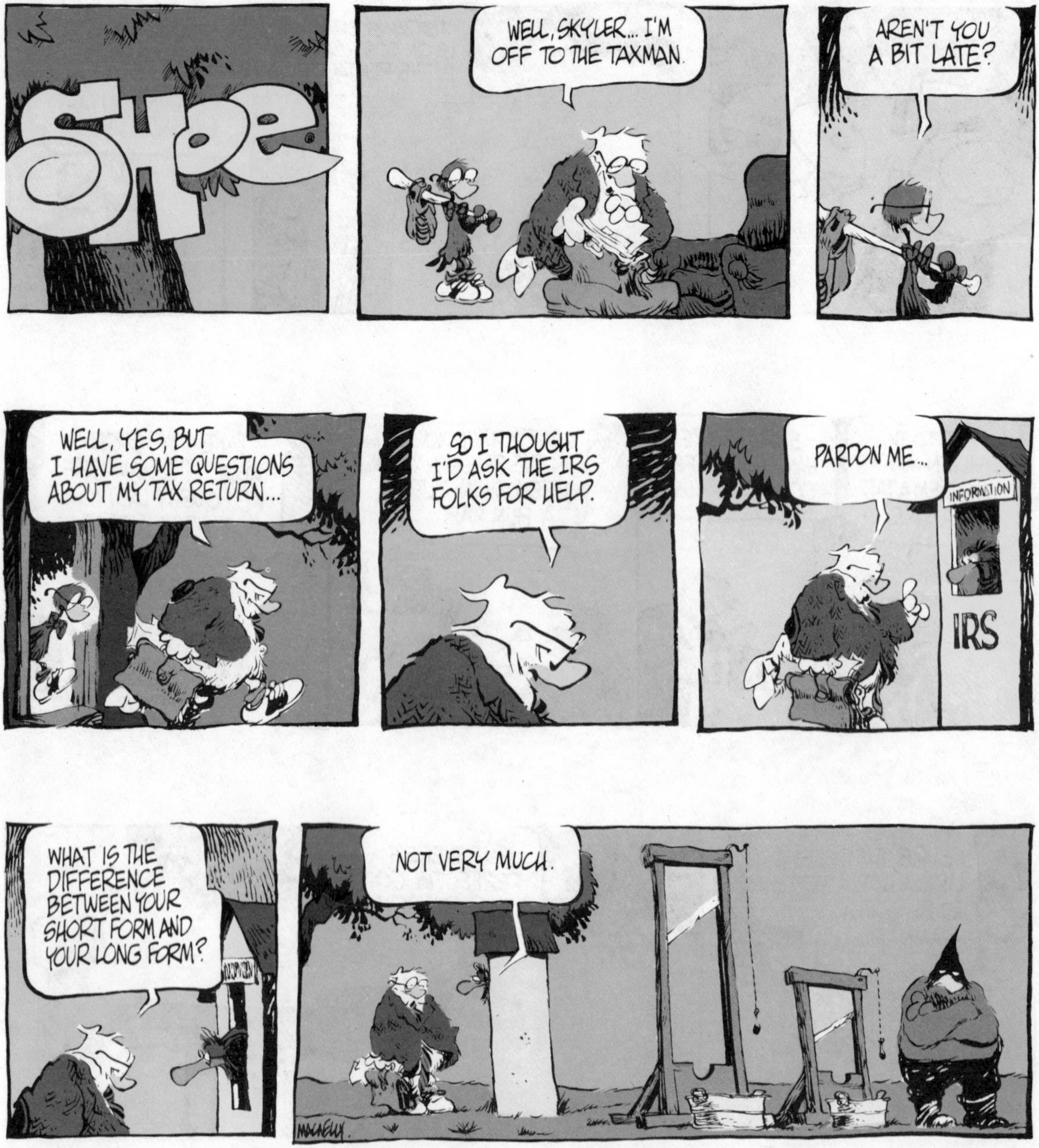
SHOE
WELL, SKYLER... I'M OFF TO THE TAXMAN.
AREN'T YOU A BIT LATE?
WELL, YES, BUT I HAVE SOME QUESTIONS ABOUT MY TAX RETURN...
SO I THOUGHT I'D ASK THE IRS FOLKS FOR HELP.
PARDON ME...
INFORMATION
IRS
WHAT IS THE DIFFERENCE BETWEEN YOUR SHORT FORM AND YOUR LONG FORM?
NOT VERY MUCH.
MACNELLY

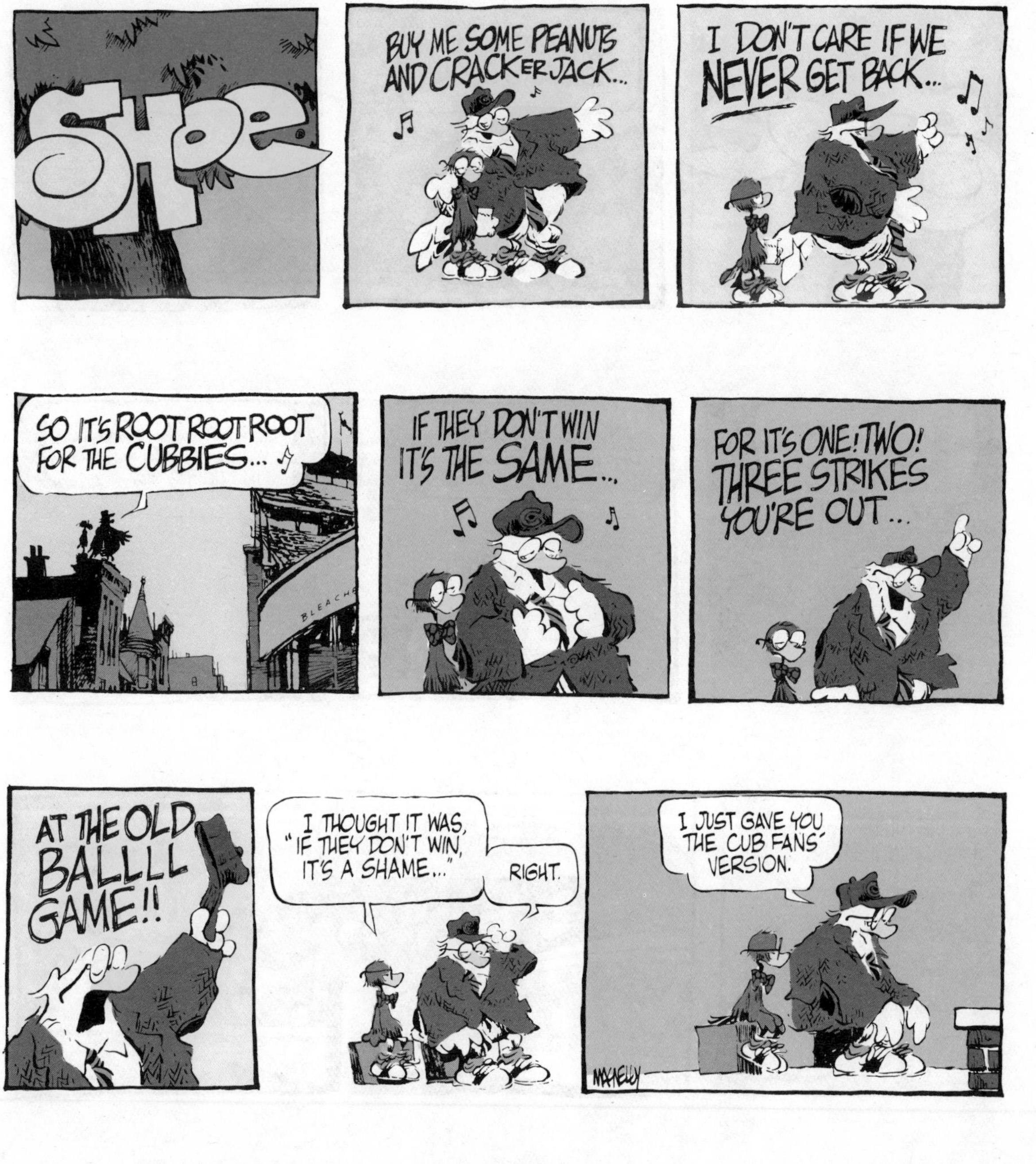
SHOE
BUY ME SOME PEANUTS AND CRACKER JACK...
I DON'T CARE IF WE NEVER GET BACK...
SO IT'S ROOT ROOT ROOT FOR THE CUBBIES...
BLEACH
IF THEY DON'T WIN IT'S THE SAME...
FOR IT'S ONE! TWO! THREE STRIKES YOU'RE OUT...
AT THE OLD BALLLL GAME!!
I THOUGHT IT WAS, "IF THEY DON'T WIN, IT'S A SHAME..."
RIGHT.
I JUST GAVE YOU THE CUB FANS' VERSION.
MACNELLY

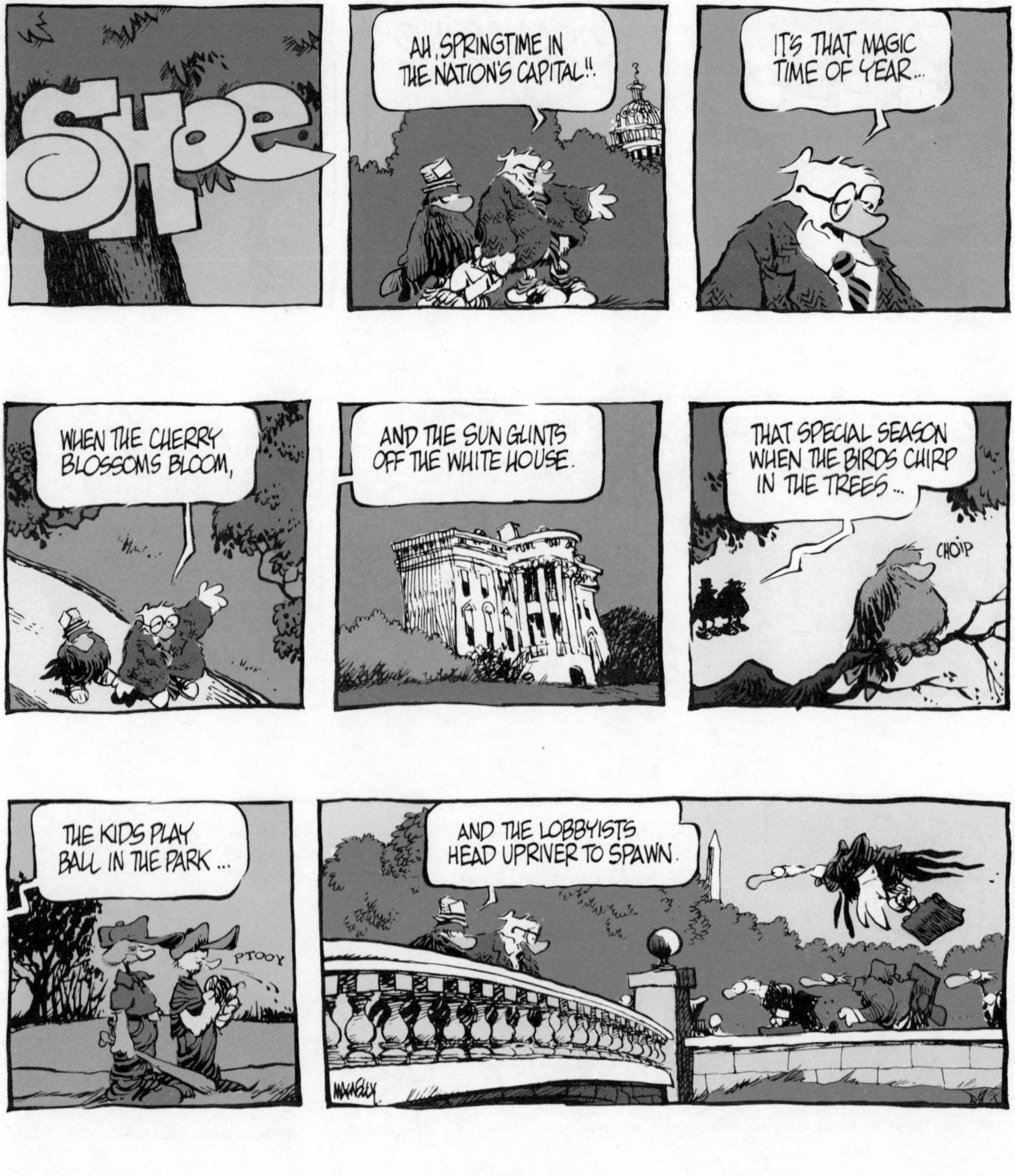

SHOE
AH, SPRINGTIME IN THE NATION'S CAPITAL!!
IT'S THAT MAGIC TIME OF YEAR...
WHEN THE CHERRY BLOSSOMS BLOOM,
AND THE SUN GLINTS OFF THE WHITE HOUSE.
THAT SPECIAL SEASON WHEN THE BIRDS CHIRP IN THE TREES...
CHOIP
THE KIDS PLAY BALL IN THE PARK...
PTOOY
AND THE LOBBYISTS HEAD UPRIVER TO SPAWN.
MACNELLY

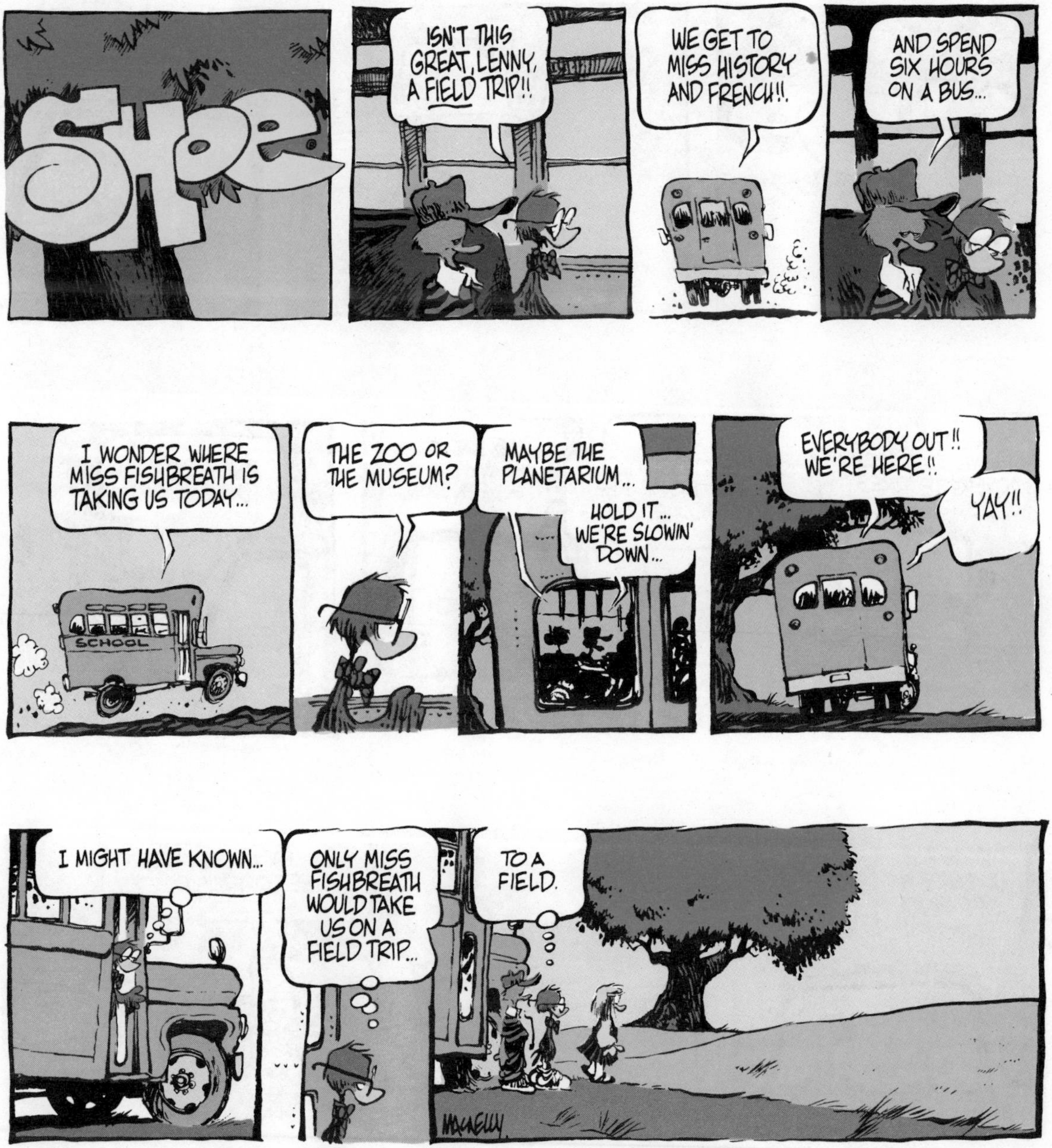
SHOE
ISN'T THIS GREAT, LENNY, A FIELD TRIP!!
WE GET TO MISS HISTORY AND FRENCH!!
AND SPEND SIX HOURS ON A BUS...
I WONDER WHERE MISS FISHBREATH IS TAKING US TODAY...
SCHOOL
THE ZOO OR THE MUSEUM?
MAYBE THE PLANETARIUM...
HOLD IT... WE'RE SLOWIN' DOWN...
EVERYBODY OUT!! WE'RE HERE!!
YAY!!
I MIGHT HAVE KNOWN...
ONLY MISS FISHBREATH WOULD TAKE US ON A FIELD TRIP...
TO A FIELD.
MACNELLY

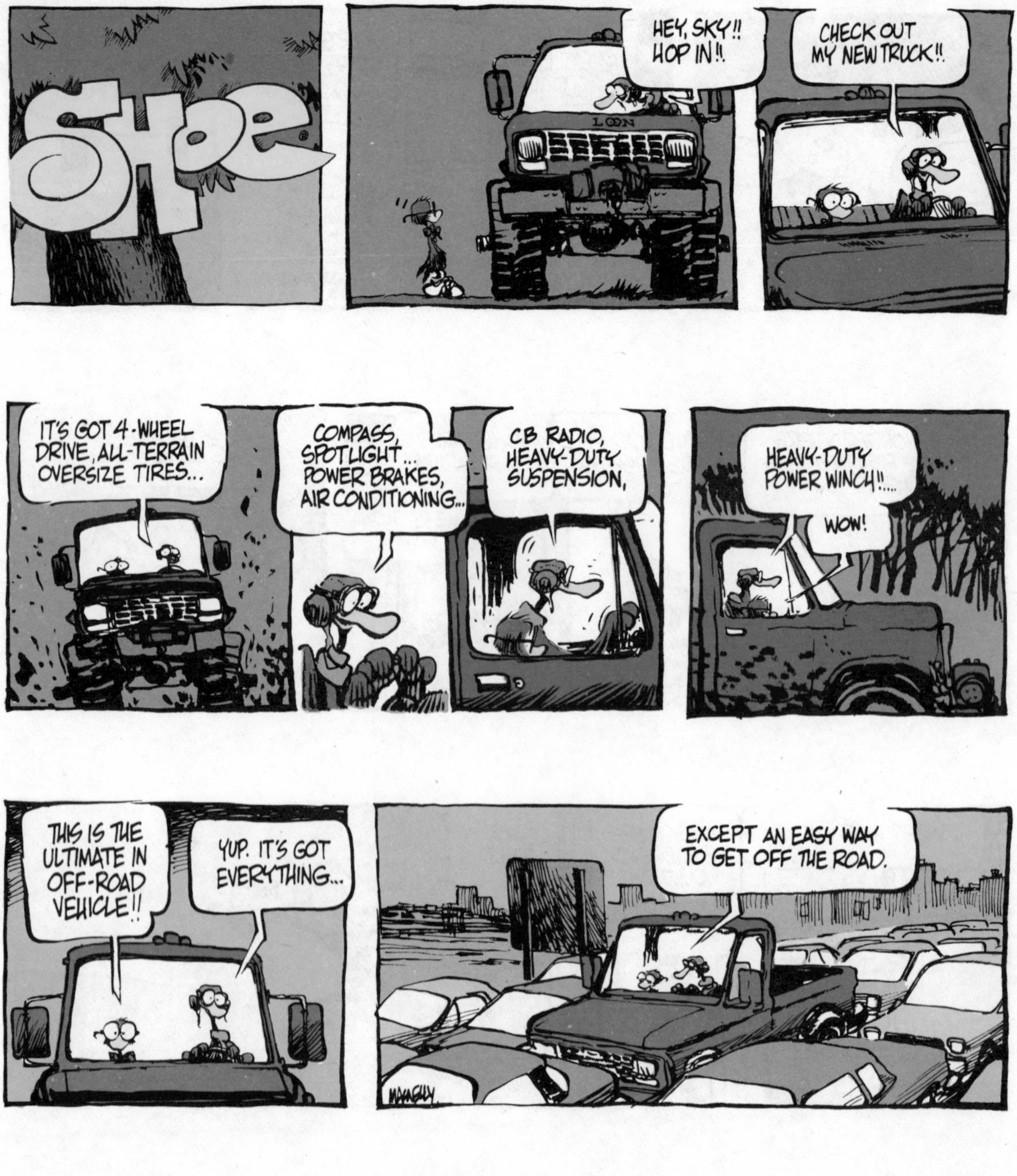
SHOE®
HEY, SKY!! HOP IN!!
CHECK OUT MY NEW TRUCK!!
IT'S GOT 4-WHEEL DRIVE, ALL-TERRAIN OVERSIZE TIRES...
COMPASS, SPOTLIGHT... POWER BRAKES, AIR CONDITIONING...
CB RADIO, HEAVY-DUTY SUSPENSION,
HEAVY-DUTY POWER WINCH!!....
WOW!
THIS IS THE ULTIMATE IN OFF-ROAD VEHICLE!!
YUP. IT'S GOT EVERYTHING...
EXCEPT AN EASY WAY TO GET OFF THE ROAD.
MACNELLY

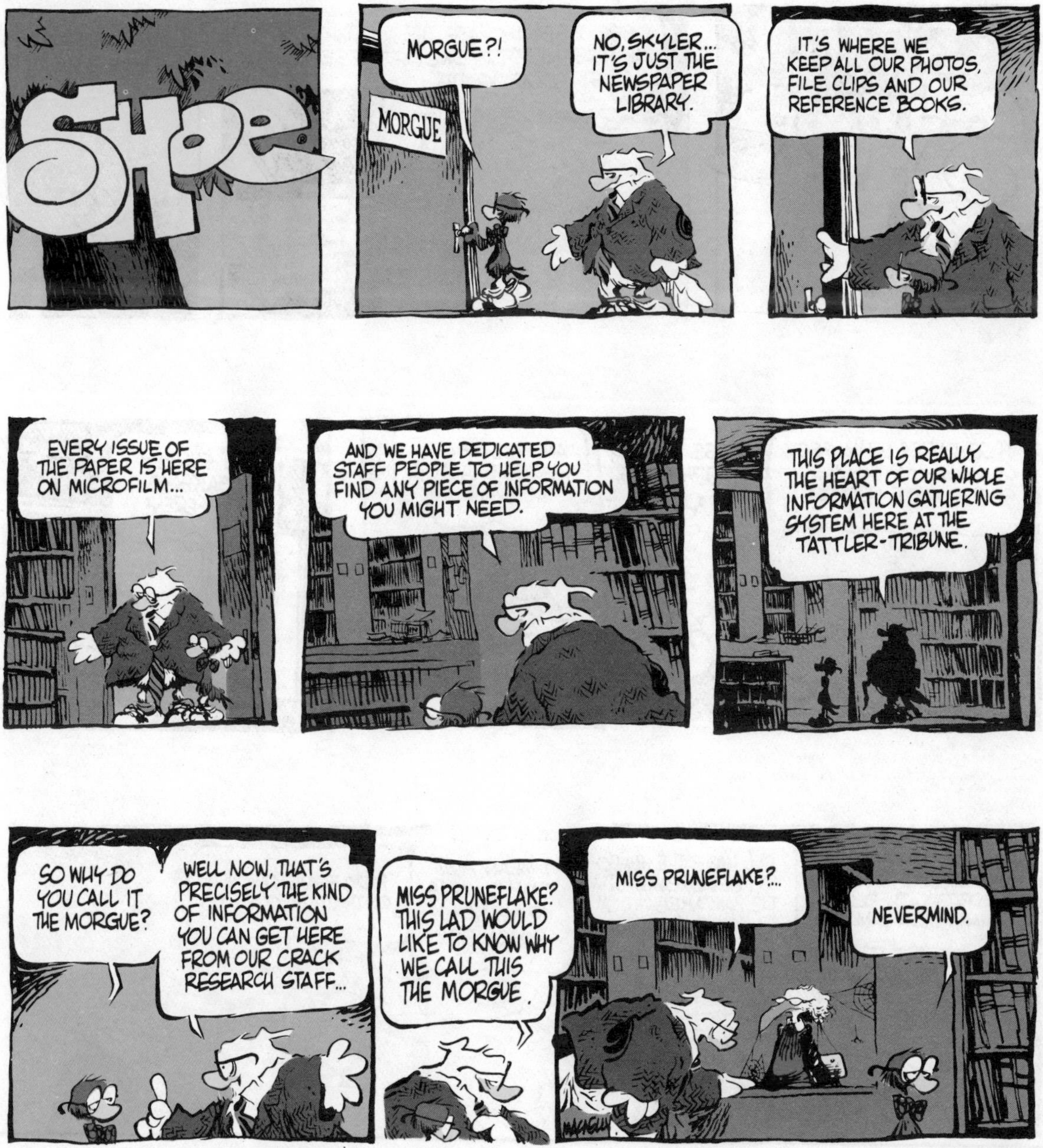

SHOE
MORGUE?!
MORGUE
NO, SKYLER... IT'S JUST THE NEWSPAPER LIBRARY.
IT'S WHERE WE KEEP ALL OUR PHOTOS, FILE CLIPS AND OUR REFERENCE BOOKS.
EVERY ISSUE OF THE PAPER IS HERE ON MICROFILM...
AND WE HAVE DEDICATED STAFF PEOPLE TO HELP YOU FIND ANY PIECE OF INFORMATION YOU MIGHT NEED.
THIS PLACE IS REALLY THE HEART OF OUR WHOLE INFORMATION GATHERING SYSTEM HERE AT THE TATTLER-TRIBUNE.
SO WHY DO YOU CALL IT THE MORGUE?
WELL NOW, THAT'S PRECISELY THE KIND OF INFORMATION YOU CAN GET HERE FROM OUR CRACK RESEARCH STAFF...
MISS PRUNEFLAKE? THIS LAD WOULD LIKE TO KNOW WHY WE CALL THIS THE MORGUE.
MISS PRUNEFLAKE?...
NEVERMIND.
MACNELLY

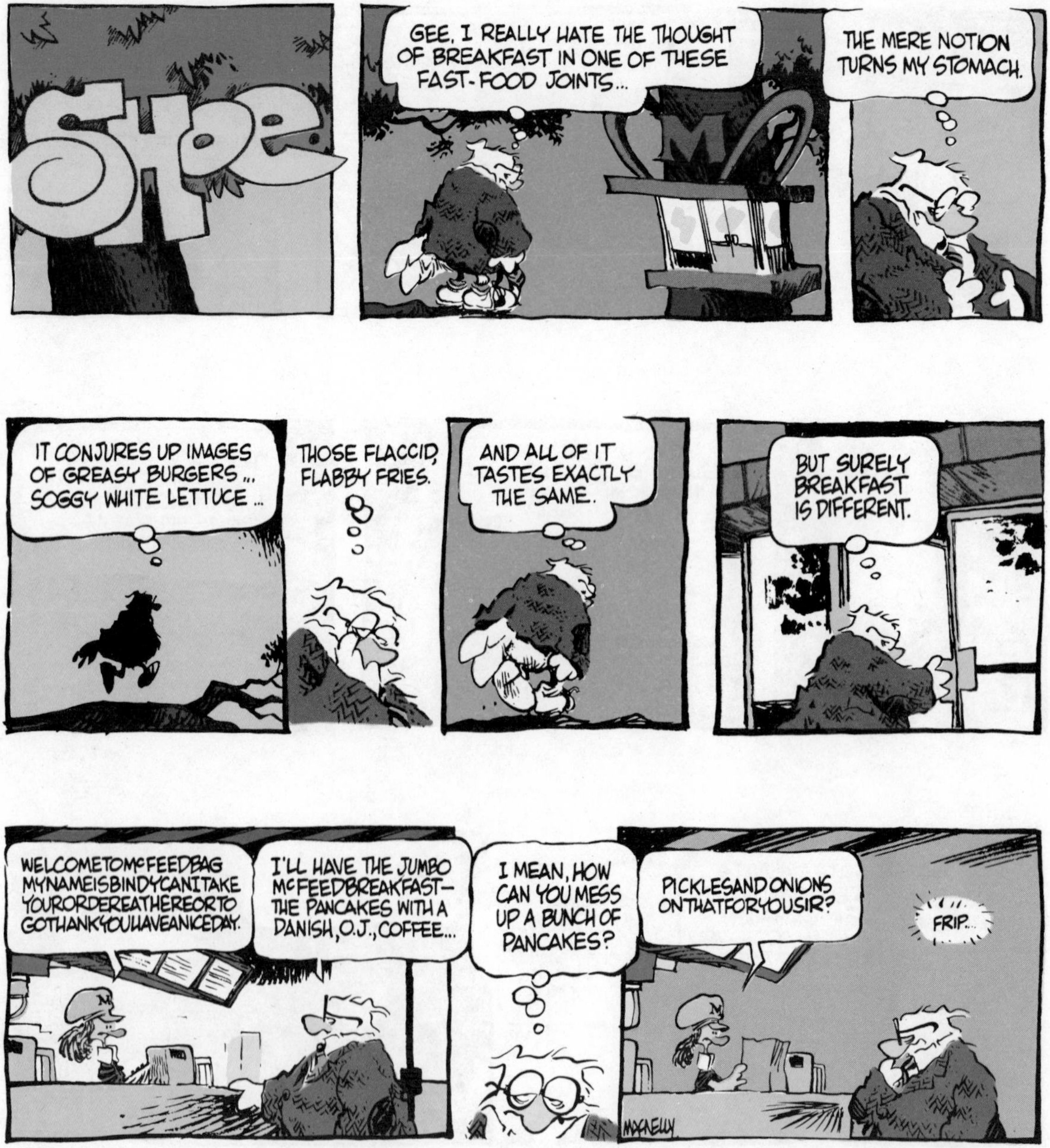
SHOE
GEE, I REALLY HATE THE THOUGHT OF BREAKFAST IN ONE OF THESE FAST-FOOD JOINTS...
THE MERE NOTION TURNS MY STOMACH.
IT CONJURES UP IMAGES OF GREASY BURGERS ... SOGGY WHITE LETTUCE ...
THOSE FLACCID, FLABBY FRIES.
AND ALL OF IT TASTES EXACTLY THE SAME.
BUT SURELY BREAKFAST IS DIFFERENT.
WELCOMETOMcFEEDBAG MYNAMEISBINDYCANITAKE YOURORDEREATHEREORTO GOTHANKYOUHAVEANICEDAY.
I'LL HAVE THE JUMBO McFEEDBREAKFAST— THE PANCAKES WITH A DANISH, O.J., COFFEE...
I MEAN, HOW CAN YOU MESS UP A BUNCH OF PANCAKES?
PICKLESANDONIONS ONTHATFORYOUSIR?
FRIP...
MACNELLY

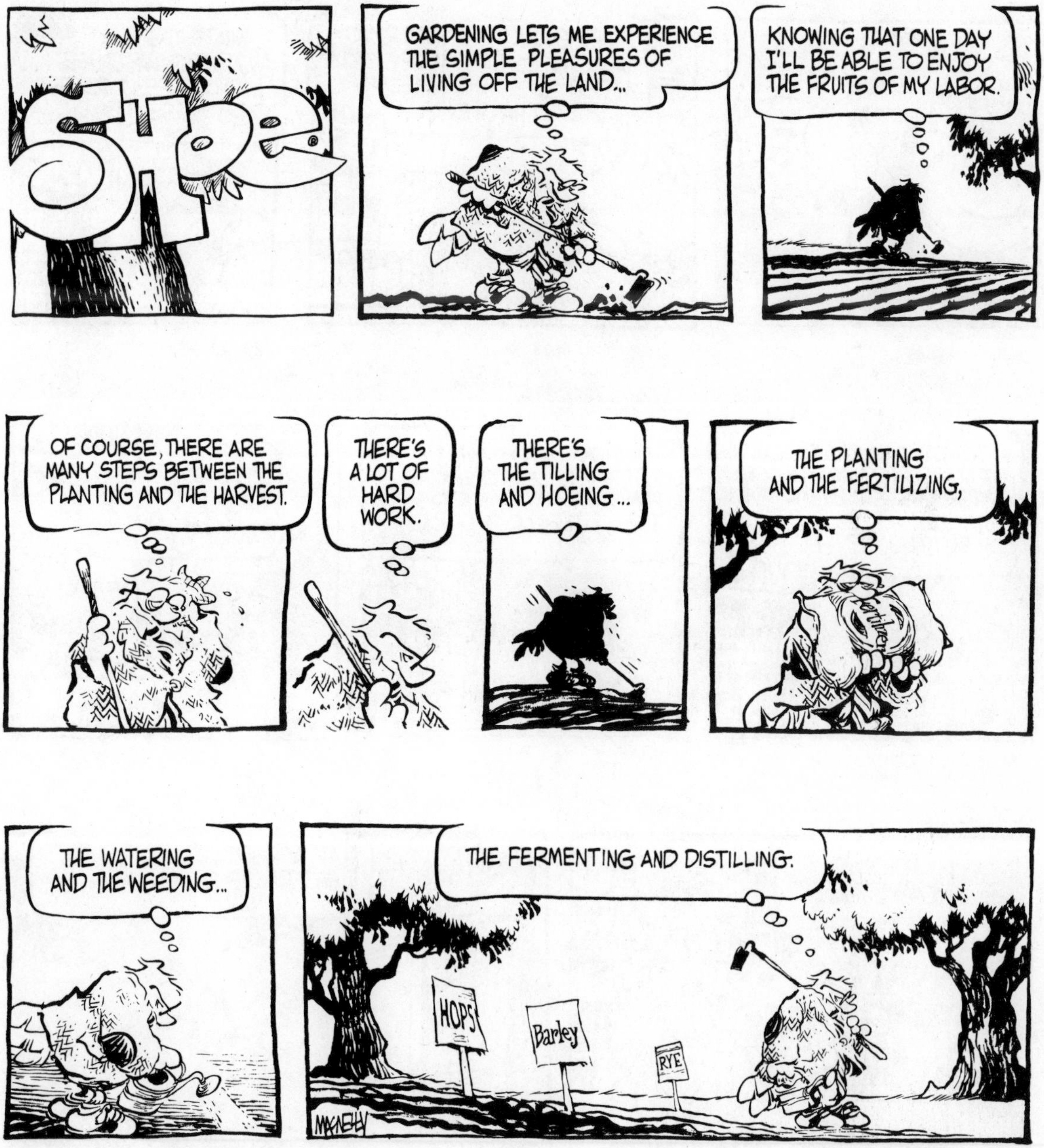
SHOE
GARDENING LETS ME EXPERIENCE THE SIMPLE PLEASURES OF LIVING OFF THE LAND...
KNOWING THAT ONE DAY I'LL BE ABLE TO ENJOY THE FRUITS OF MY LABOR.
OF COURSE, THERE ARE MANY STEPS BETWEEN THE PLANTING AND THE HARVEST.
THERE'S A LOT OF HARD WORK.
THERE'S THE TILLING AND HOEING...
THE PLANTING AND THE FERTILIZING,
Fertilizer
THE WATERING AND THE WEEDING...
THE FERMENTING AND DISTILLING.
HOPS
Barley
RYE
MACNELLY

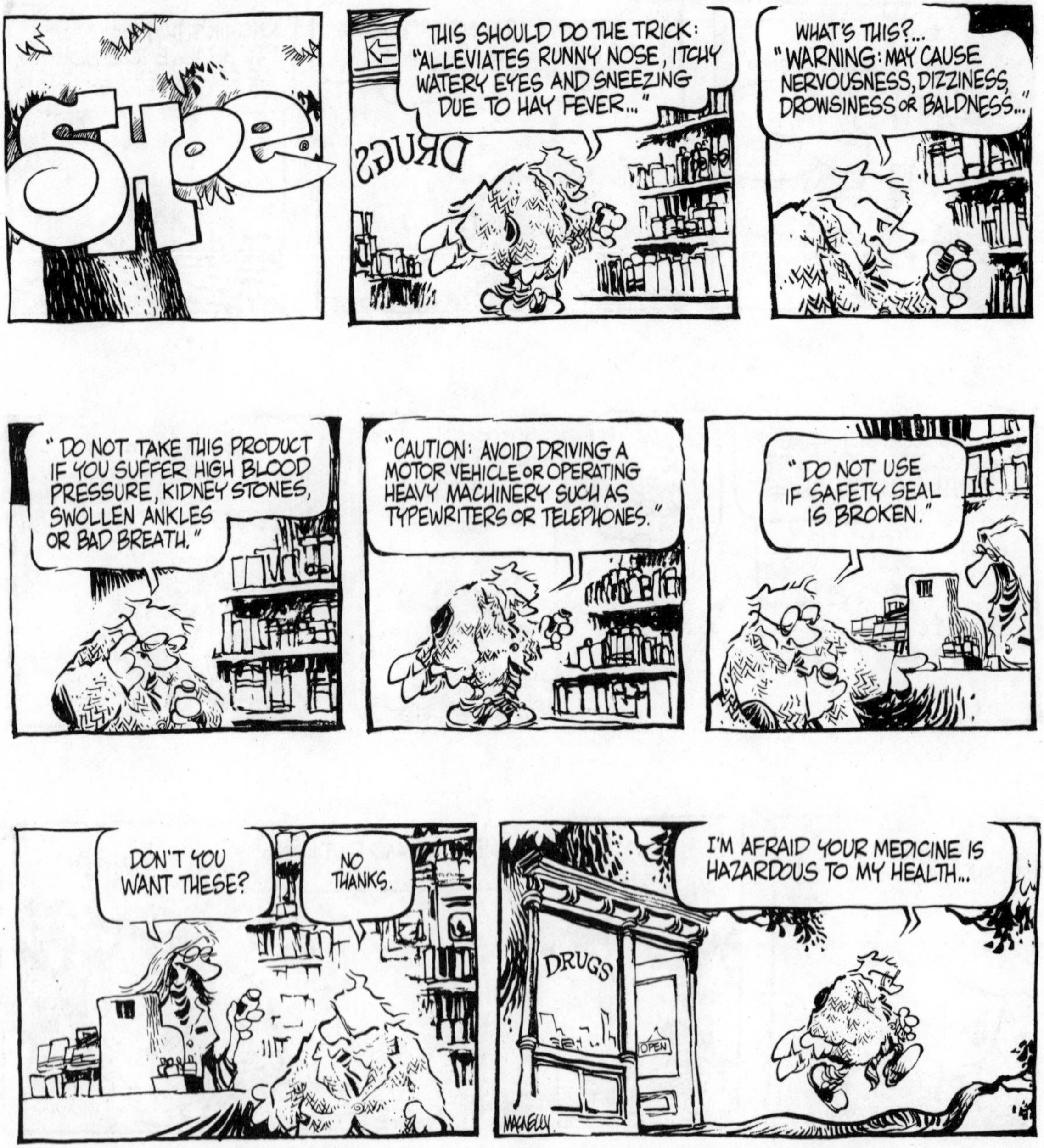
SHOE®
THIS SHOULD DO THE TRICK: "ALLEVIATES RUNNY NOSE, ITCHY WATERY EYES AND SNEEZING DUE TO HAY FEVER..."
DRUGS
WHAT'S THIS?... "WARNING: MAY CAUSE NERVOUSNESS, DIZZINESS, DROWSINESS OR BALDNESS..."
"DO NOT TAKE THIS PRODUCT IF YOU SUFFER HIGH BLOOD PRESSURE, KIDNEY STONES, SWOLLEN ANKLES OR BAD BREATH."
"CAUTION: AVOID DRIVING A MOTOR VEHICLE OR OPERATING HEAVY MACHINERY SUCH AS TYPEWRITERS OR TELEPHONES."
"DO NOT USE IF SAFETY SEAL IS BROKEN."
DON'T YOU WANT THESE?
NO THANKS.
I'M AFRAID YOUR MEDICINE IS HAZARDOUS TO MY HEALTH...
DRUGS
OPEN
MACNELLY

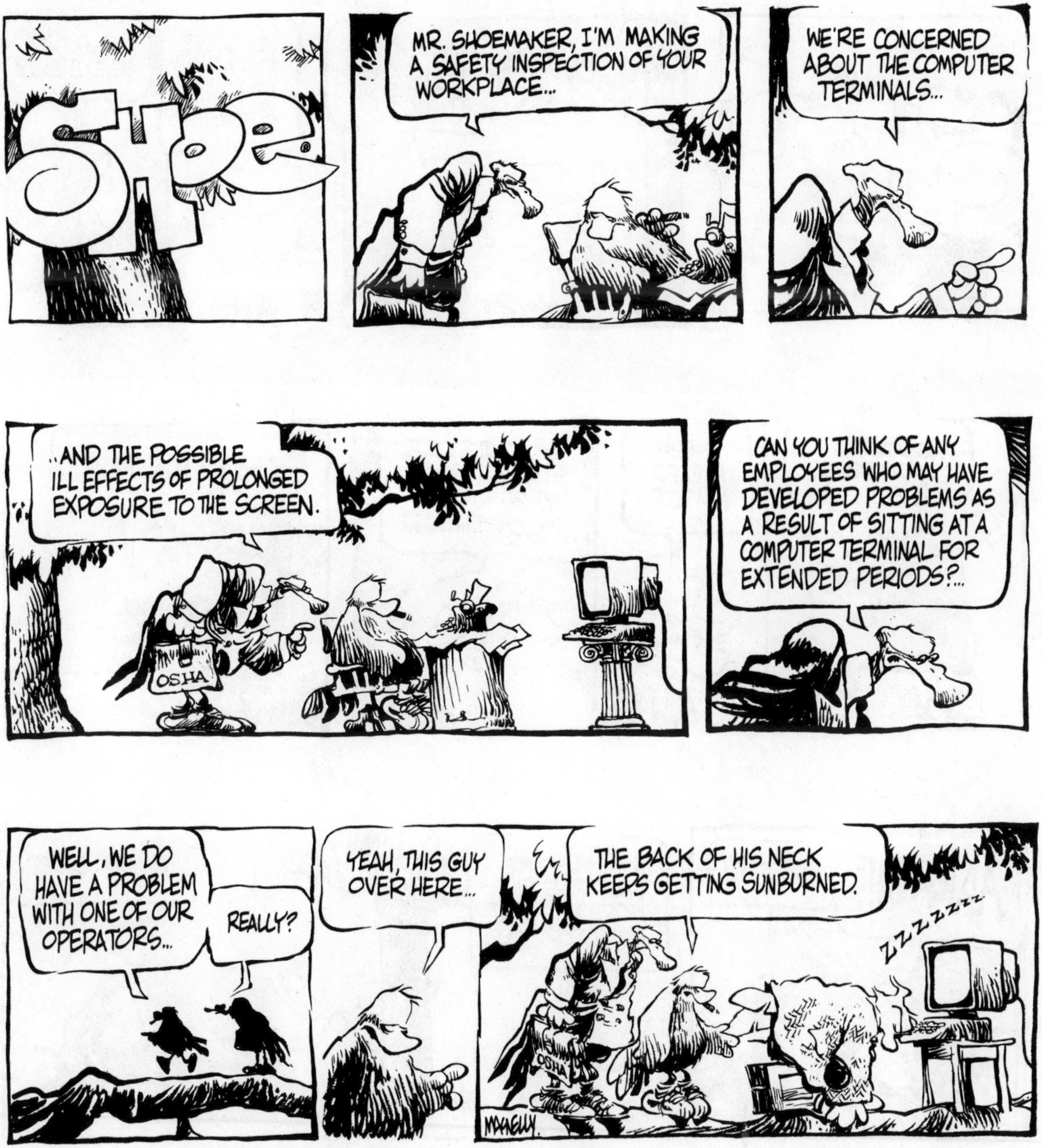
SHOE
MR. SHOEMAKER, I'M MAKING A SAFETY INSPECTION OF YOUR WORKPLACE...
WE'RE CONCERNED ABOUT THE COMPUTER TERMINALS...
..AND THE POSSIBLE ILL EFFECTS OF PROLONGED EXPOSURE TO THE SCREEN.
OSHA
CAN YOU THINK OF ANY EMPLOYEES WHO MAY HAVE DEVELOPED PROBLEMS AS A RESULT OF SITTING AT A COMPUTER TERMINAL FOR EXTENDED PERIODS?...
WELL, WE DO HAVE A PROBLEM WITH ONE OF OUR OPERATORS...
REALLY?
YEAH, THIS GUY OVER HERE...
THE BACK OF HIS NECK KEEPS GETTING SUNBURNED.
ZZZZZZZ
OSHA
MACNELLY

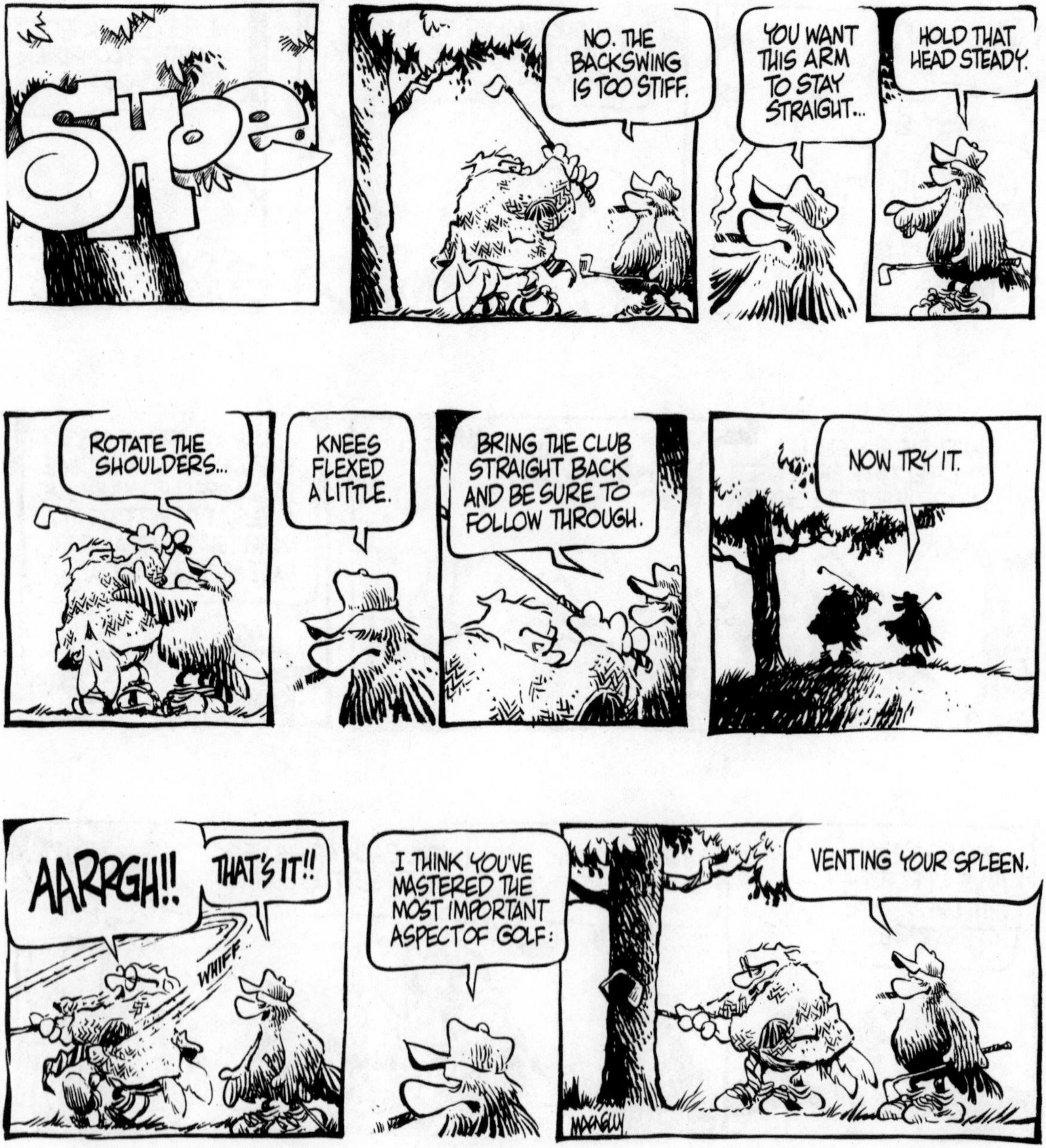
SHOE
NO. THE BACKSWING IS TOO STIFF.
YOU WANT THIS ARM TO STAY STRAIGHT...
HOLD THAT HEAD STEADY.
ROTATE THE SHOULDERS...
KNEES FLEXED A LITTLE.
BRING THE CLUB STRAIGHT BACK AND BE SURE TO FOLLOW THROUGH.
NOW TRY IT.
AARRGH!!
THAT'S IT!!
WHIFF
I THINK YOU'VE MASTERED THE MOST IMPORTANT ASPECT OF GOLF:
VENTING YOUR SPLEEN.
MACNELLY

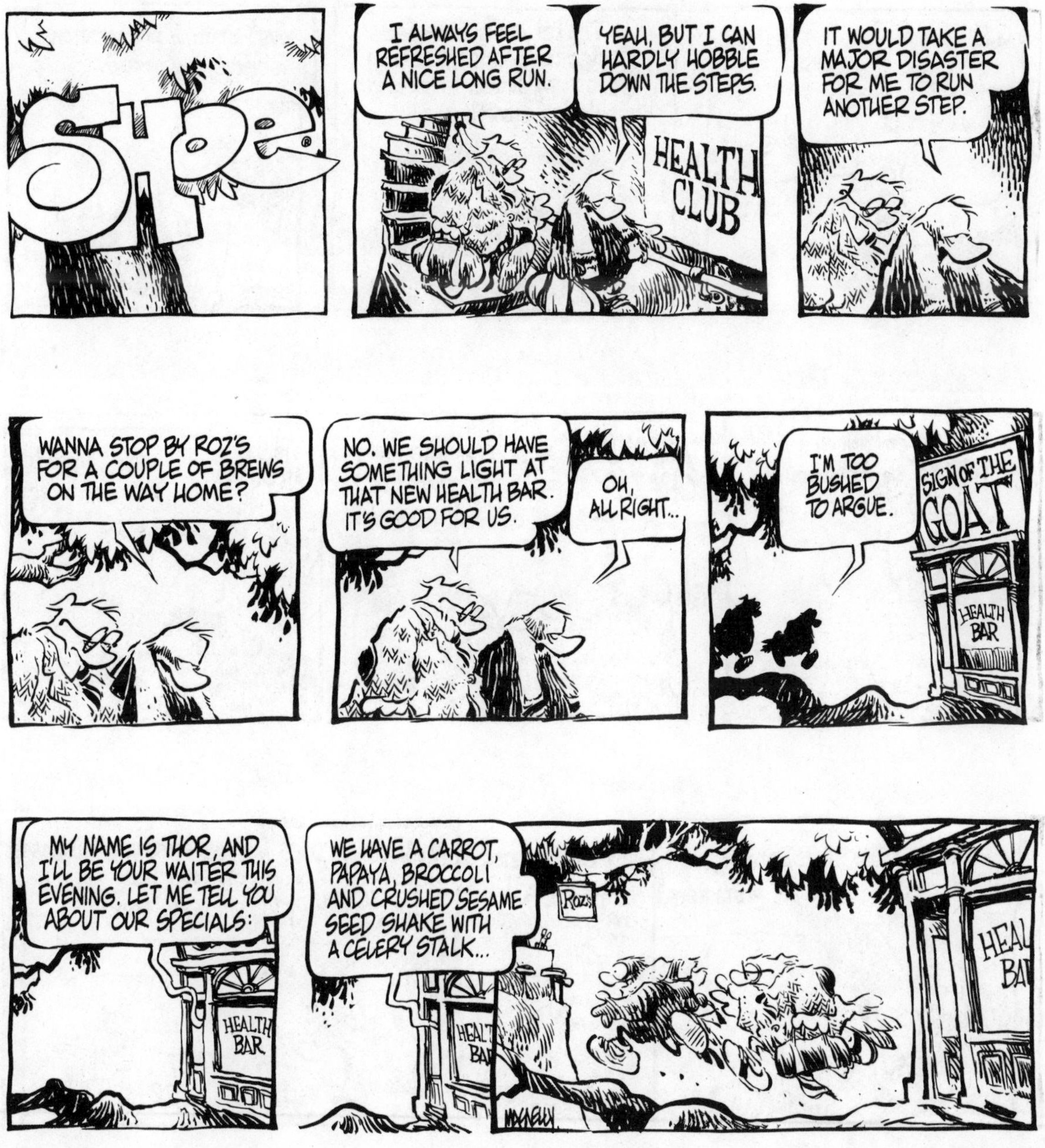
SHOE®
I ALWAYS FEEL REFRESHED AFTER A NICE LONG RUN.
YEAH, BUT I CAN HARDLY HOBBLE DOWN THE STEPS.
HEALTH CLUB
IT WOULD TAKE A MAJOR DISASTER FOR ME TO RUN ANOTHER STEP.
WANNA STOP BY ROZ'S FOR A COUPLE OF BREWS ON THE WAY HOME?
NO. WE SHOULD HAVE SOMETHING LIGHT AT THAT NEW HEALTH BAR. IT'S GOOD FOR US.
OH, ALL RIGHT...
I'M TOO BUSHED TO ARGUE.
SIGN OF THE GOAT
HEALTH BAR
MY NAME IS THOR, AND I'LL BE YOUR WAITER THIS EVENING. LET ME TELL YOU ABOUT OUR SPECIALS:
HEALTH BAR
WE HAVE A CARROT, PAPAYA, BROCCOLI AND CRUSHED SESAME SEED SHAKE WITH A CELERY STALK...
ROZ'S
MACNELLY

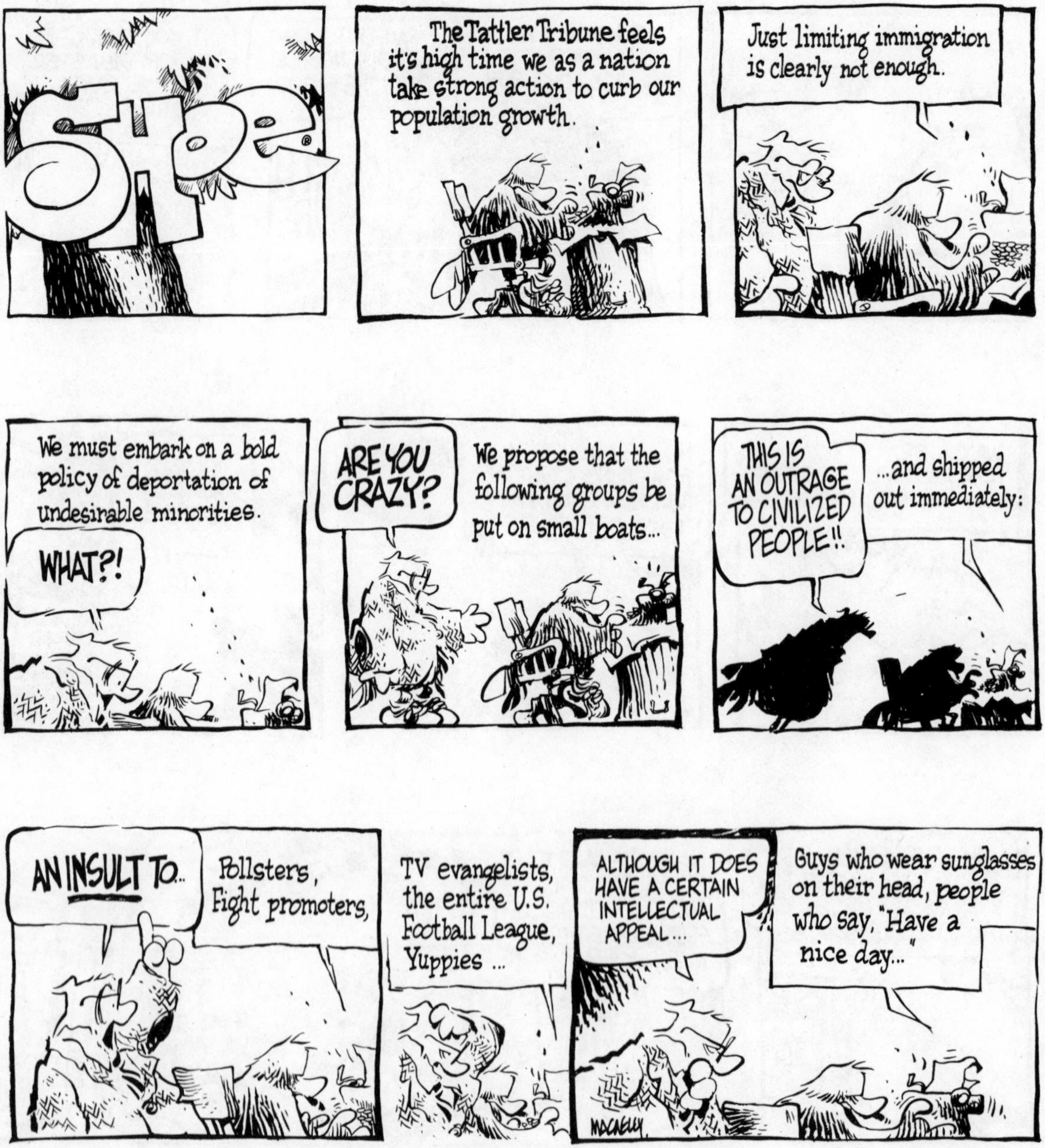
SHOE®
The Tattler Tribune feels it's high time we as a nation take strong action to curb our population growth.
Just limiting immigration is clearly not enough.
We must embark on a bold policy of deportation of undesirable minorities.
WHAT?!
ARE YOU CRAZY?
We propose that the following groups be put on small boats...
THIS IS AN OUTRAGE TO CIVILIZED PEOPLE!!
...and shipped out immediately:
AN INSULT TO...
Pollsters, Fight promoters,
TV evangelists, the entire U.S. Football League, Yuppies ...
ALTHOUGH IT DOES HAVE A CERTAIN INTELLECTUAL APPEAL...
Guys who wear sunglasses on their head, people who say, "Have a nice day..."
MACNELLY

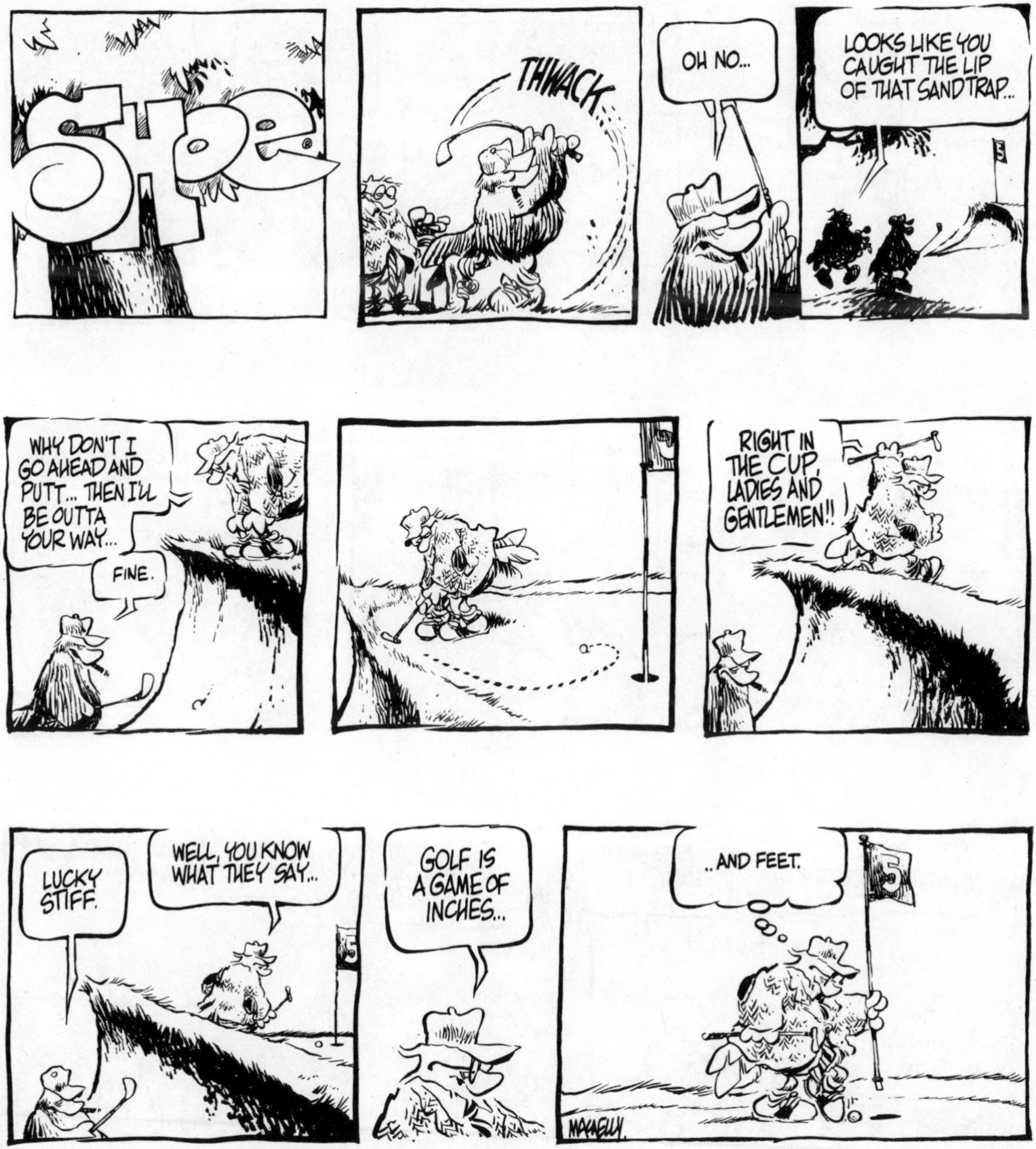
SHOE®
THWACK
OH NO...
LOOKS LIKE YOU CAUGHT THE LIP OF THAT SANDTRAP...
5
WHY DON'T I GO AHEAD AND PUTT... THEN I'LL BE OUTTA YOUR WAY...
FINE.
RIGHT IN THE CUP, LADIES AND GENTLEMEN!!
LUCKY STIFF.
WELL, YOU KNOW WHAT THEY SAY...
5
GOLF IS A GAME OF INCHES...
..AND FEET.
5
MACNELLY.

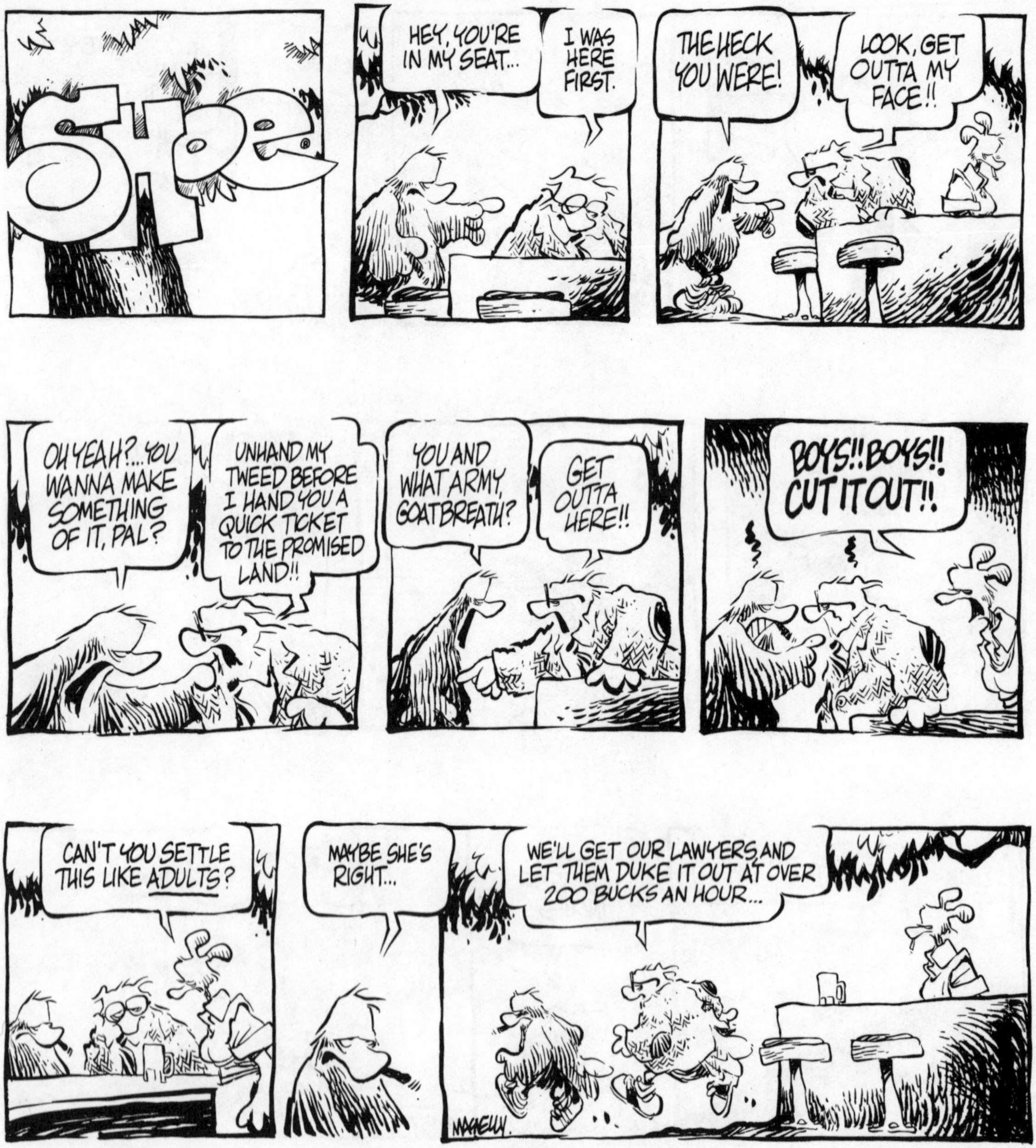
SHOE®
HEY, YOU'RE IN MY SEAT...
I WAS HERE FIRST.
THE HECK YOU WERE!
LOOK, GET OUTTA MY FACE!!
OH YEAH?...YOU WANNA MAKE SOMETHING OF IT, PAL?
UNHAND MY TWEED BEFORE I HAND YOU A QUICK TICKET TO THE PROMISED LAND!!
YOU AND WHAT ARMY, GOATBREATH?
GET OUTTA HERE!!
BOYS!! BOYS!! CUT IT OUT!!
CAN'T YOU SETTLE THIS LIKE ADULTS?
MAYBE SHE'S RIGHT...
WE'LL GET OUR LAWYERS AND LET THEM DUKE IT OUT AT OVER 200 BUCKS AN HOUR...
MACNELLY

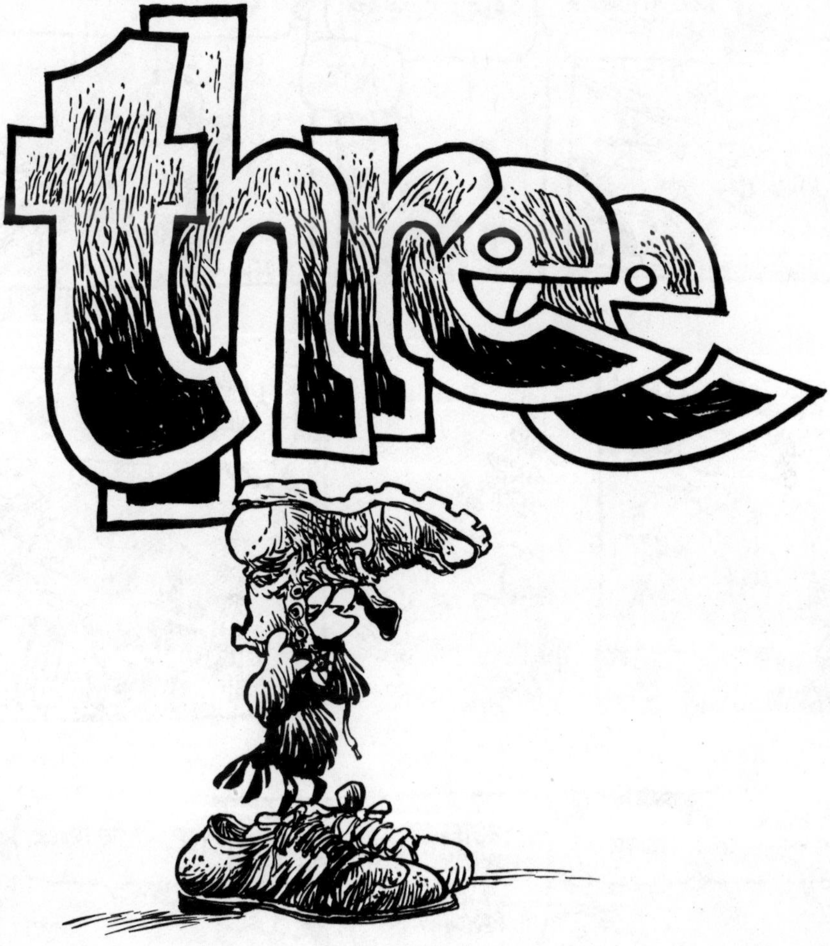
three

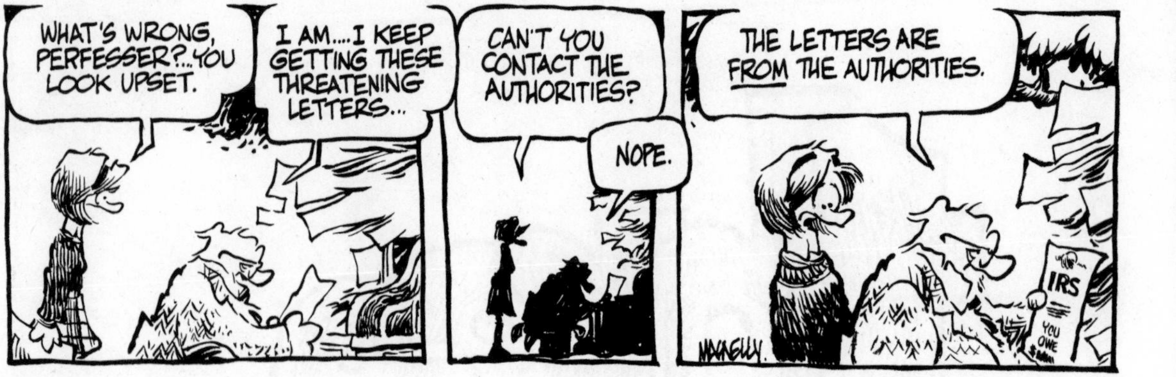
WHAT'S WRONG, PERFESSER?...YOU LOOK UPSET.
I AM....I KEEP GETTING THESE THREATENING LETTERS...
CAN'T YOU CONTACT THE AUTHORITIES?
NOPE.
THE LETTERS ARE FROM THE AUTHORITIES.
IRS
YOU OWE
MACNELLY

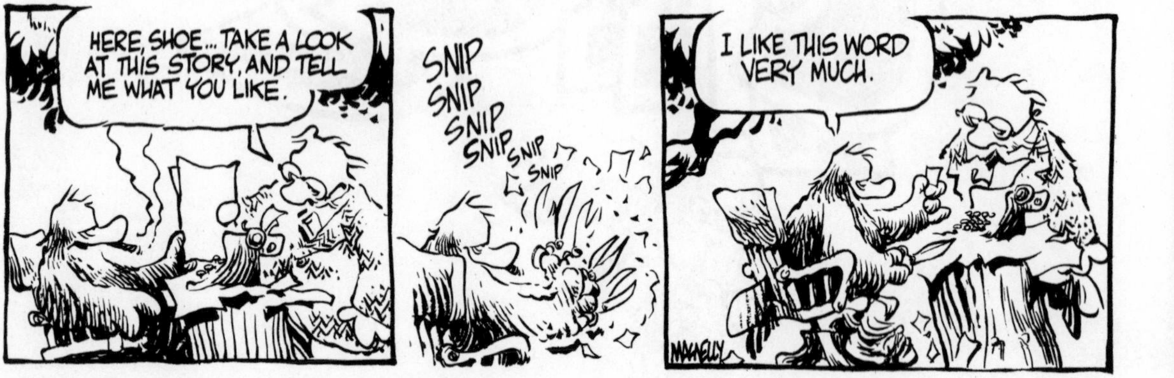
HERE, SHOE... TAKE A LOOK AT THIS STORY, AND TELL ME WHAT YOU LIKE.
SNIP SNIP SNIP SNIP SNIP SNIP
I LIKE THIS WORD VERY MUCH.
MACNELLY

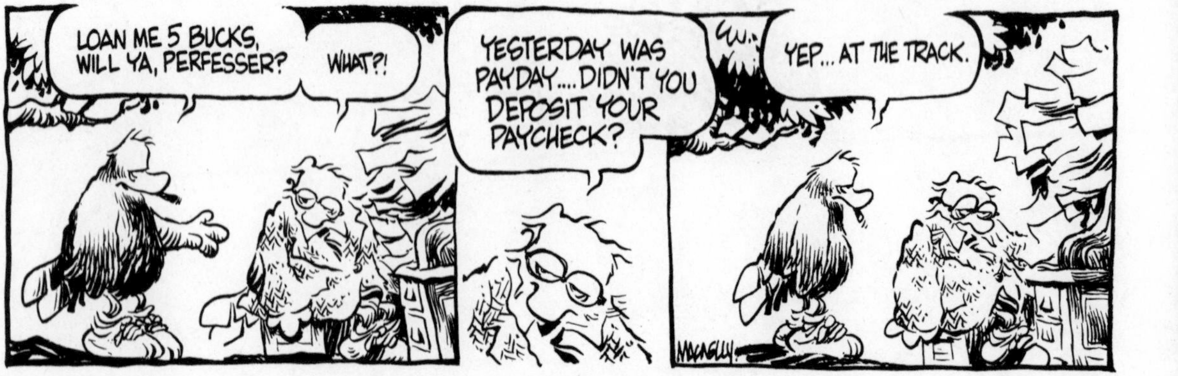
LOAN ME 5 BUCKS, WILL YA, PERFESSER?
WHAT?!
YESTERDAY WAS PAYDAY.... DIDN'T YOU DEPOSIT YOUR PAYCHECK?
YEP... AT THE TRACK.
MACNELLY

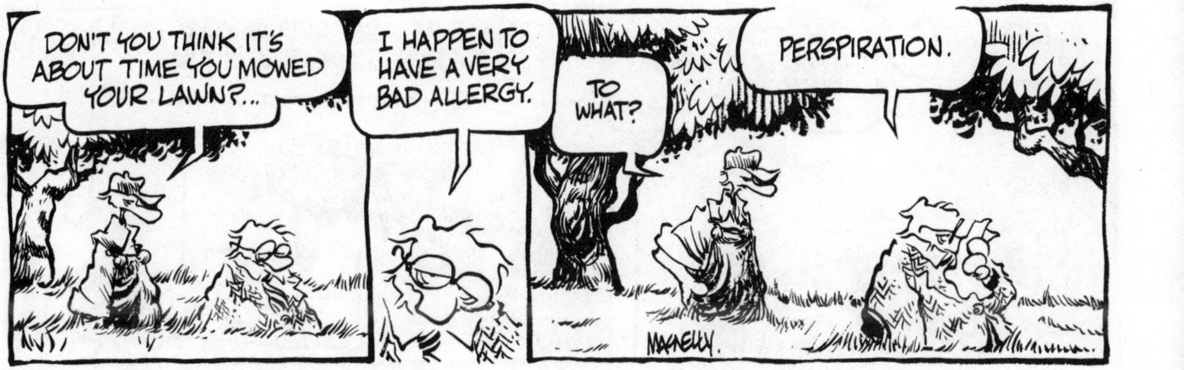
DON'T YOU THINK IT'S ABOUT TIME YOU MOWED YOUR LAWN?...
I HAPPEN TO HAVE A VERY BAD ALLERGY.
TO WHAT?
PERSPIRATION.
MACNELLY

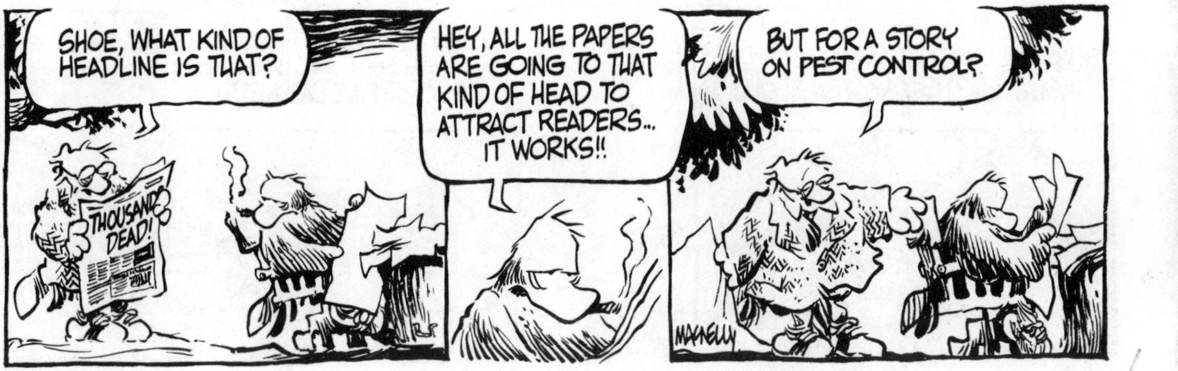
SHOE, WHAT KIND OF HEADLINE IS THAT?
THOUSAND DEAD!
HEY, ALL THE PAPERS ARE GOING TO THAT KIND OF HEAD TO ATTRACT READERS... IT WORKS!!
BUT FOR A STORY ON PEST CONTROL?
MACNELLY

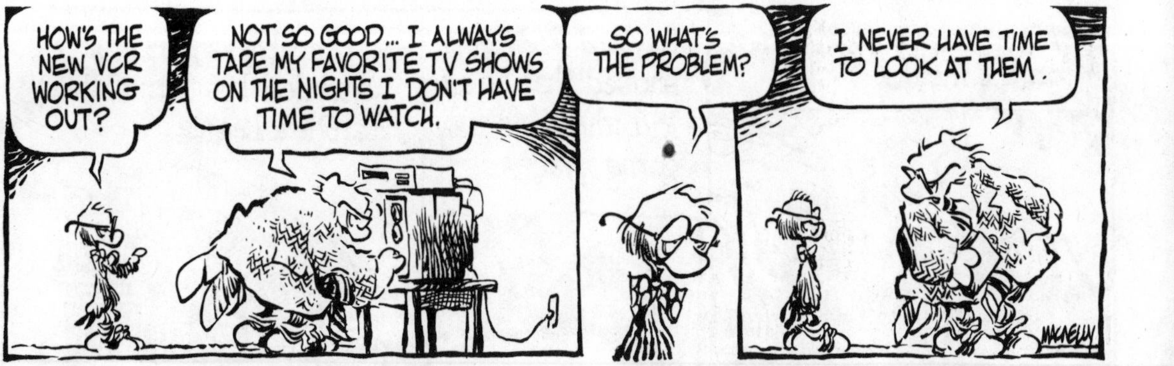
HOW'S THE NEW VCR WORKING OUT?
NOT SO GOOD... I ALWAYS TAPE MY FAVORITE TV SHOWS ON THE NIGHTS I DON'T HAVE TIME TO WATCH.
SO WHAT'S THE PROBLEM?
I NEVER HAVE TIME TO LOOK AT THEM.
MACNELLY

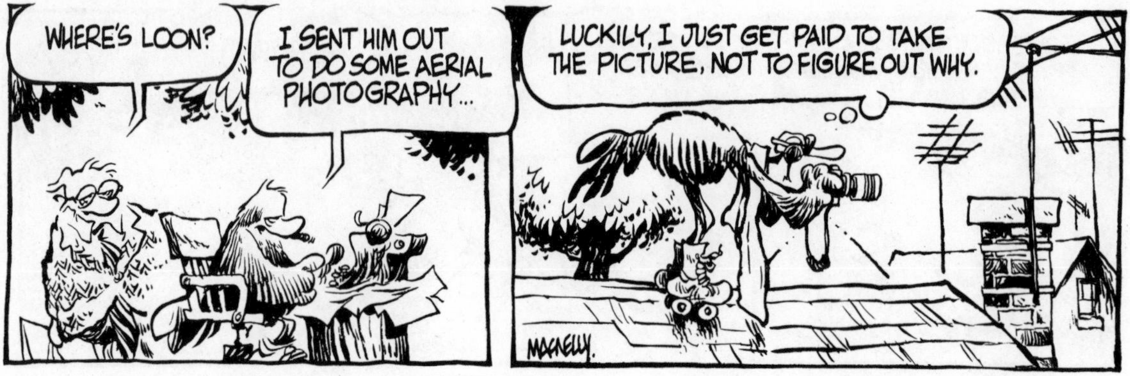
WHERE'S LOON?
I SENT HIM OUT TO DO SOME AERIAL PHOTOGRAPHY...
LUCKILY, I JUST GET PAID TO TAKE THE PICTURE, NOT TO FIGURE OUT WHY.
MACNELLY.

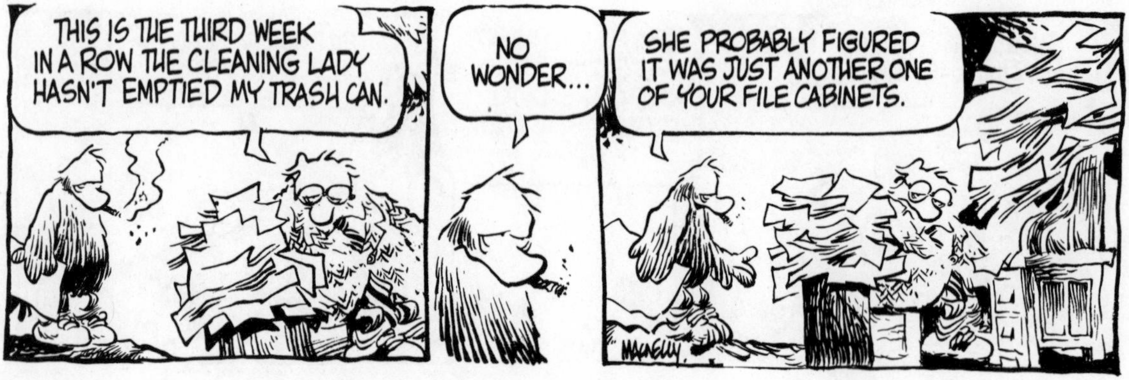
THIS IS THE THIRD WEEK IN A ROW THE CLEANING LADY HASN'T EMPTIED MY TRASH CAN.
NO WONDER...
SHE PROBABLY FIGURED IT WAS JUST ANOTHER ONE OF YOUR FILE CABINETS.
MACNELLY.

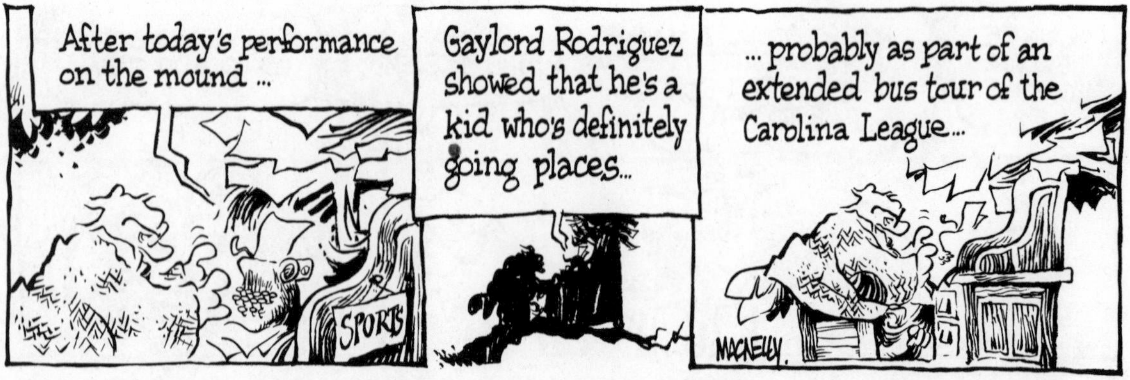
After today's performance on the mound ...
SPORTS
Gaylord Rodriguez showed that he's a kid who's definitely going places...
... probably as part of an extended bus tour of the Carolina League...
MACNELLY.

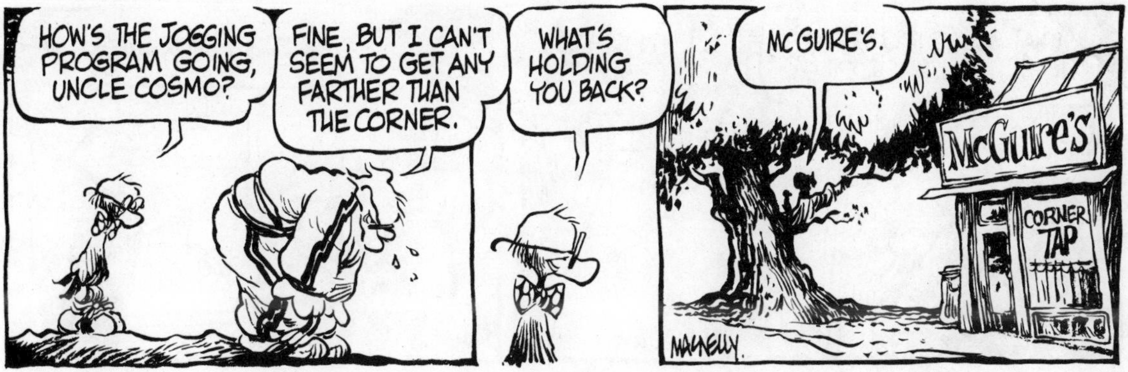
HOW'S THE JOGGING PROGRAM GOING, UNCLE COSMO?
FINE, BUT I CAN'T SEEM TO GET ANY FARTHER THAN THE CORNER.
WHAT'S HOLDING YOU BACK?
MC GUIRE'S.
McGuire's
CORNER TAP
MACNELLY

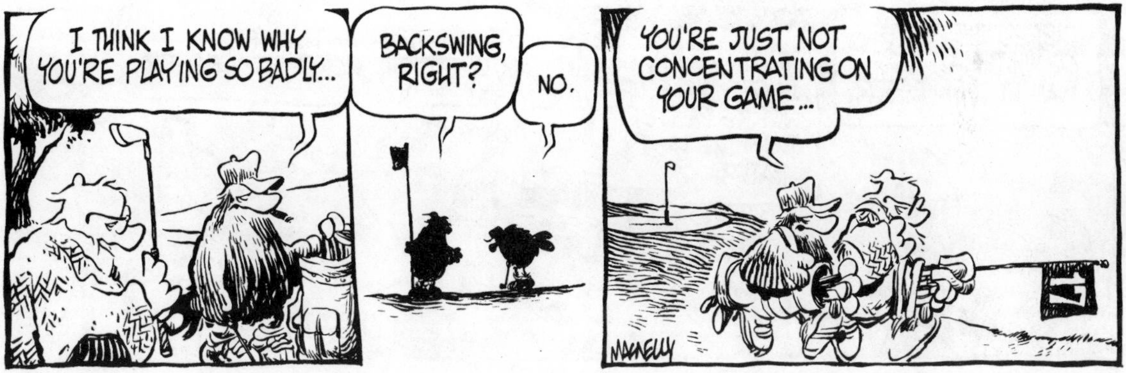
I THINK I KNOW WHY YOU'RE PLAYING SO BADLY...
BACKSWING, RIGHT?
NO.
YOU'RE JUST NOT CONCENTRATING ON YOUR GAME...
MACNELLY

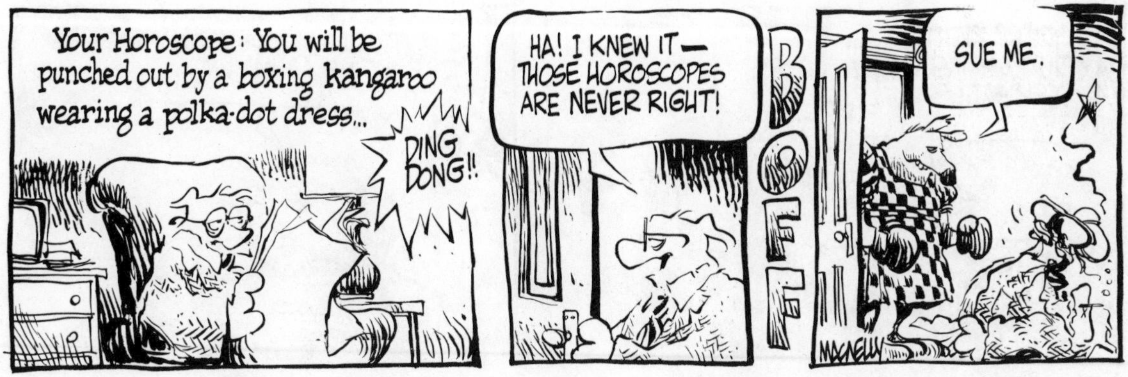
Your Horoscope: You will be punched out by a boxing kangaroo wearing a polka-dot dress...
DING DONG!!
HA! I KNEW IT— THOSE HOROSCOPES ARE NEVER RIGHT!
BOFF
SUE ME.
MACNELLY

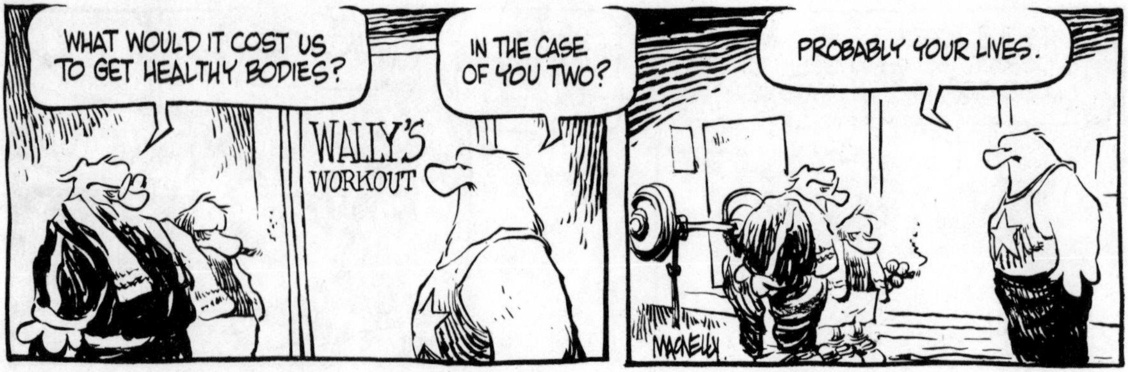
WHAT WOULD IT COST US TO GET HEALTHY BODIES?
WALLY'S WORKOUT
IN THE CASE OF YOU TWO?
PROBABLY YOUR LIVES.

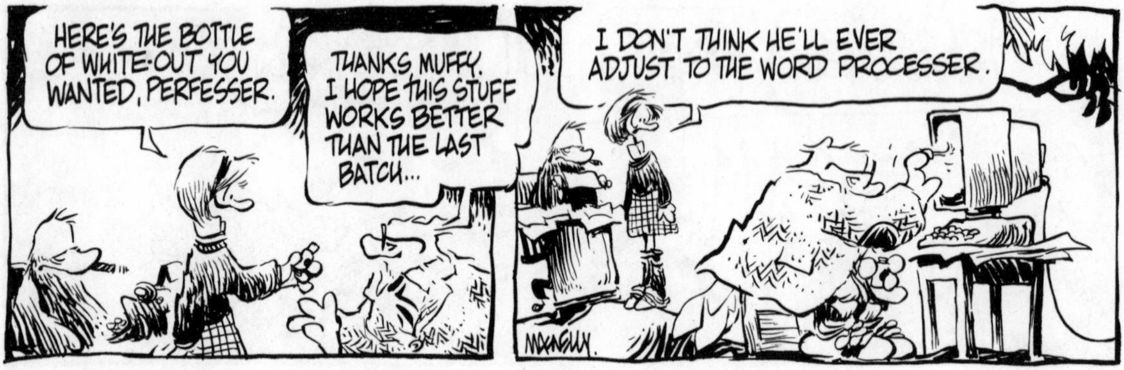
HERE'S THE BOTTLE OF WHITE-OUT YOU WANTED, PERFESSER.
THANKS MUFFY. I HOPE THIS STUFF WORKS BETTER THAN THE LAST BATCH...
I DON'T THINK HE'LL EVER ADJUST TO THE WORD PROCESSER.

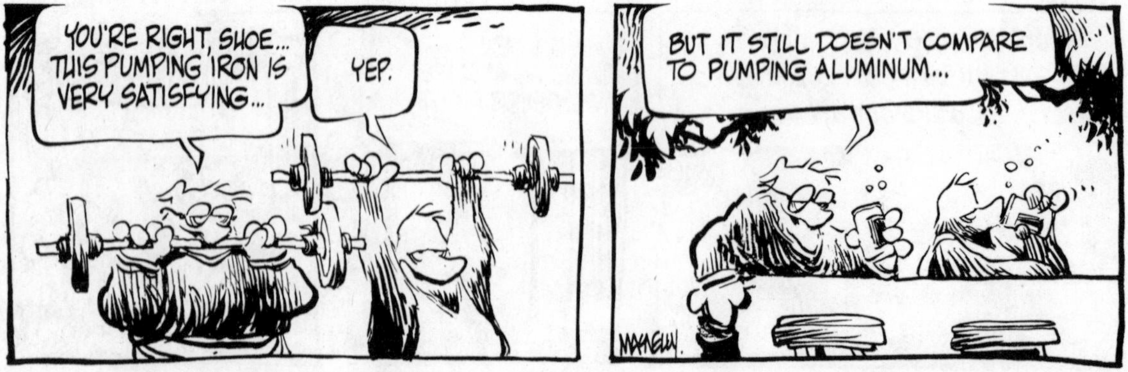
YOU'RE RIGHT, SHOE... THIS PUMPING IRON IS VERY SATISFYING...
YEP.
BUT IT STILL DOESN'T COMPARE TO PUMPING ALUMINUM...

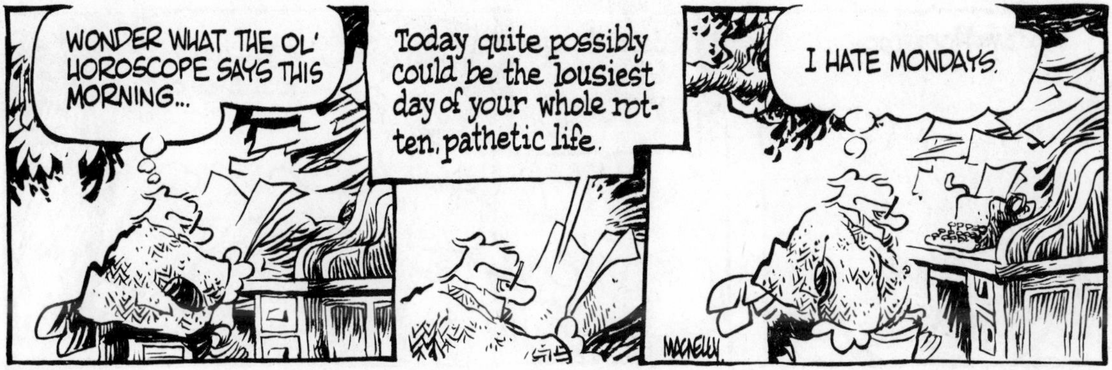
WONDER WHAT THE OL' HOROSCOPE SAYS THIS MORNING...
Today quite possibly could be the lousiest day of your whole rotten, pathetic life.
I HATE MONDAYS.

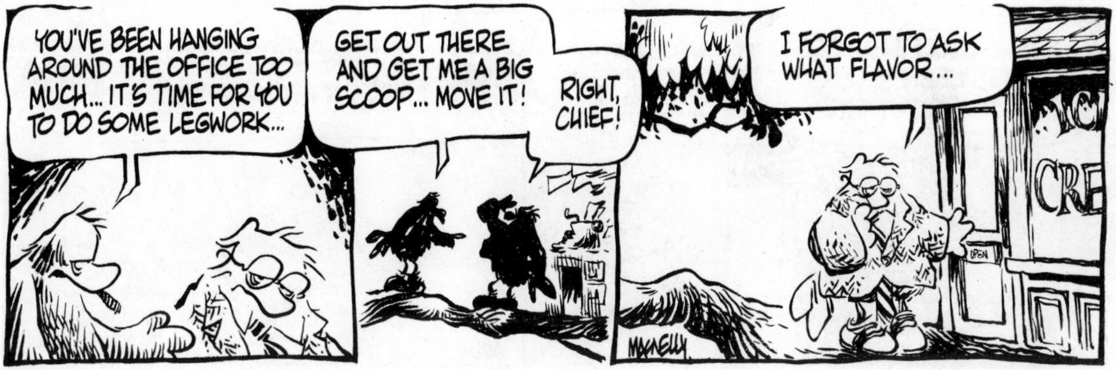
YOU'VE BEEN HANGING AROUND THE OFFICE TOO MUCH... IT'S TIME FOR YOU TO DO SOME LEGWORK...
GET OUT THERE AND GET ME A BIG SCOOP... MOVE IT!
RIGHT, CHIEF!
I FORGOT TO ASK WHAT FLAVOR...

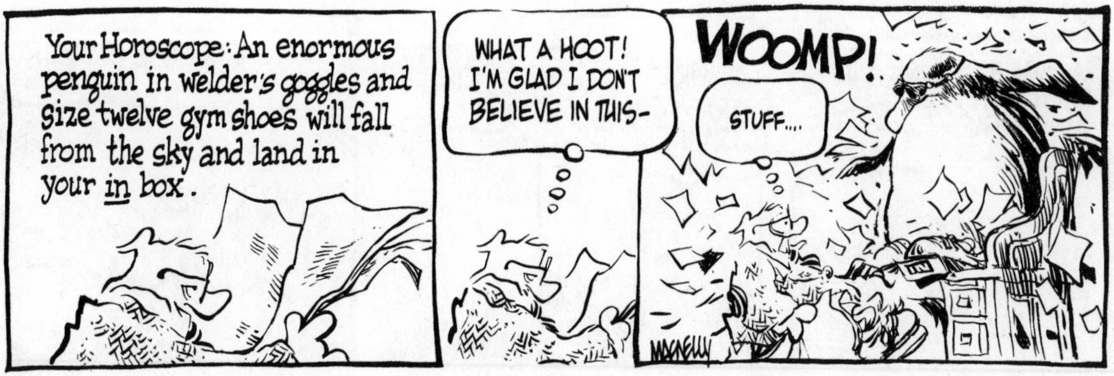
Your Horoscope: An enormous penguin in welder's goggles and size twelve gym shoes will fall from the sky and land in your in box.
WHAT A HOOT! I'M GLAD I DON'T BELIEVE IN THIS-
WOOMP!
STUFF....

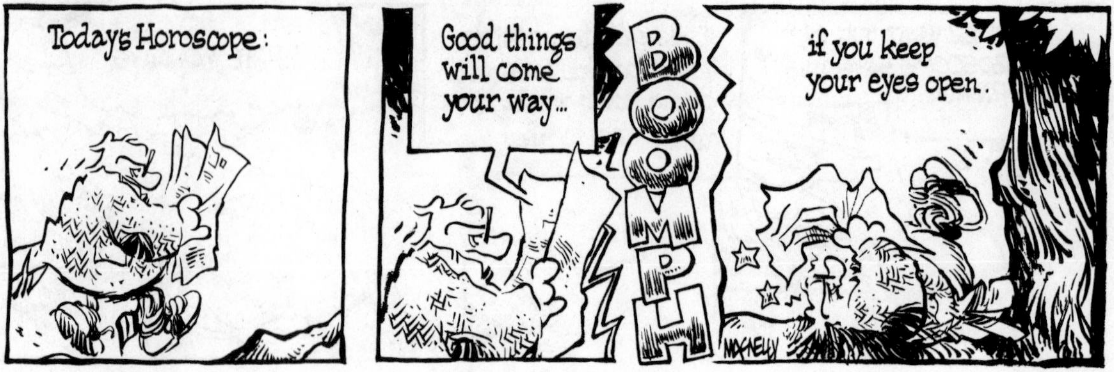
Today's Horoscope:
Good things will come your way...
BOOOMPH
if you keep your eyes open.
MACNELLY

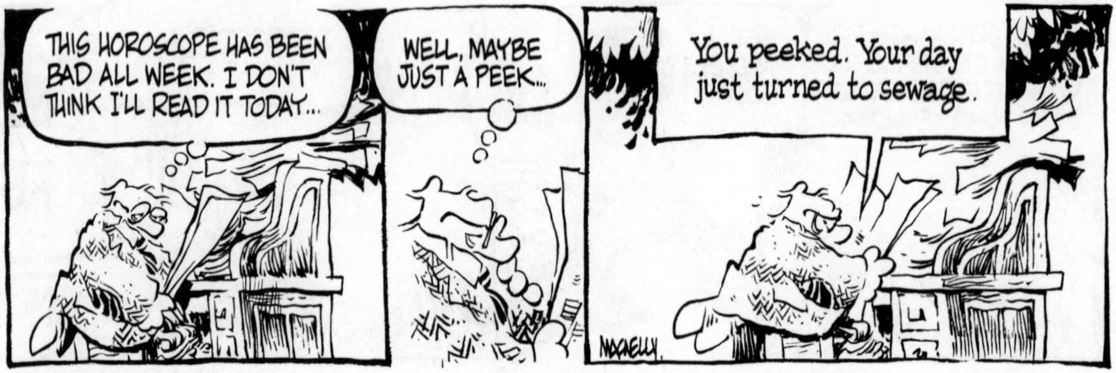
THIS HOROSCOPE HAS BEEN BAD ALL WEEK. I DON'T THINK I'LL READ IT TODAY...
WELL, MAYBE JUST A PEEK...
You peeked. Your day just turned to sewage.
MACNELLY

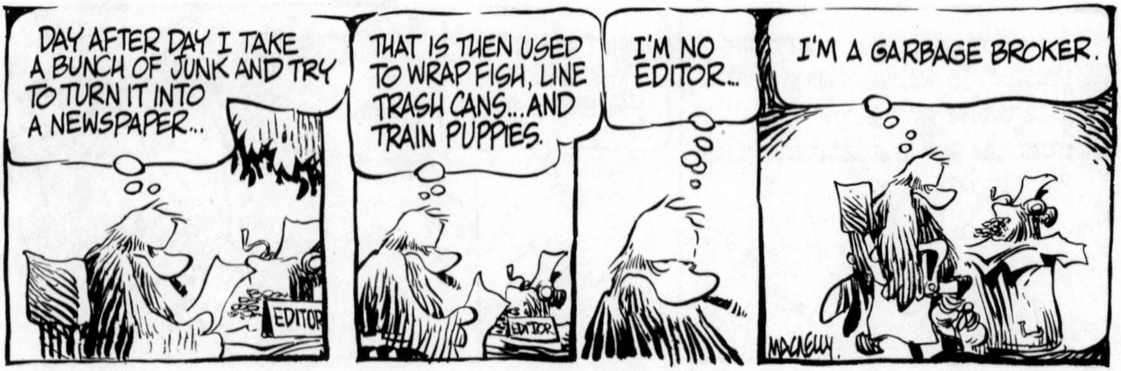
DAY AFTER DAY I TAKE A BUNCH OF JUNK AND TRY TO TURN IT INTO A NEWSPAPER...
EDITOR
THAT IS THEN USED TO WRAP FISH, LINE TRASH CANS... AND TRAIN PUPPIES.
EDITOR
I'M NO EDITOR...
I'M A GARBAGE BROKER.
MACNELLY

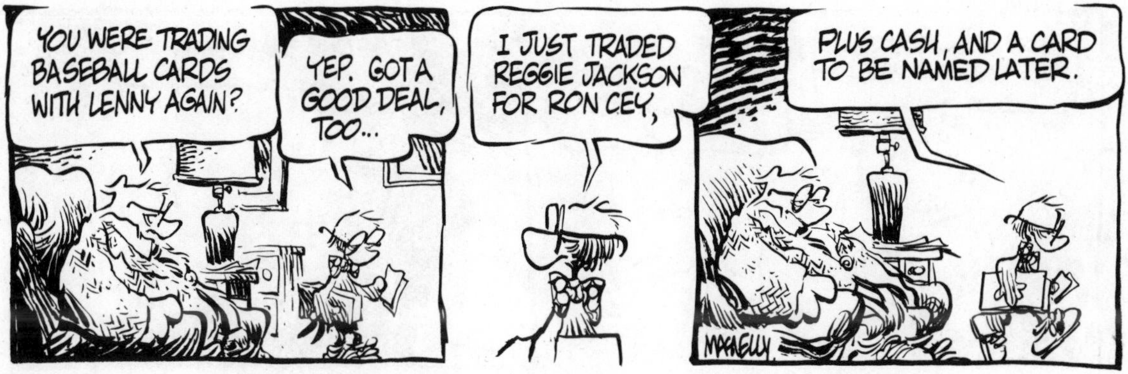
YOU WERE TRADING BASEBALL CARDS WITH LENNY AGAIN?
YEP. GOT A GOOD DEAL, TOO...
I JUST TRADED REGGIE JACKSON FOR RON CEY,
PLUS CASH, AND A CARD TO BE NAMED LATER.
MACNELLY

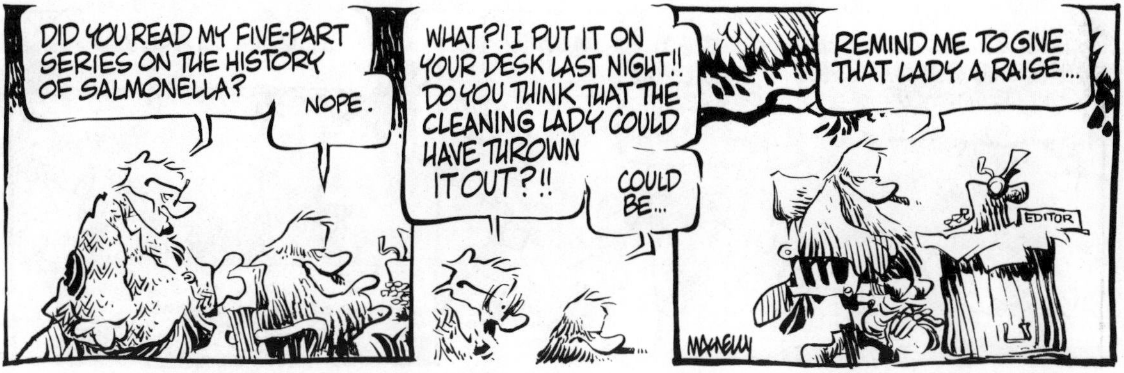
DID YOU READ MY FIVE-PART SERIES ON THE HISTORY OF SALMONELLA?
NOPE.
WHAT?! I PUT IT ON YOUR DESK LAST NIGHT!! DO YOU THINK THAT THE CLEANING LADY COULD HAVE THROWN IT OUT?!!
COULD BE...
REMIND ME TO GIVE THAT LADY A RAISE...
EDITOR
MACNELLY

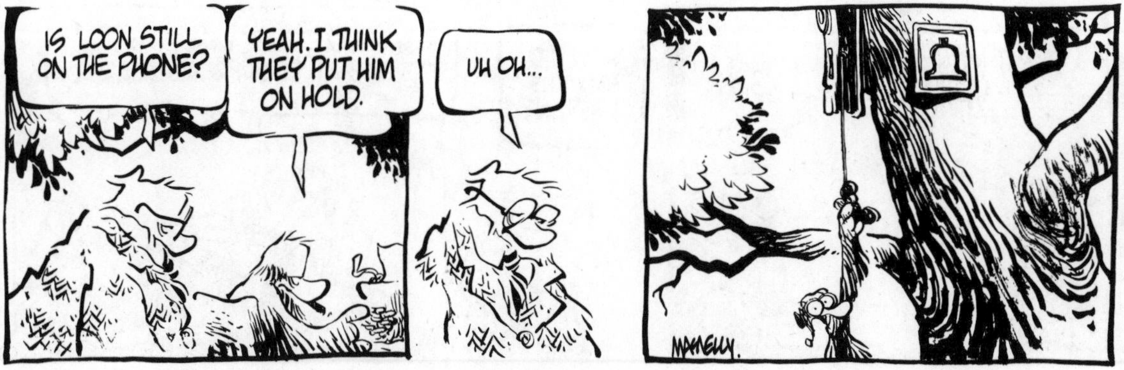
IS LOON STILL ON THE PHONE?
YEAH. I THINK THEY PUT HIM ON HOLD.
UH OH...
MACNELLY.

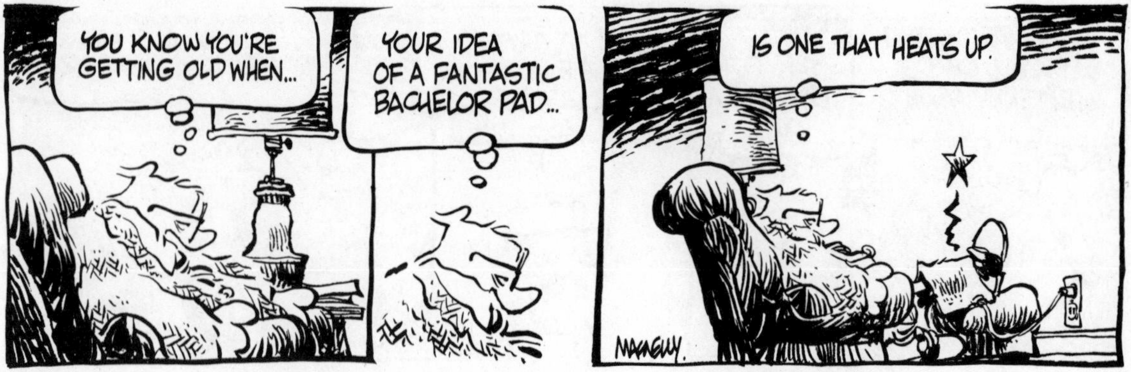
YOU KNOW YOU'RE GETTING OLD WHEN...
YOUR IDEA OF A FANTASTIC BACHELOR PAD...
IS ONE THAT HEATS UP.
MACNELLY

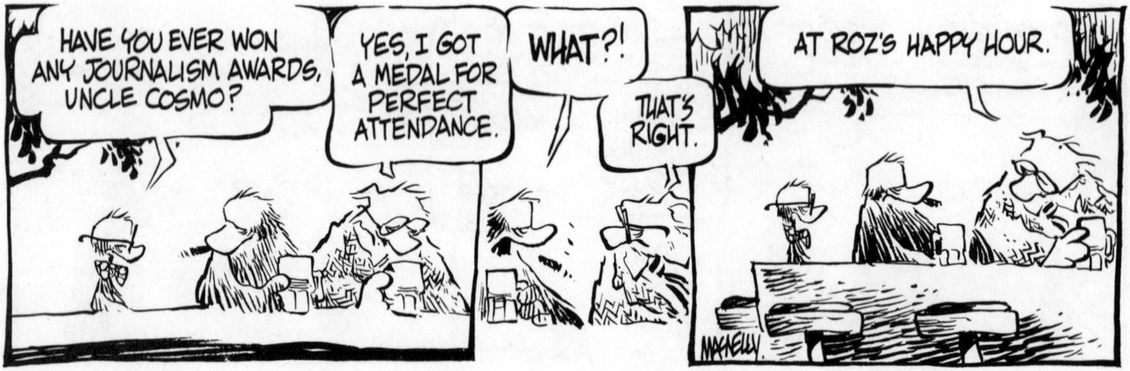
HAVE YOU EVER WON ANY JOURNALISM AWARDS, UNCLE COSMO?
YES, I GOT A MEDAL FOR PERFECT ATTENDANCE.
WHAT?!
THAT'S RIGHT.
AT ROZ'S HAPPY HOUR.
MACNELLY

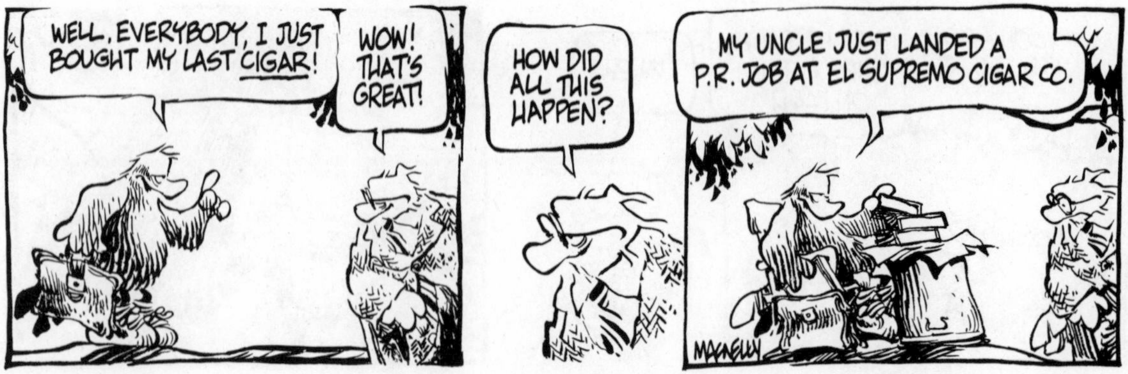
WELL, EVERYBODY, I JUST BOUGHT MY LAST CIGAR!
WOW! THAT'S GREAT!
HOW DID ALL THIS HAPPEN?
MY UNCLE JUST LANDED A P.R. JOB AT EL SUPREMO CIGAR CO.
MACNELLY

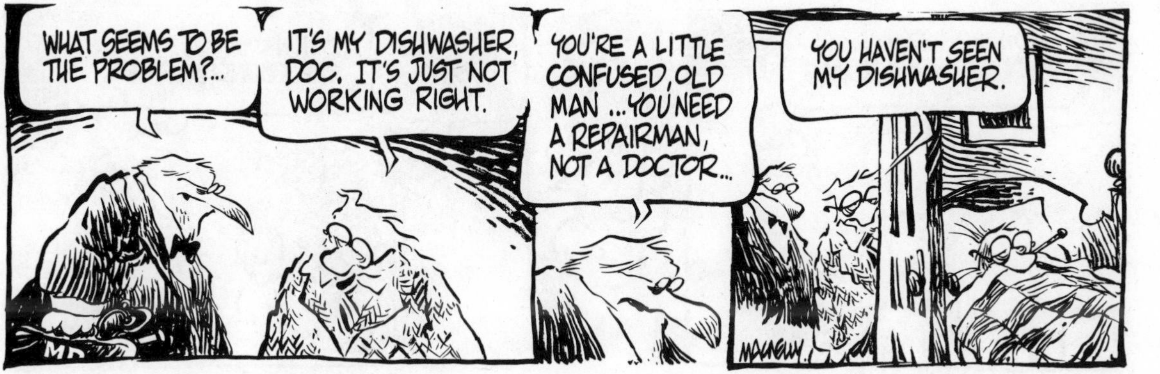
WHAT SEEMS TO BE THE PROBLEM?...
IT'S MY DISHWASHER, DOC. IT'S JUST NOT WORKING RIGHT.
YOU'RE A LITTLE CONFUSED, OLD MAN ...YOU NEED A REPAIRMAN, NOT A DOCTOR...
YOU HAVEN'T SEEN MY DISHWASHER.
MACNELLY

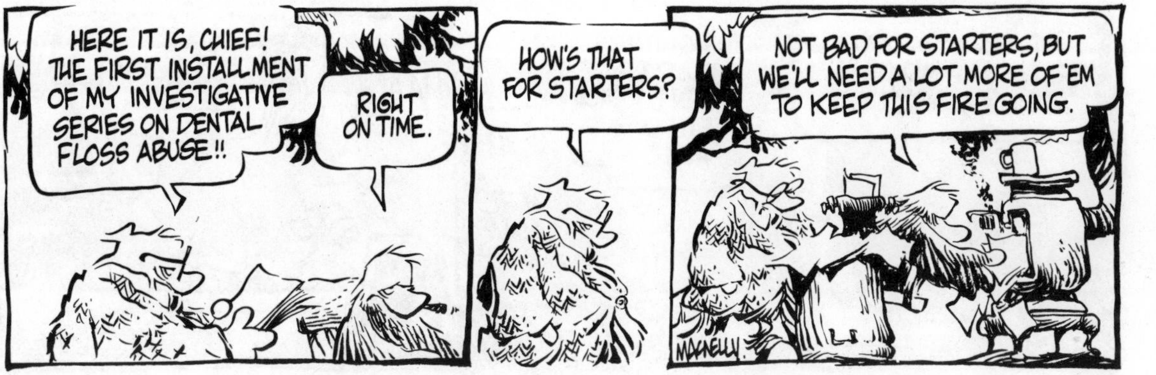
HERE IT IS, CHIEF! THE FIRST INSTALLMENT OF MY INVESTIGATIVE SERIES ON DENTAL FLOSS ABUSE!!
RIGHT ON TIME.
HOW'S THAT FOR STARTERS?
NOT BAD FOR STARTERS, BUT WE'LL NEED A LOT MORE OF 'EM TO KEEP THIS FIRE GOING.
MACNELLY

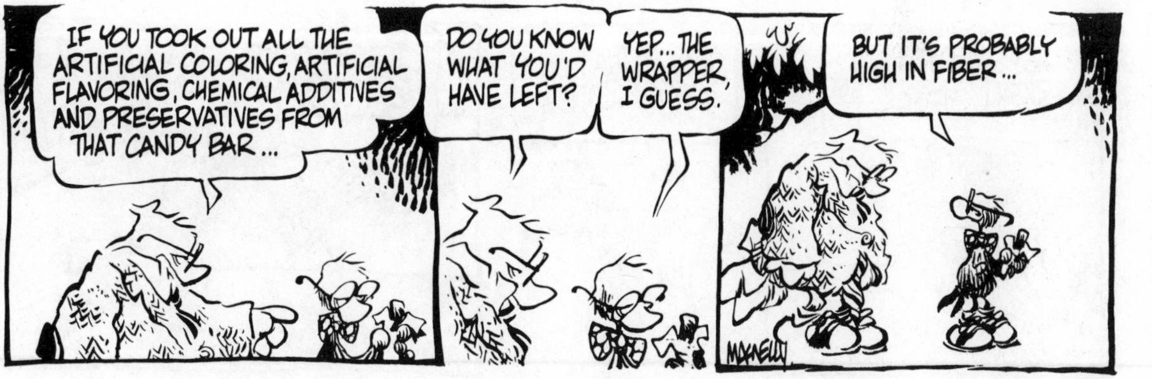
IF YOU TOOK OUT ALL THE ARTIFICIAL COLORING, ARTIFICIAL FLAVORING, CHEMICAL ADDITIVES AND PRESERVATIVES FROM THAT CANDY BAR ...
DO YOU KNOW WHAT YOU'D HAVE LEFT?
YEP... THE WRAPPER, I GUESS.
BUT IT'S PROBABLY HIGH IN FIBER ...
MACNELLY

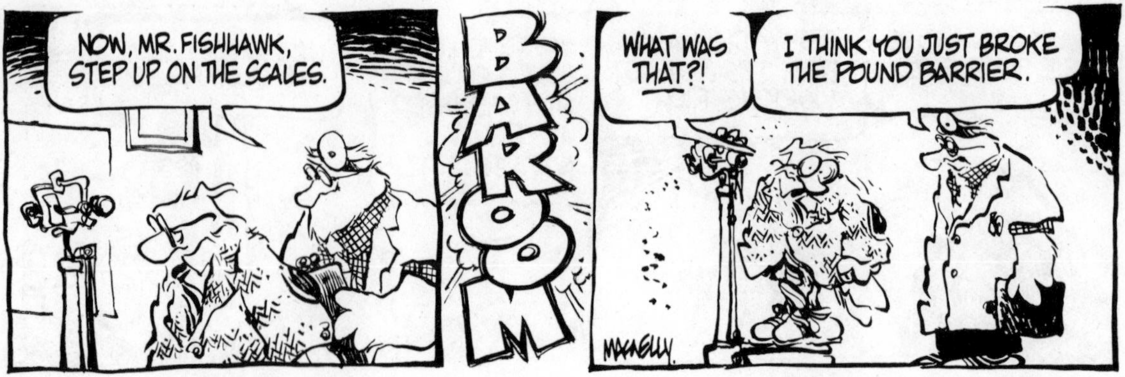
NOW, MR. FISHHAWK, STEP UP ON THE SCALES.
BAROOM
WHAT WAS THAT?!
I THINK YOU JUST BROKE THE POUND BARRIER.
MACNELLY

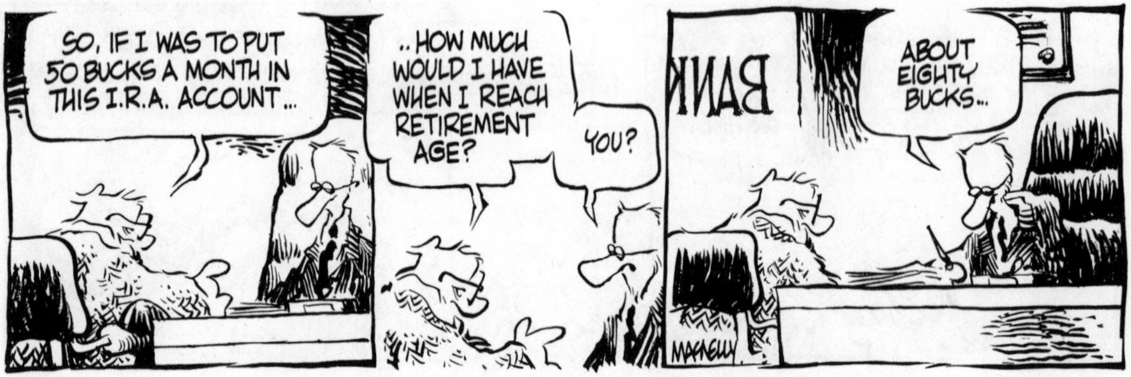
SO, IF I WAS TO PUT 50 BUCKS A MONTH IN THIS I.R.A. ACCOUNT...
..HOW MUCH WOULD I HAVE WHEN I REACH RETIREMENT AGE?
YOU?
BANK
ABOUT EIGHTY BUCKS...
MACNELLY

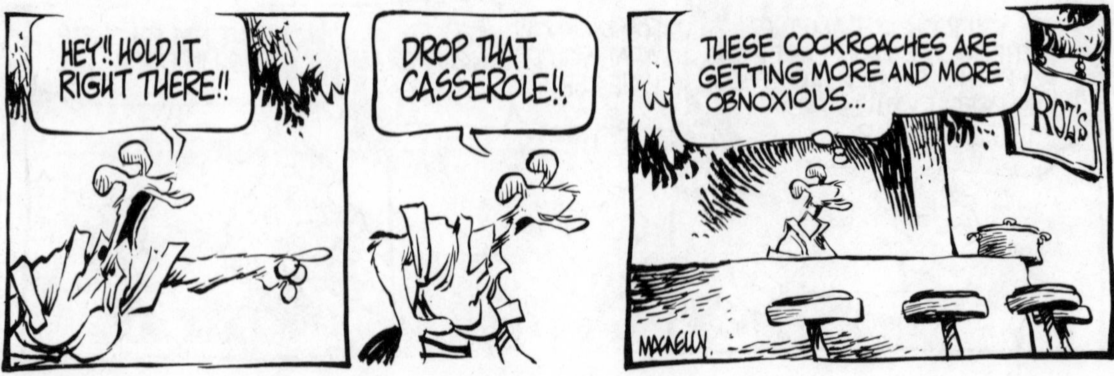
HEY!! HOLD IT RIGHT THERE!!
DROP THAT CASSEROLE!!
THESE COCKROACHES ARE GETTING MORE AND MORE OBNOXIOUS...
ROZ'S
MACNELLY

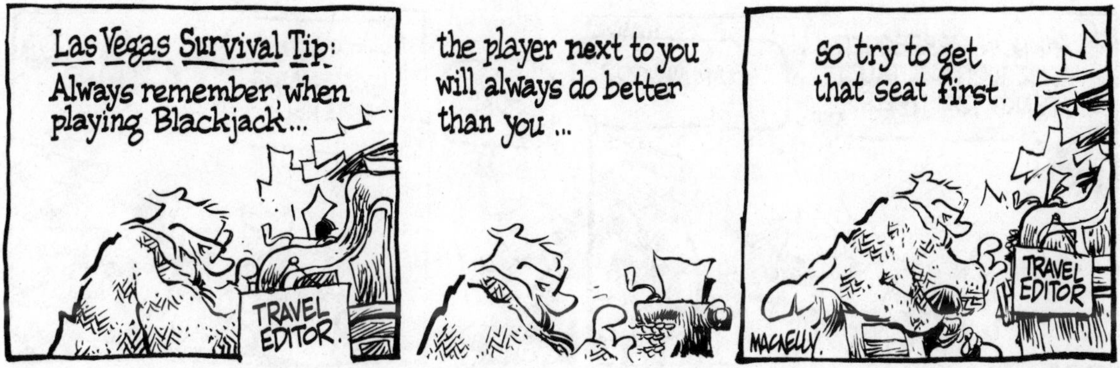
Las Vegas Survival Tip: Always remember, when playing Blackjack...
TRAVEL EDITOR.
the player next to you will always do better than you ...
so try to get that seat first.
TRAVEL EDITOR
MACNELLY

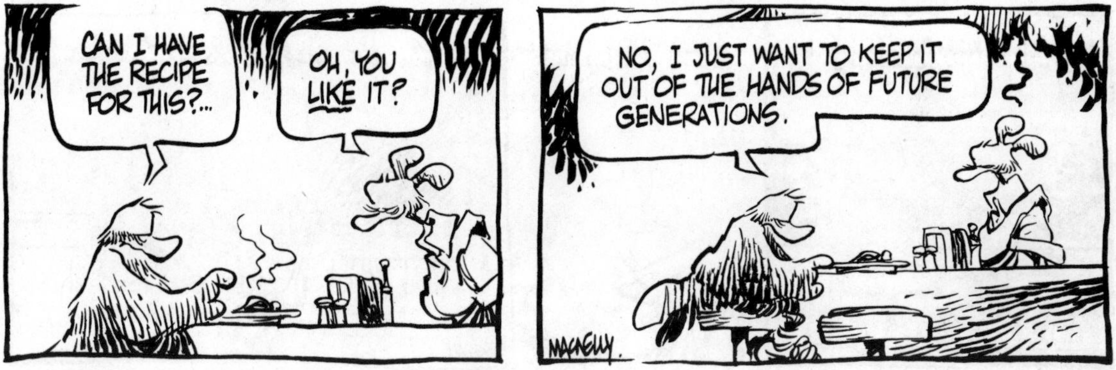
CAN I HAVE THE RECIPE FOR THIS?...
OH, YOU LIKE IT?
NO, I JUST WANT TO KEEP IT OUT OF THE HANDS OF FUTURE GENERATIONS.
MACNELLY

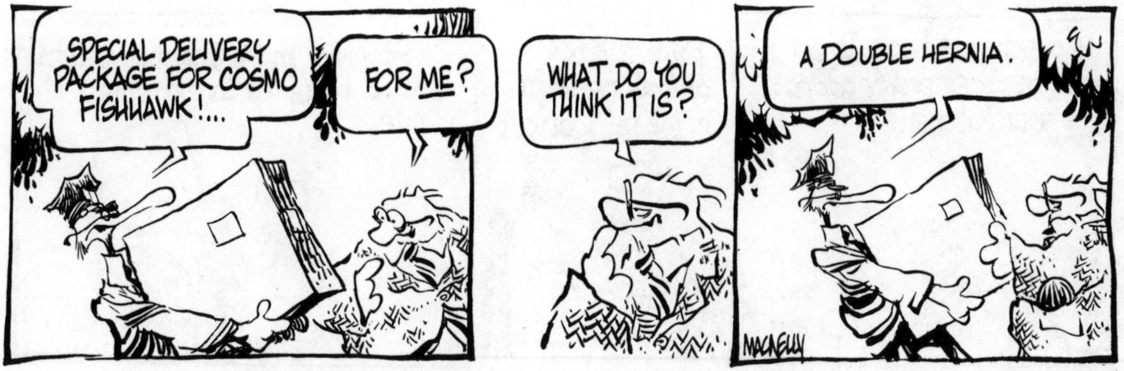
SPECIAL DELIVERY PACKAGE FOR COSMO FISHHAWK!...
FOR ME?
WHAT DO YOU THINK IT IS?
A DOUBLE HERNIA.
MACNELLY

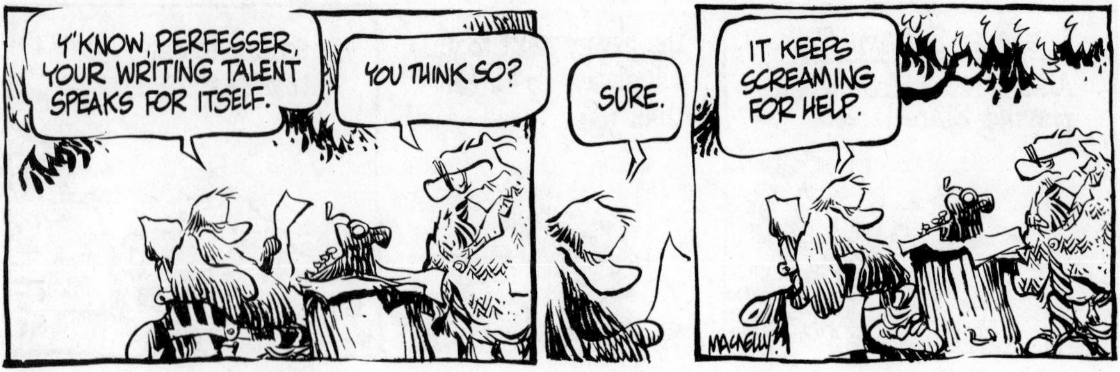
Y'KNOW, PERFESSER, YOUR WRITING TALENT SPEAKS FOR ITSELF.
YOU THINK SO?
SURE.
IT KEEPS SCREAMING FOR HELP.
MACNELLY

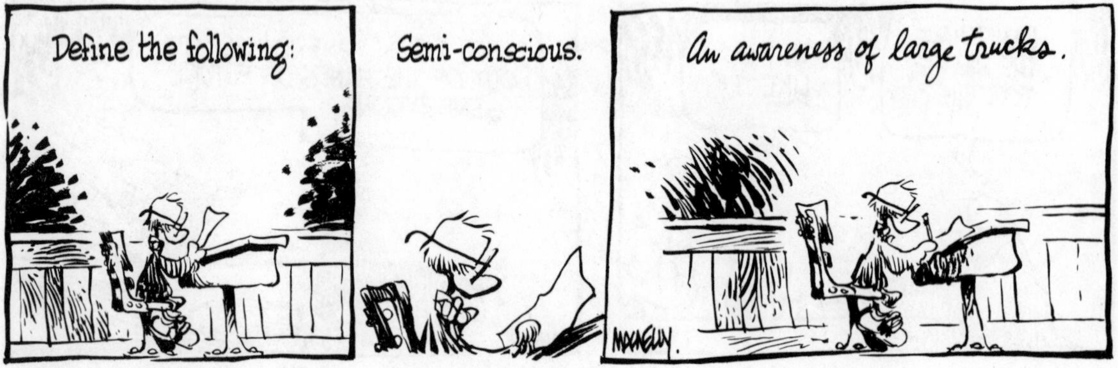
Define the following:
Semi-conscious.
An awareness of large trucks.
MACNELLY.

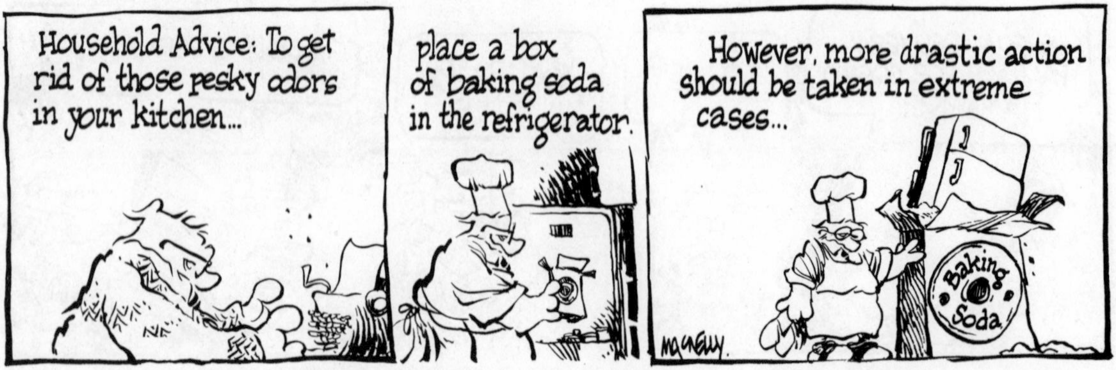
Household Advice: To get rid of those pesky odors in your kitchen...
place a box of baking soda in the refrigerator.
However, more drastic action should be taken in extreme cases...
Baking Soda
MACNELLY.

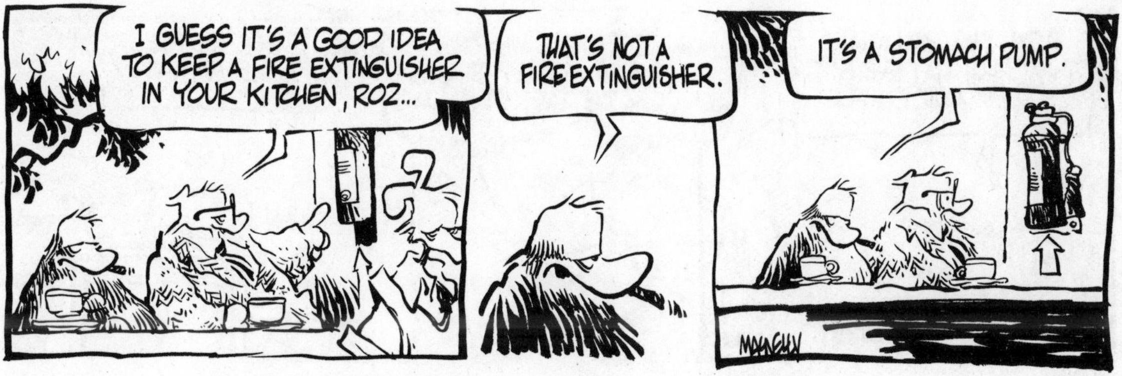
I GUESS IT'S A GOOD IDEA TO KEEP A FIRE EXTINGUISHER IN YOUR KITCHEN, ROZ...
THAT'S NOT A FIRE EXTINGUISHER.
IT'S A STOMACH PUMP.
MACNELLY

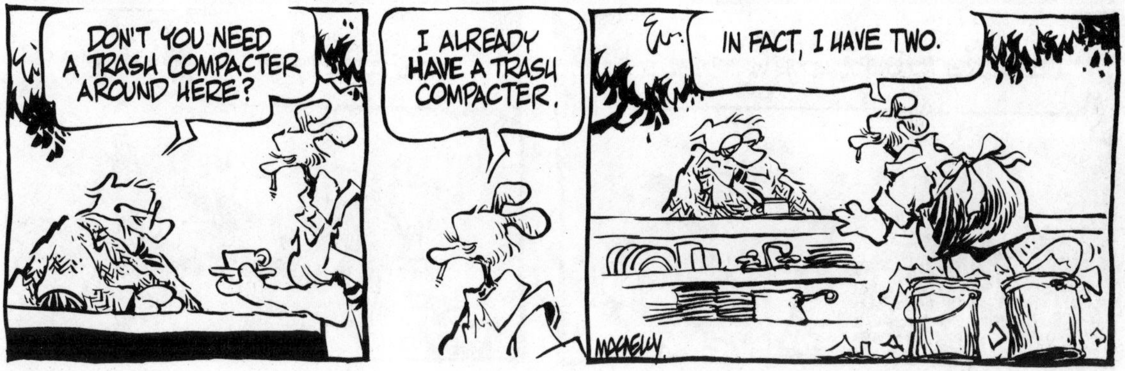
DON'T YOU NEED A TRASH COMPACTER AROUND HERE?
I ALREADY HAVE A TRASH COMPACTER.
IN FACT, I HAVE TWO.
MACNELLY

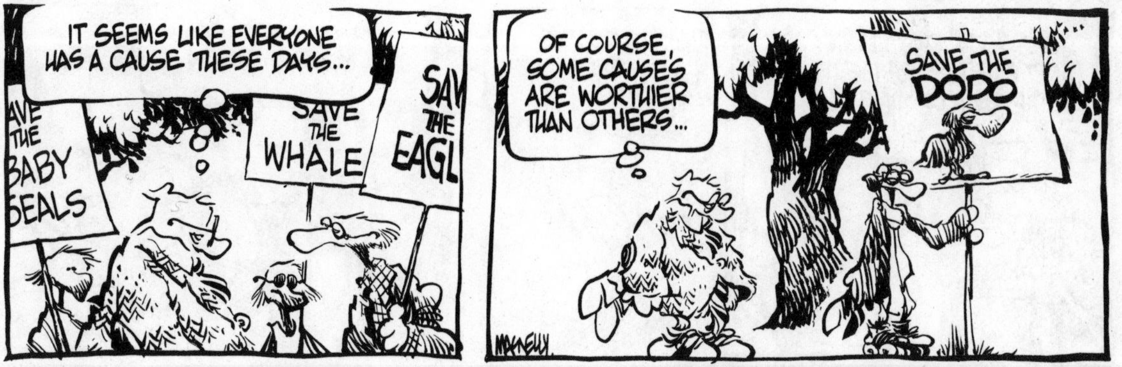
IT SEEMS LIKE EVERYONE HAS A CAUSE THESE DAYS...
AVE THE BABY SEALS
SAVE THE WHALE
SAV THE EAGL
OF COURSE, SOME CAUSES ARE WORTHIER THAN OTHERS...
SAVE THE DODO
MACNELLY

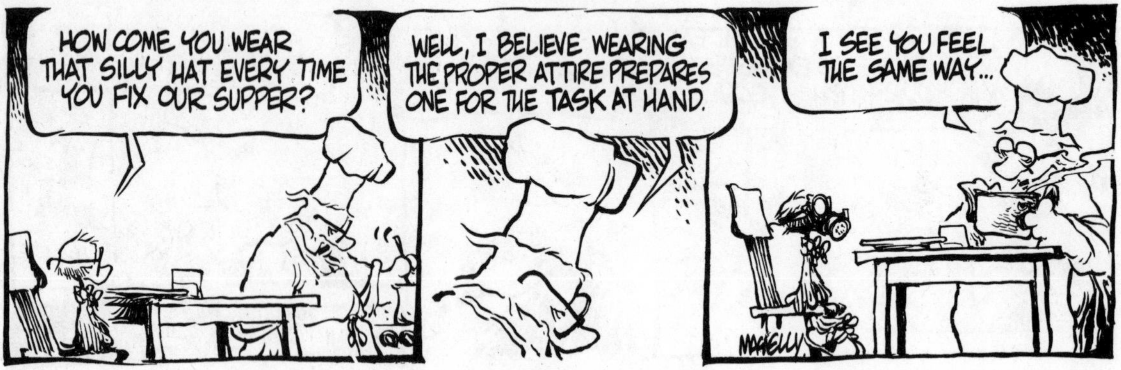
HOW COME YOU WEAR THAT SILLY HAT EVERY TIME YOU FIX OUR SUPPER?
WELL, I BELIEVE WEARING THE PROPER ATTIRE PREPARES ONE FOR THE TASK AT HAND.
I SEE YOU FEEL THE SAME WAY...
MACNELLY

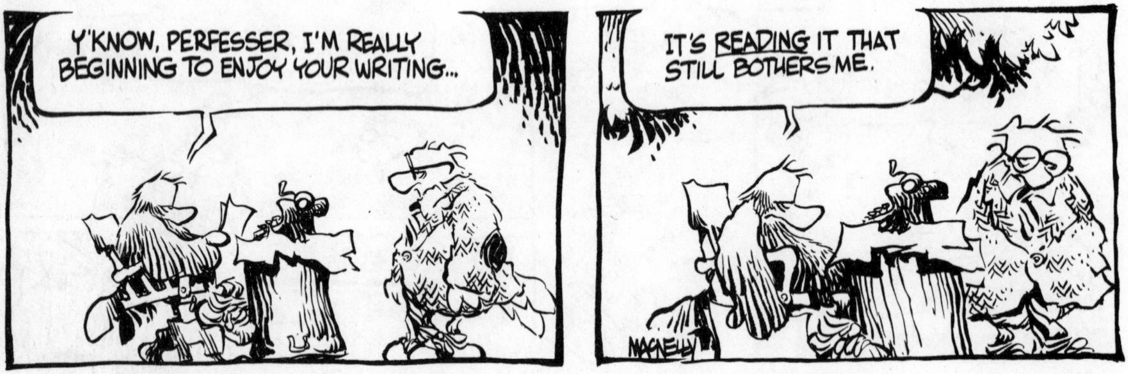
Y'KNOW, PERFESSER, I'M REALLY BEGINNING TO ENJOY YOUR WRITING...
IT'S READING IT THAT STILL BOTHERS ME.
MACNELLY

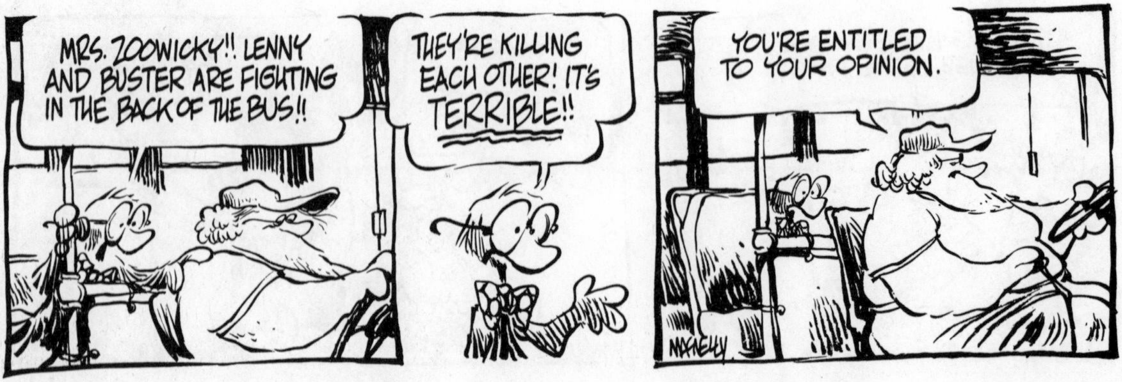
MRS. ZOOWICKY!! LENNY AND BUSTER ARE FIGHTING IN THE BACK OF THE BUS!!
THEY'RE KILLING EACH OTHER! IT'S TERRIBLE!!
YOU'RE ENTITLED TO YOUR OPINION.
MACNELLY

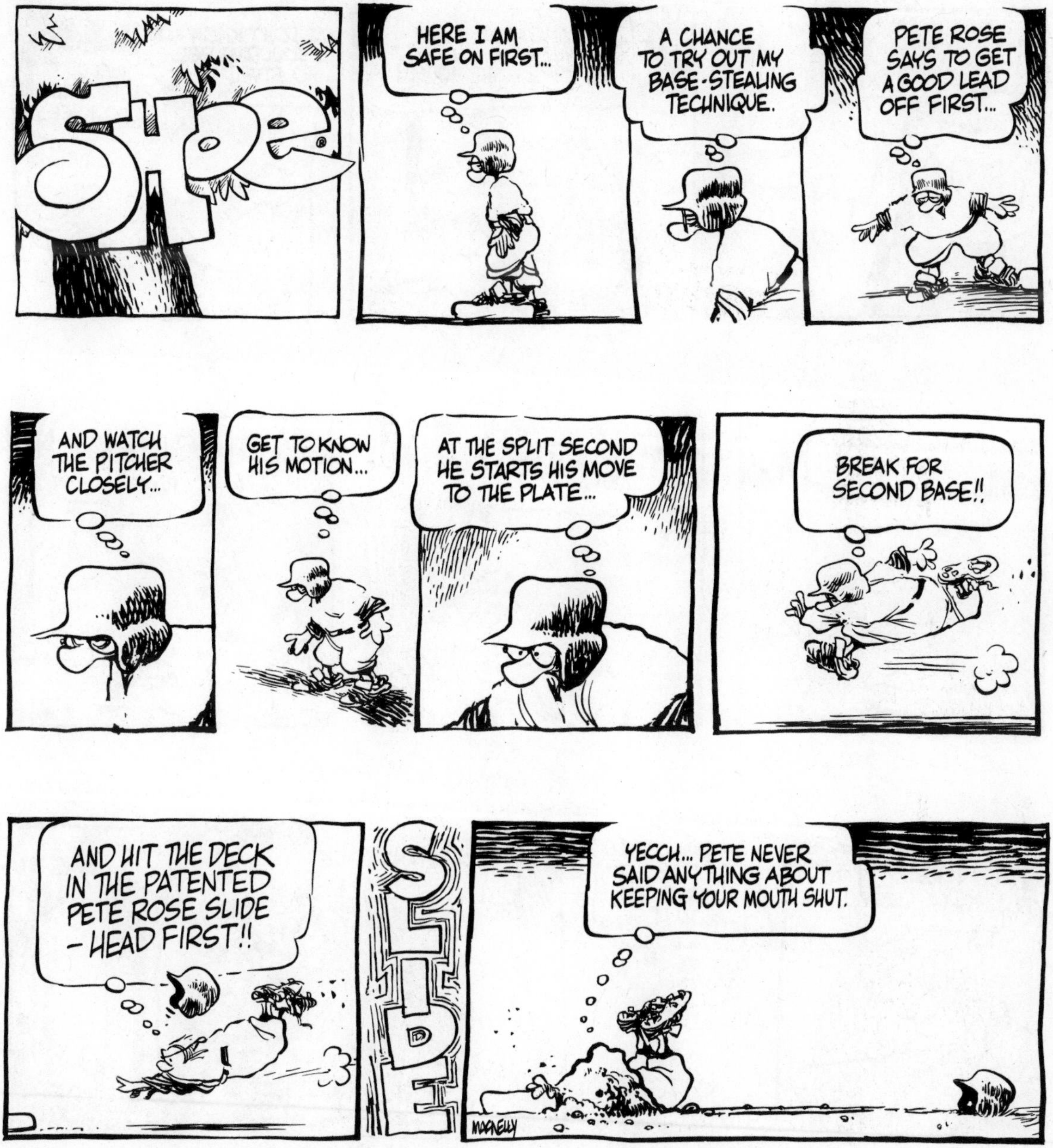
SHOE
HERE I AM SAFE ON FIRST...
A CHANCE TO TRY OUT MY BASE-STEALING TECHNIQUE.
PETE ROSE SAYS TO GET A GOOD LEAD OFF FIRST...
AND WATCH THE PITCHER CLOSELY...
GET TO KNOW HIS MOTION...
AT THE SPLIT SECOND HE STARTS HIS MOVE TO THE PLATE...
BREAK FOR SECOND BASE!!
AND HIT THE DECK IN THE PATENTED PETE ROSE SLIDE – HEAD FIRST!!
SLIDE
YECCH... PETE NEVER SAID ANYTHING ABOUT KEEPING YOUR MOUTH SHUT.
MACNELLY

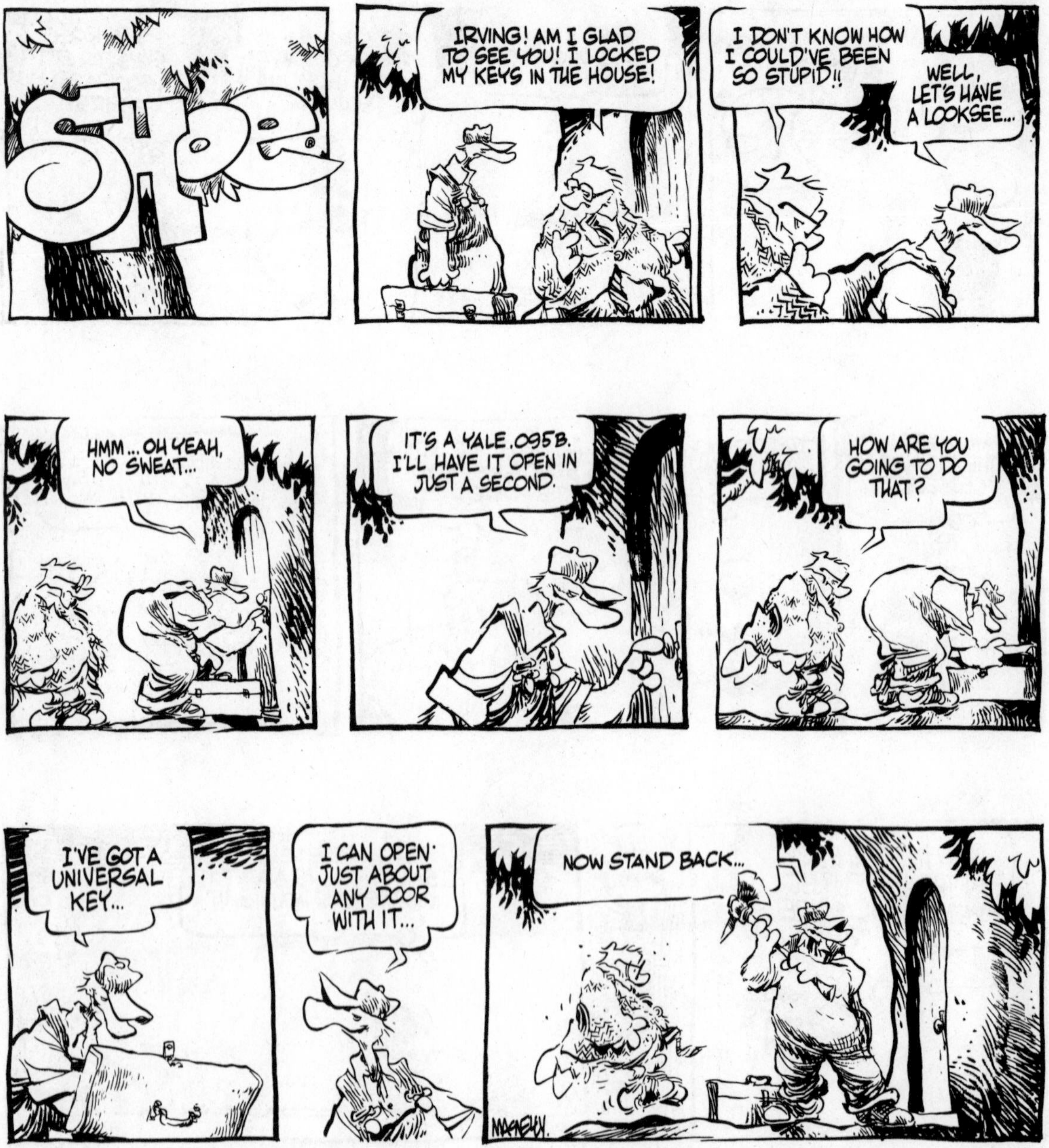
SHOE
IRVING! AM I GLAD TO SEE YOU! I LOCKED MY KEYS IN THE HOUSE!
I DON'T KNOW HOW I COULD'VE BEEN SO STUPID!!
WELL, LET'S HAVE A LOOKSEE...
HMM... OH YEAH, NO SWEAT...
IT'S A YALE .095B. I'LL HAVE IT OPEN IN JUST A SECOND.
HOW ARE YOU GOING TO DO THAT?
I'VE GOT A UNIVERSAL KEY...
I CAN OPEN JUST ABOUT ANY DOOR WITH IT...
NOW STAND BACK...
MACNELLY

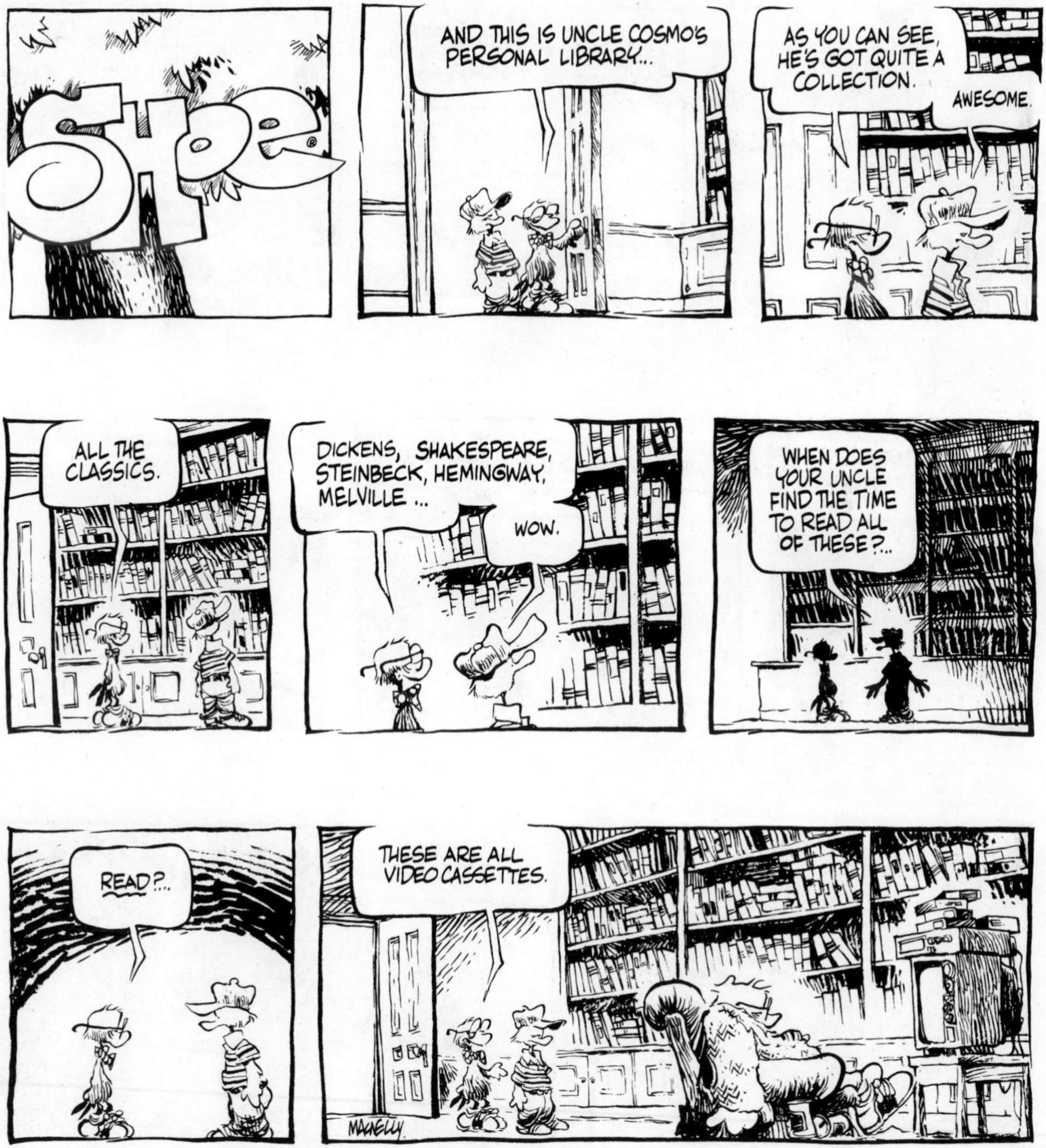
SHOE®
AND THIS IS UNCLE COSMO'S PERSONAL LIBRARY...
AS YOU CAN SEE, HE'S GOT QUITE A COLLECTION.
AWESOME.
ALL THE CLASSICS.
DICKENS, SHAKESPEARE, STEINBECK, HEMINGWAY, MELVILLE ...
WOW.
WHEN DOES YOUR UNCLE FIND THE TIME TO READ ALL OF THESE?...
READ?...
THESE ARE ALL VIDEO CASSETTES.
MACNELLY

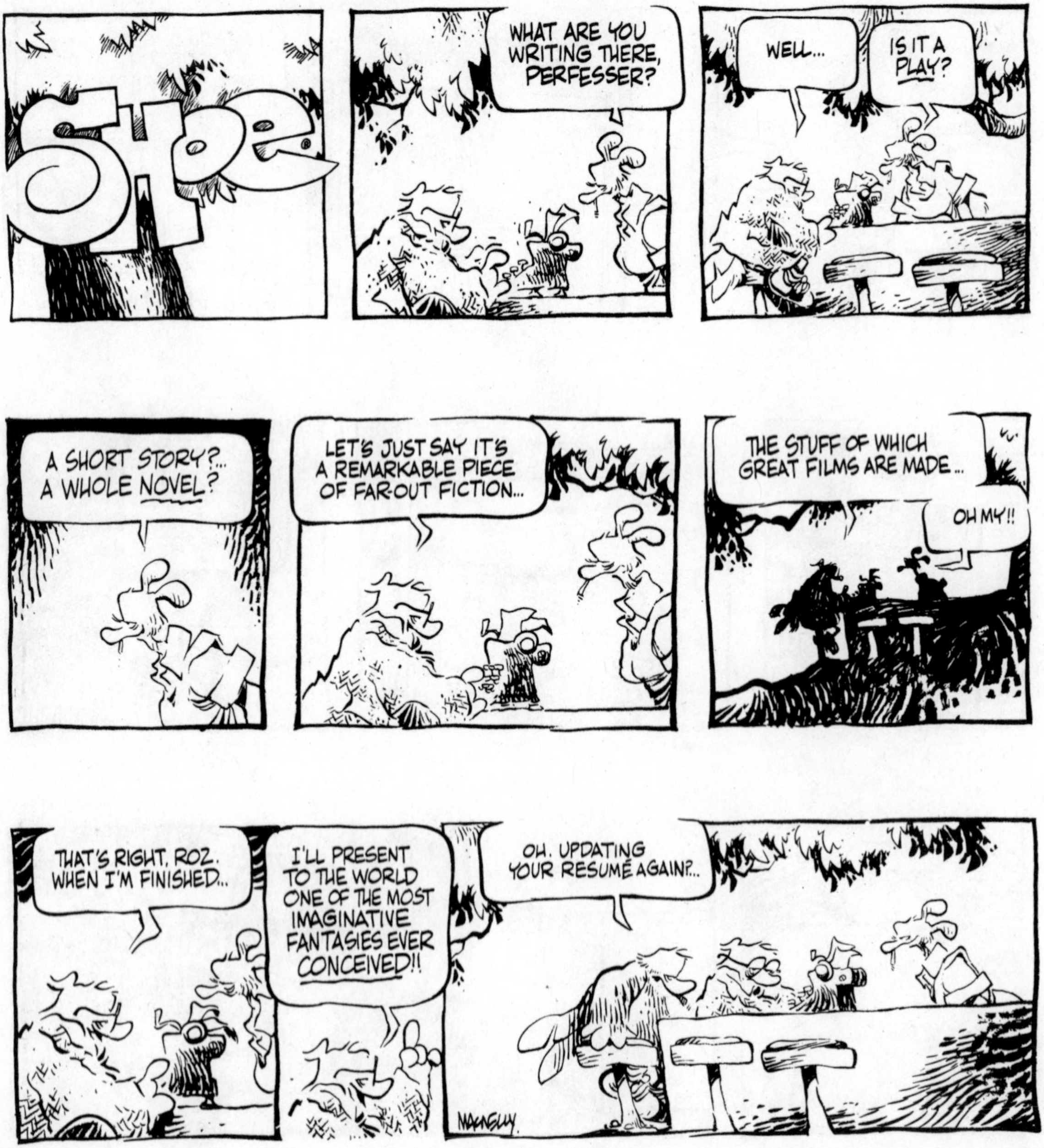
SHOE
WHAT ARE YOU WRITING THERE, PERFESSER?
WELL...
IS IT A PLAY?
A SHORT STORY?... A WHOLE NOVEL?
LET'S JUST SAY IT'S A REMARKABLE PIECE OF FAR-OUT FICTION...
THE STUFF OF WHICH GREAT FILMS ARE MADE...
OH MY!!
THAT'S RIGHT, ROZ. WHEN I'M FINISHED...
I'LL PRESENT TO THE WORLD ONE OF THE MOST IMAGINATIVE FANTASIES EVER CONCEIVED!!
OH. UPDATING YOUR RESUMÉ AGAIN?...
MACNELLY

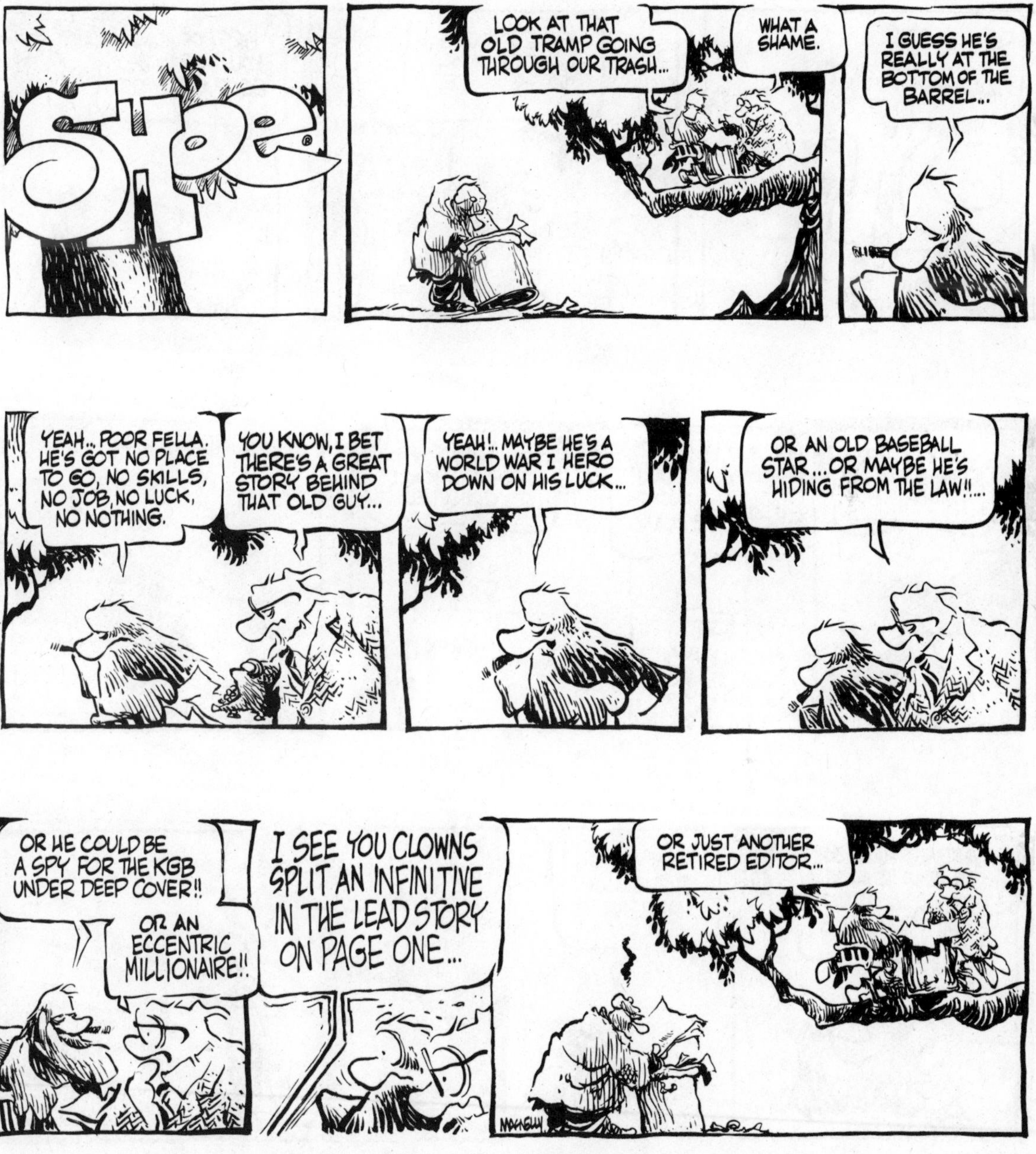
SHOE®
LOOK AT THAT OLD TRAMP GOING THROUGH OUR TRASH...
WHAT A SHAME.
I GUESS HE'S REALLY AT THE BOTTOM OF THE BARREL...
YEAH... POOR FELLA. HE'S GOT NO PLACE TO GO, NO SKILLS, NO JOB, NO LUCK, NO NOTHING.
YOU KNOW, I BET THERE'S A GREAT STORY BEHIND THAT OLD GUY...
YEAH!.. MAYBE HE'S A WORLD WAR I HERO DOWN ON HIS LUCK...
OR AN OLD BASEBALL STAR ... OR MAYBE HE'S HIDING FROM THE LAW!!...
OR HE COULD BE A SPY FOR THE KGB UNDER DEEP COVER!!
OR AN ECCENTRIC MILLIONAIRE!!
I SEE YOU CLOWNS SPLIT AN INFINITIVE IN THE LEAD STORY ON PAGE ONE...
OR JUST ANOTHER RETIRED EDITOR...
MACNELLY

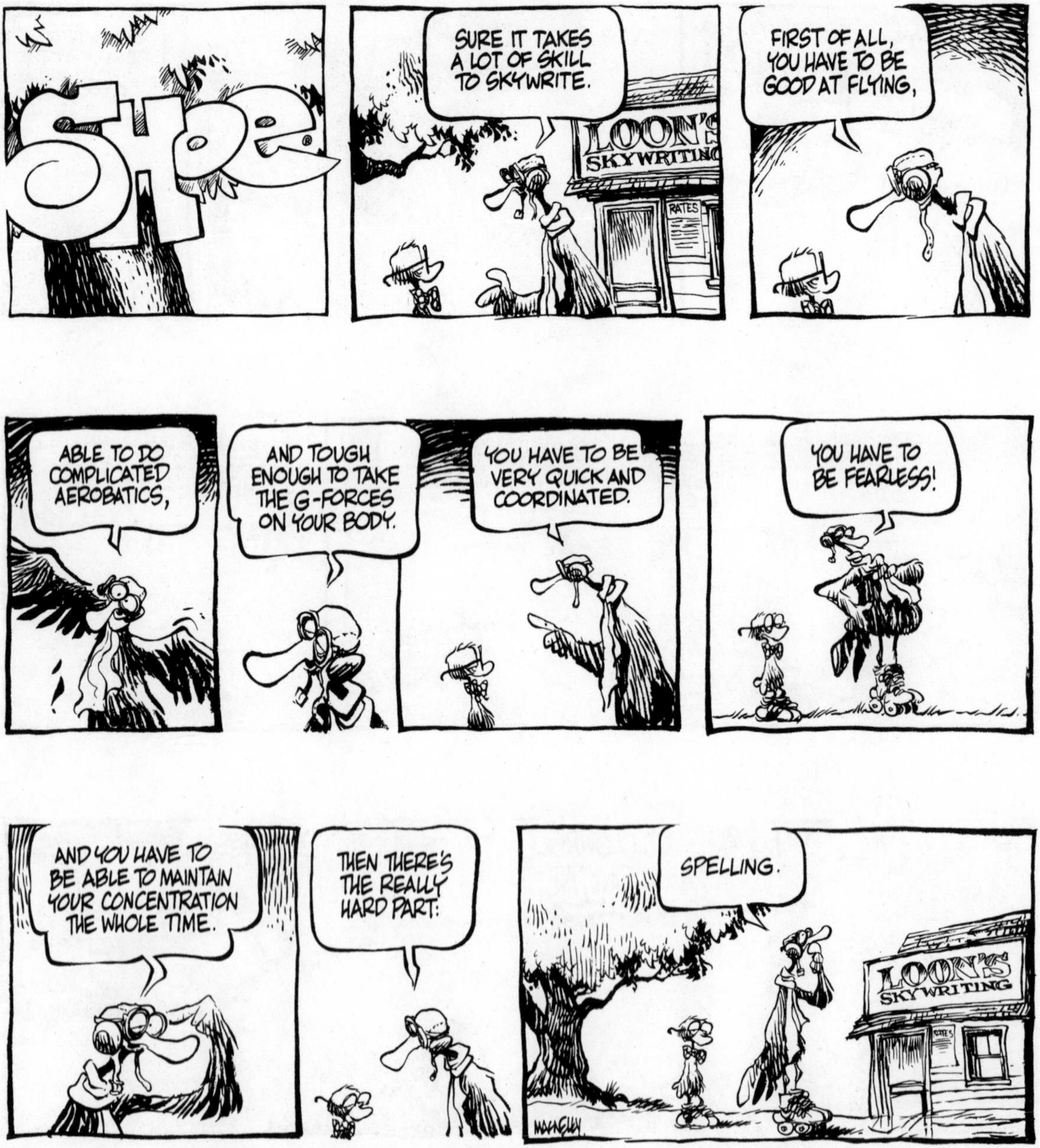
SHOE
SURE IT TAKES A LOT OF SKILL TO SKYWRITE.
LOON'S SKYWRITING
RATES
FIRST OF ALL, YOU HAVE TO BE GOOD AT FLYING,
ABLE TO DO COMPLICATED AEROBATICS,
AND TOUGH ENOUGH TO TAKE THE G-FORCES ON YOUR BODY.
YOU HAVE TO BE VERY QUICK AND COORDINATED.
YOU HAVE TO BE FEARLESS!
AND YOU HAVE TO BE ABLE TO MAINTAIN YOUR CONCENTRATION THE WHOLE TIME.
THEN THERE'S THE REALLY HARD PART:
SPELLING.
LOON'S SKYWRITING
RATES
MACNELLY

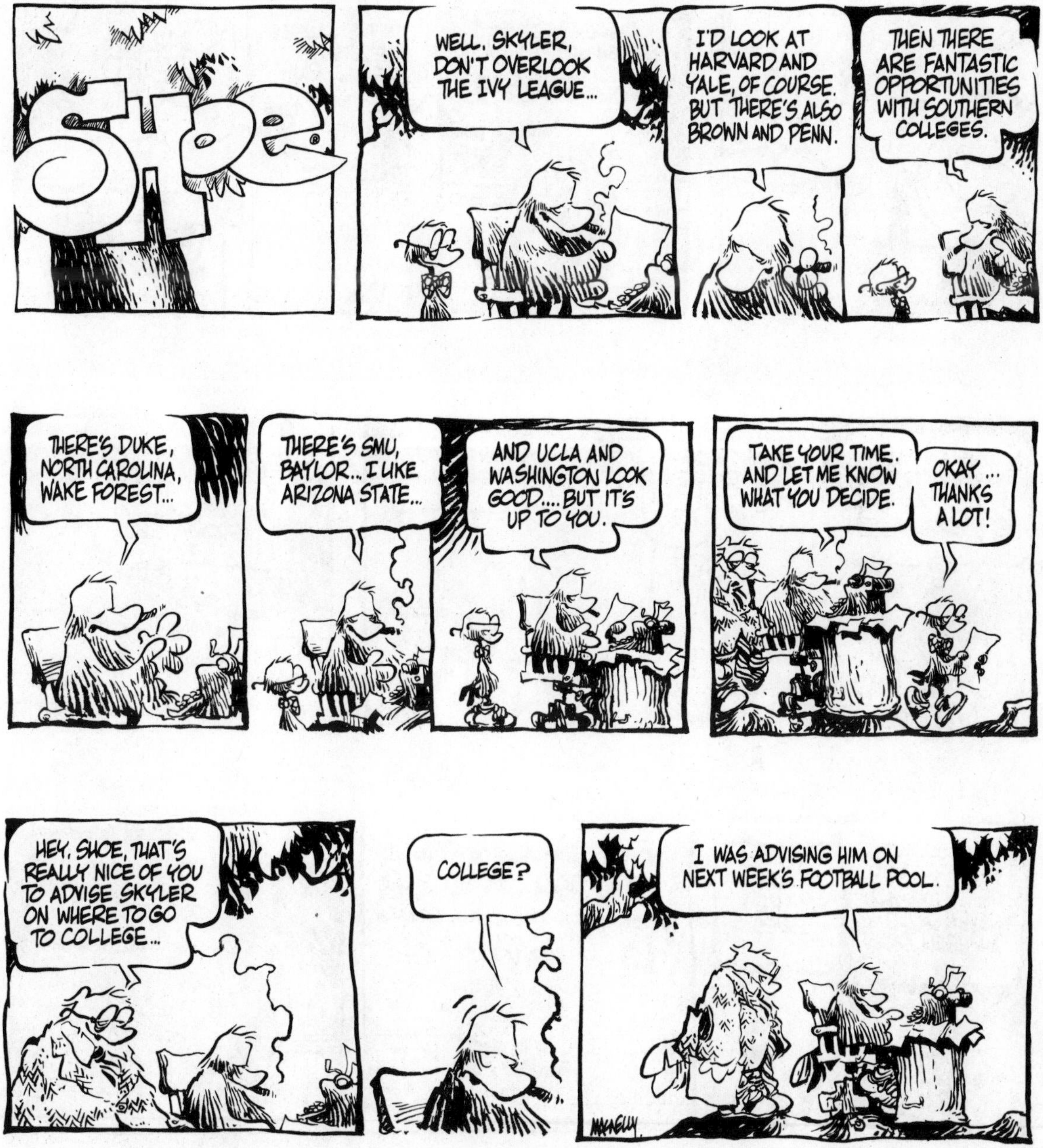
SHOE®
WELL, SKYLER, DON'T OVERLOOK THE IVY LEAGUE...
I'D LOOK AT HARVARD AND YALE, OF COURSE. BUT THERE'S ALSO BROWN AND PENN.
THEN THERE ARE FANTASTIC OPPORTUNITIES WITH SOUTHERN COLLEGES.
THERE'S DUKE, NORTH CAROLINA, WAKE FOREST...
THERE'S SMU, BAYLOR... I LIKE ARIZONA STATE...
AND UCLA AND WASHINGTON LOOK GOOD.... BUT IT'S UP TO YOU.
TAKE YOUR TIME. AND LET ME KNOW WHAT YOU DECIDE.
OKAY ... THANKS A LOT!
HEY, SHOE, THAT'S REALLY NICE OF YOU TO ADVISE SKYLER ON WHERE TO GO TO COLLEGE...
COLLEGE?
I WAS ADVISING HIM ON NEXT WEEK'S FOOTBALL POOL.
MACNELLY

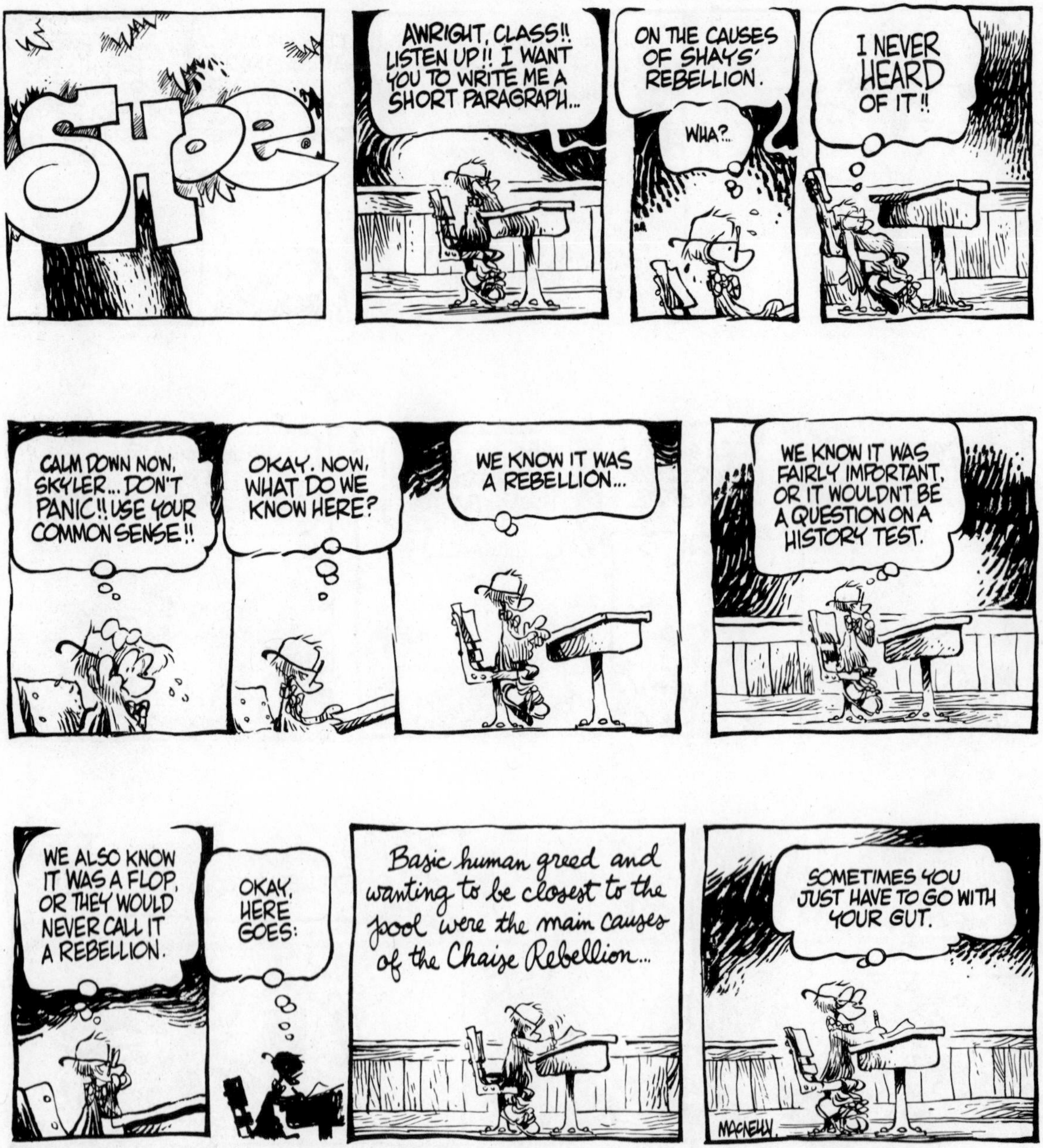
SHOE®
AWRIGHT, CLASS!! LISTEN UP!! I WANT YOU TO WRITE ME A SHORT PARAGRAPH...
ON THE CAUSES OF SHAYS' REBELLION.
WHA?...
I NEVER HEARD OF IT!!
CALM DOWN NOW, SKYLER... DON'T PANIC!! USE YOUR COMMON SENSE!!
OKAY. NOW, WHAT DO WE KNOW HERE?
WE KNOW IT WAS A REBELLION...
WE KNOW IT WAS FAIRLY IMPORTANT, OR IT WOULDN'T BE A QUESTION ON A HISTORY TEST.
WE ALSO KNOW IT WAS A FLOP, OR THEY WOULD NEVER CALL IT A REBELLION.
OKAY, HERE GOES:
Basic human greed and wanting to be closest to the pool were the main causes of the Chaise Rebellion...
SOMETIMES YOU JUST HAVE TO GO WITH YOUR GUT.
MACNELLY

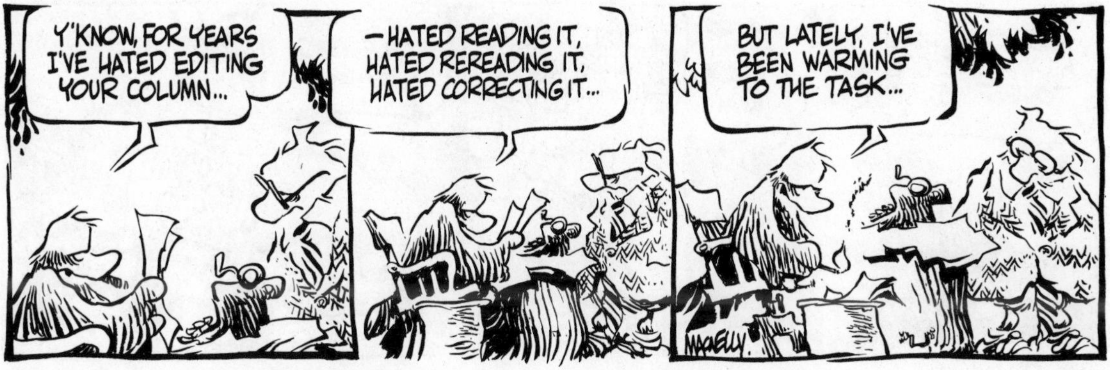
Y'KNOW, FOR YEARS I'VE HATED EDITING YOUR COLUMN...
—HATED READING IT, HATED REREADING IT, HATED CORRECTING IT...
BUT LATELY, I'VE BEEN WARMING TO THE TASK...

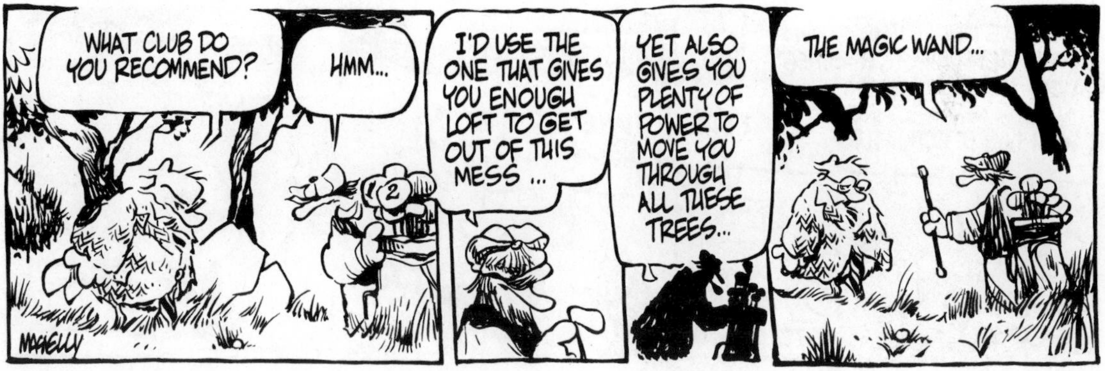
WHAT CLUB DO YOU RECOMMEND?
HMM...
I'D USE THE ONE THAT GIVES YOU ENOUGH LOFT TO GET OUT OF THIS MESS ...
YET ALSO GIVES YOU PLENTY OF POWER TO MOVE YOU THROUGH ALL THESE TREES...
THE MAGIC WAND...

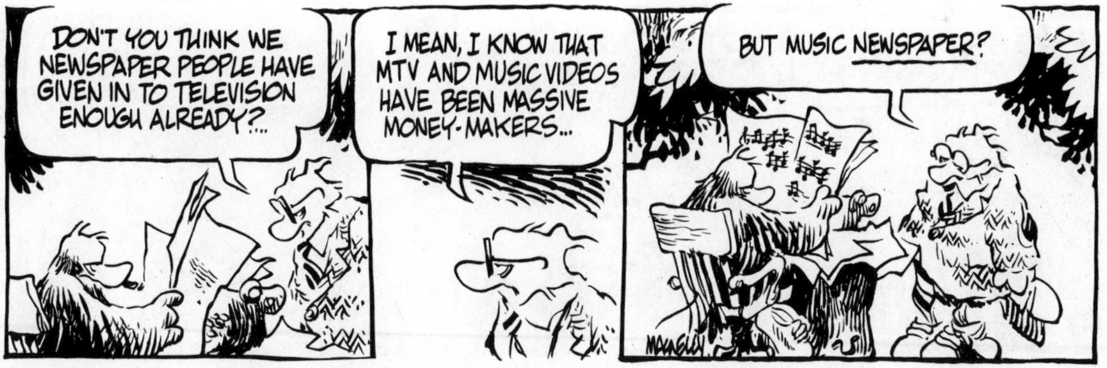
DON'T YOU THINK WE NEWSPAPER PEOPLE HAVE GIVEN IN TO TELEVISION ENOUGH ALREADY?...
I MEAN, I KNOW THAT MTV AND MUSIC VIDEOS HAVE BEEN MASSIVE MONEY-MAKERS...
BUT MUSIC NEWSPAPER?

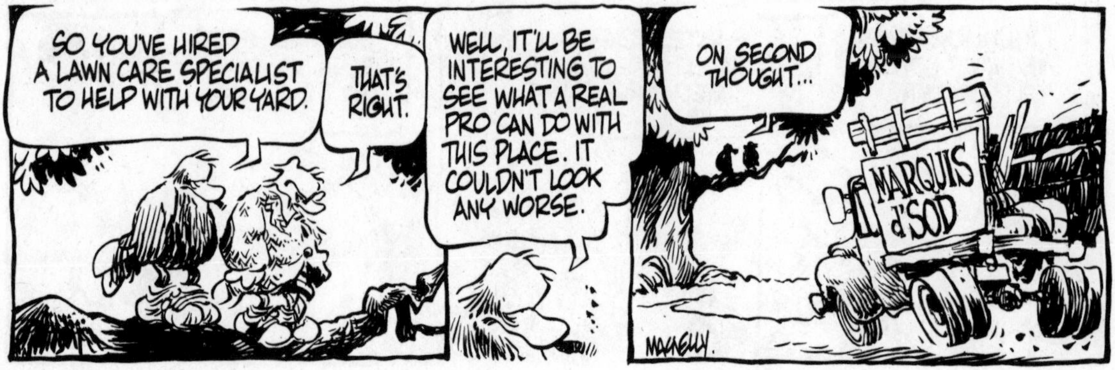
SO YOU'VE HIRED A LAWN CARE SPECIALIST TO HELP WITH YOUR YARD.
THAT'S RIGHT.
WELL, IT'LL BE INTERESTING TO SEE WHAT A REAL PRO CAN DO WITH THIS PLACE. IT COULDN'T LOOK ANY WORSE.
ON SECOND THOUGHT...
MARQUIS d'SOD
MACNELLY

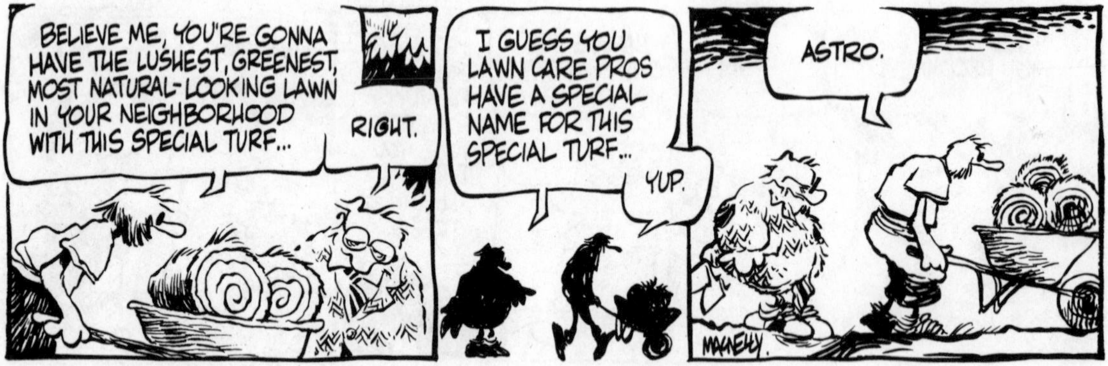
BELIEVE ME, YOU'RE GONNA HAVE THE LUSHEST, GREENEST, MOST NATURAL-LOOKING LAWN IN YOUR NEIGHBORHOOD WITH THIS SPECIAL TURF...
RIGHT.
I GUESS YOU LAWN CARE PROS HAVE A SPECIAL NAME FOR THIS SPECIAL TURF...
YUP.
ASTRO.
MACNELLY

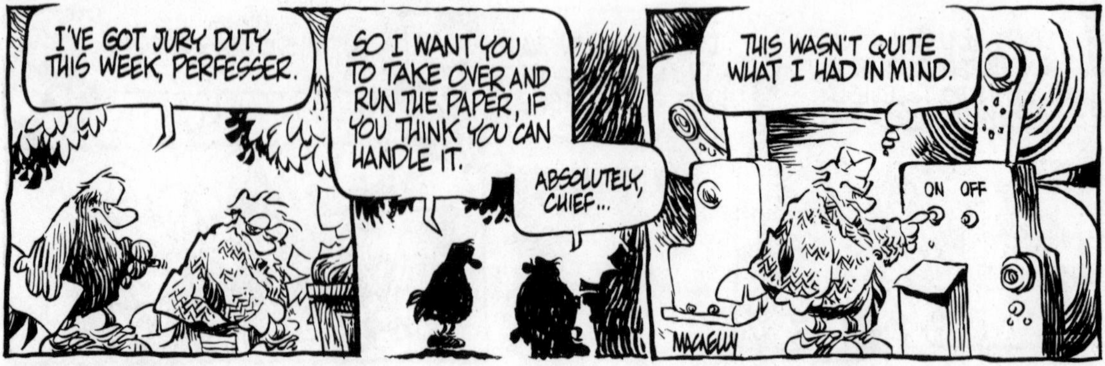
I'VE GOT JURY DUTY THIS WEEK, PERFESSER.
SO I WANT YOU TO TAKE OVER AND RUN THE PAPER, IF YOU THINK YOU CAN HANDLE IT.
ABSOLUTELY, CHIEF...
THIS WASN'T QUITE WHAT I HAD IN MIND.
ON OFF
MACNELLY

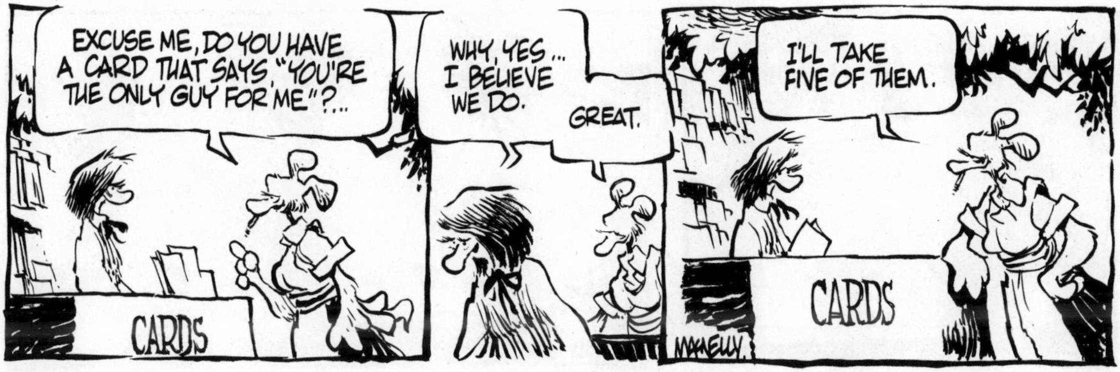
EXCUSE ME, DO YOU HAVE A CARD THAT SAYS, "YOU'RE THE ONLY GUY FOR ME"?...
CARDS
WHY, YES... I BELIEVE WE DO.
GREAT.
I'LL TAKE FIVE OF THEM.
CARDS
MACNELLY

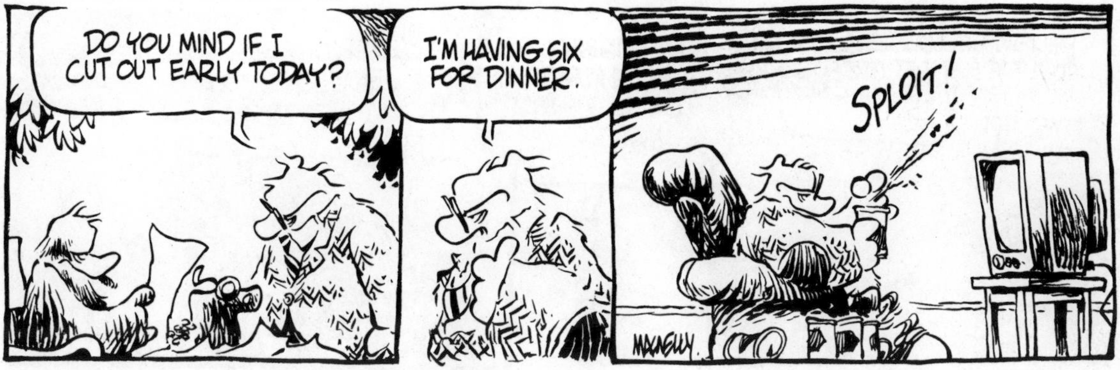
DO YOU MIND IF I CUT OUT EARLY TODAY?
I'M HAVING SIX FOR DINNER.
SPLOIT!
MACNELLY

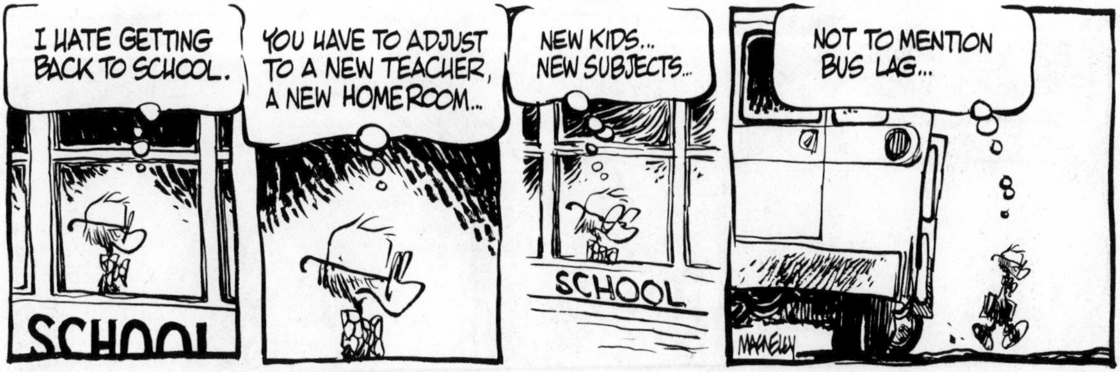
I HATE GETTING BACK TO SCHOOL.
SCHOOL
YOU HAVE TO ADJUST TO A NEW TEACHER, A NEW HOMEROOM...
NEW KIDS... NEW SUBJECTS...
SCHOOL
NOT TO MENTION BUS LAG...
MACNELLY

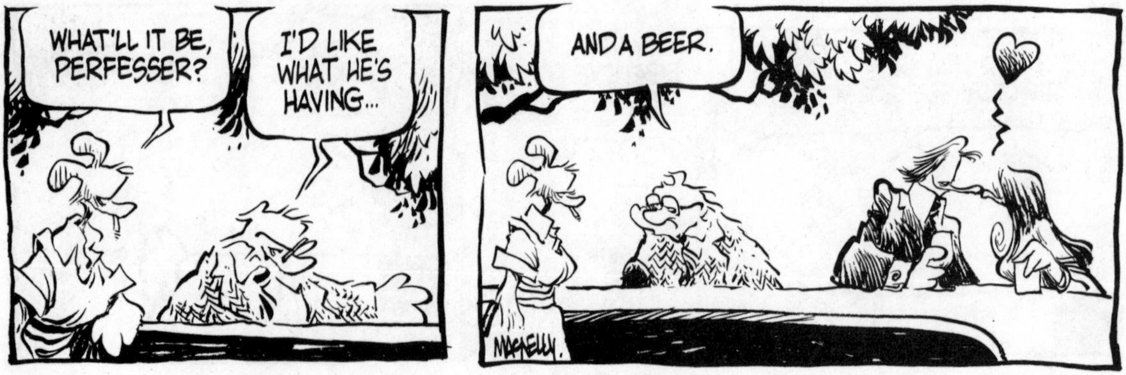
WHAT'LL IT BE, PERFESSER?
I'D LIKE WHAT HE'S HAVING...
AND A BEER.

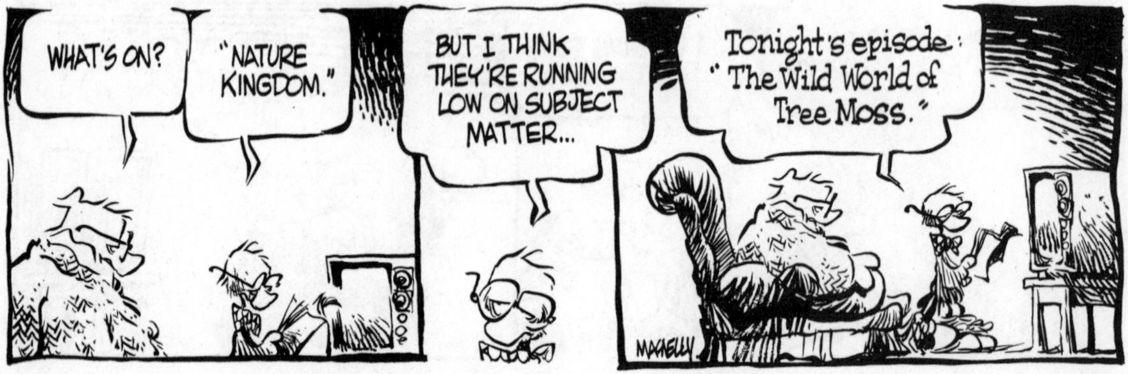
WHAT'S ON?
"NATURE KINGDOM."
BUT I THINK THEY'RE RUNNING LOW ON SUBJECT MATTER...
Tonight's episode: "The Wild World of Tree Moss."

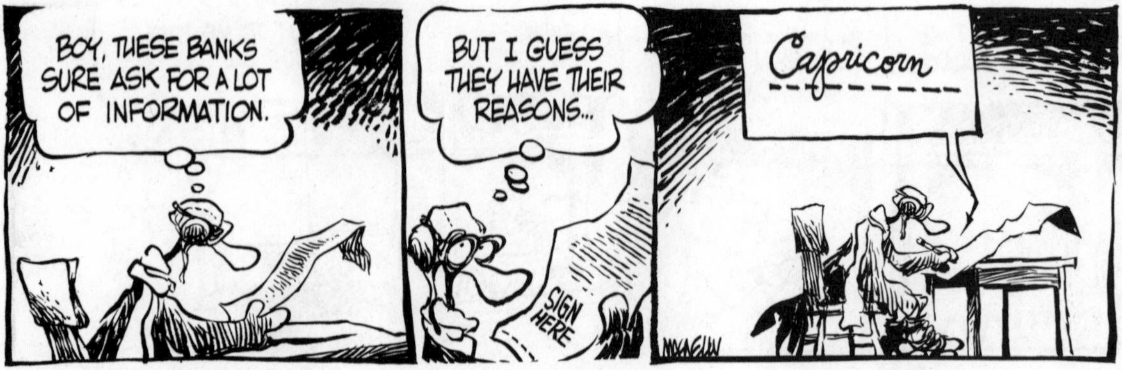
BOY, THESE BANKS SURE ASK FOR A LOT OF INFORMATION.
BUT I GUESS THEY HAVE THEIR REASONS...
SIGN HERE
Capricorn

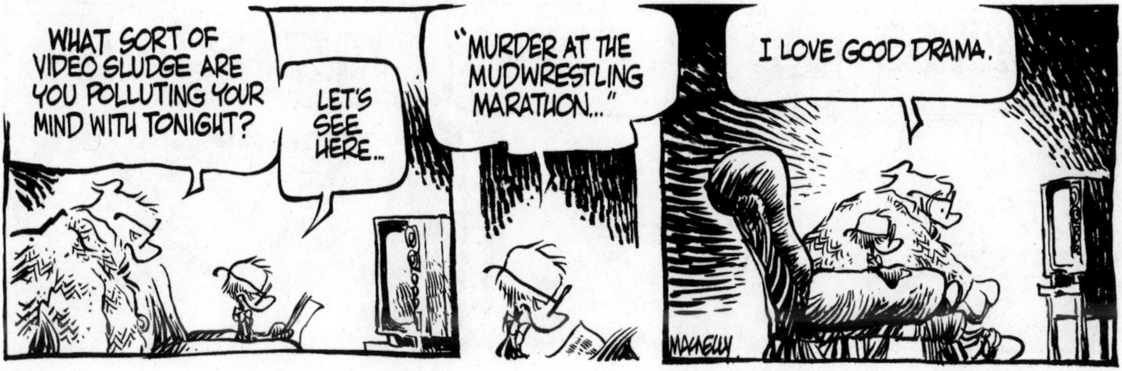
WHAT SORT OF VIDEO SLUDGE ARE YOU POLLUTING YOUR MIND WITH TONIGHT?
LET'S SEE HERE...
"MURDER AT THE MUDWRESTLING MARATHON..."
I LOVE GOOD DRAMA.

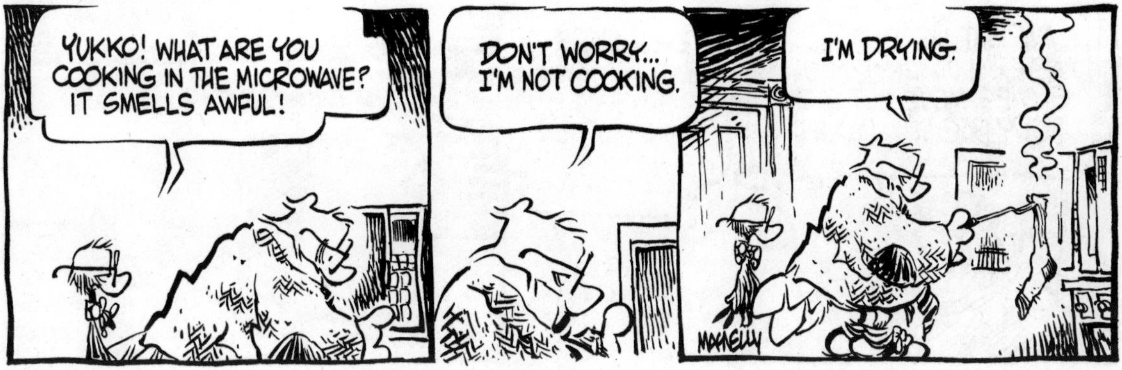
YUKKO! WHAT ARE YOU COOKING IN THE MICROWAVE? IT SMELLS AWFUL!
DON'T WORRY... I'M NOT COOKING.
I'M DRYING.

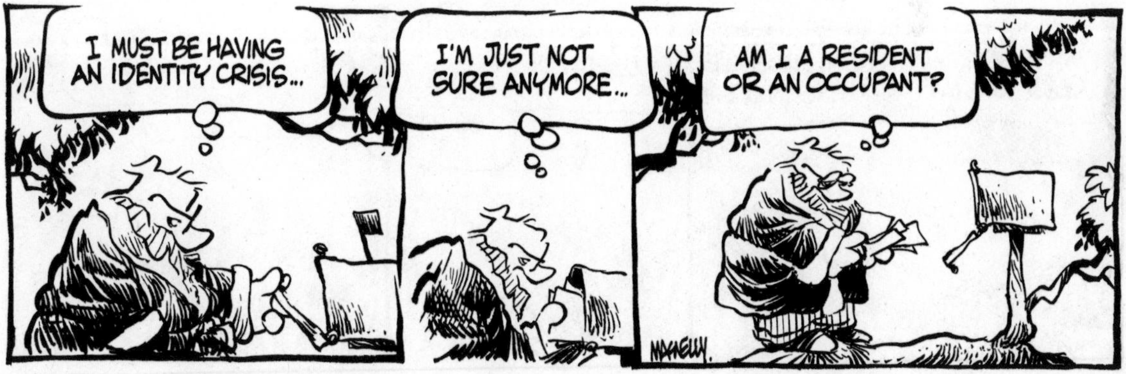
I MUST BE HAVING AN IDENTITY CRISIS...
I'M JUST NOT SURE ANYMORE...
AM I A RESIDENT OR AN OCCUPANT?

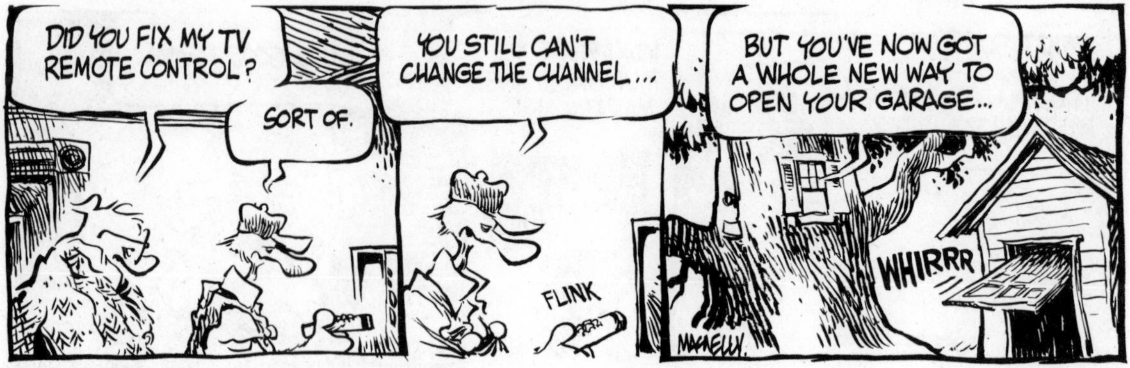
DID YOU FIX MY TV REMOTE CONTROL?
SORT OF.
YOU STILL CAN'T CHANGE THE CHANNEL...
FLINK
BUT YOU'VE NOW GOT A WHOLE NEW WAY TO OPEN YOUR GARAGE...
WHIRRR
MACNELLY.

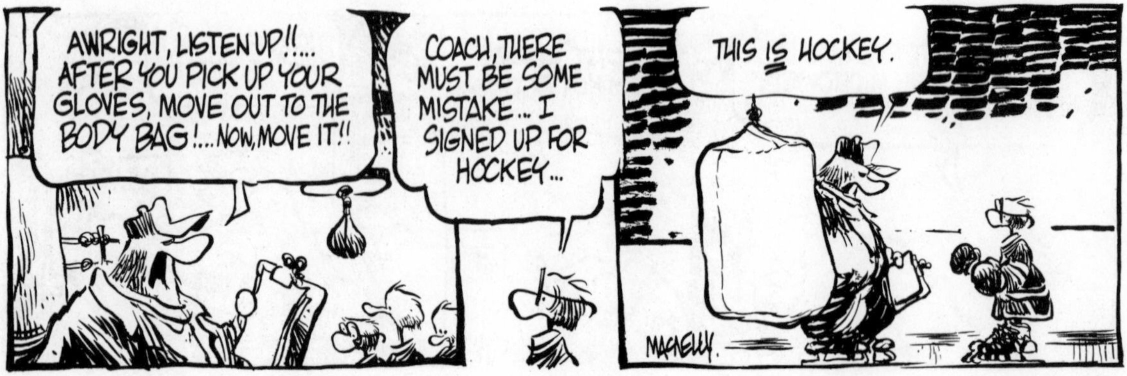
AWRIGHT, LISTEN UP!!.... AFTER YOU PICK UP YOUR GLOVES, MOVE OUT TO THE BODY BAG!...NOW, MOVE IT!!
COACH, THERE MUST BE SOME MISTAKE... I SIGNED UP FOR HOCKEY...
THIS IS HOCKEY.
MACNELLY.

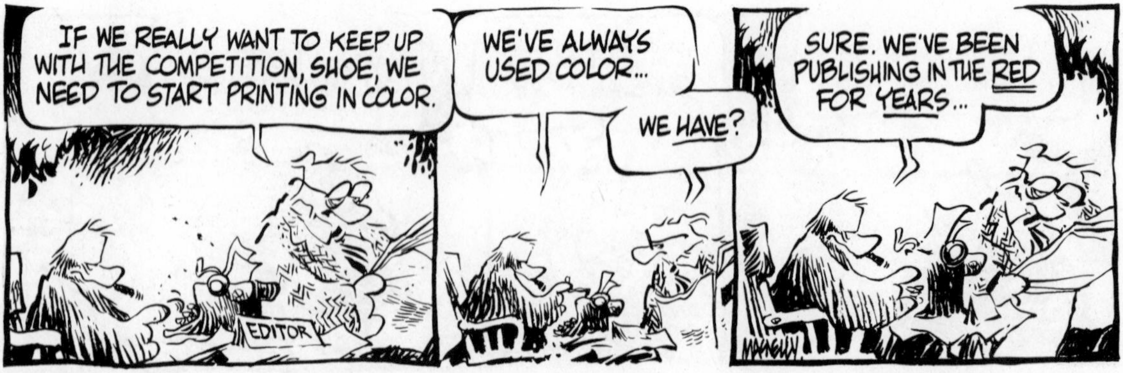
IF WE REALLY WANT TO KEEP UP WITH THE COMPETITION, SHOE, WE NEED TO START PRINTING IN COLOR.
EDITOR
WE'VE ALWAYS USED COLOR...
WE HAVE?
SURE. WE'VE BEEN PUBLISHING IN THE RED FOR YEARS...
MACNELLY.

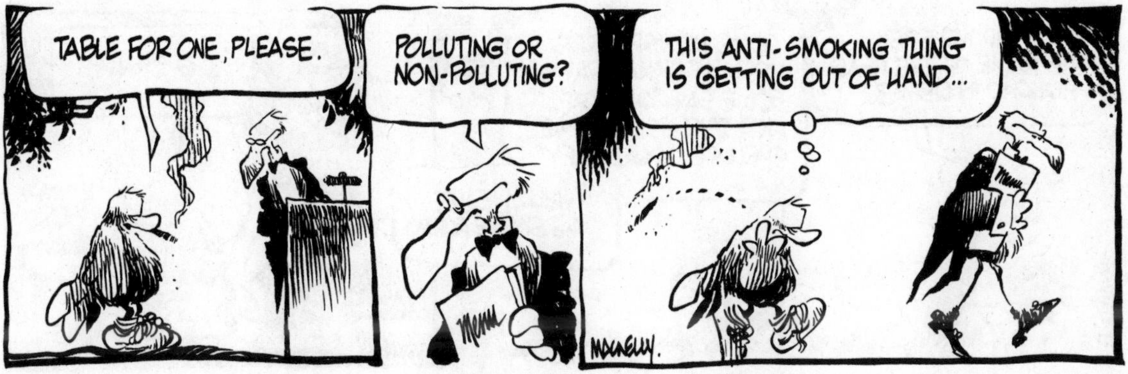
TABLE FOR ONE, PLEASE.
POLLUTING OR NON-POLLUTING?
THIS ANTI-SMOKING THING IS GETTING OUT OF HAND...
MENU

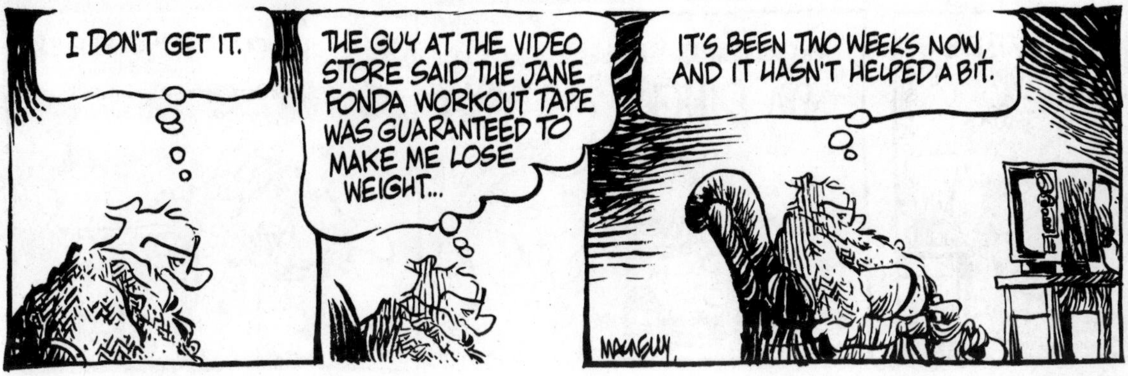
I DON'T GET IT.
THE GUY AT THE VIDEO STORE SAID THE JANE FONDA WORKOUT TAPE WAS GUARANTEED TO MAKE ME LOSE WEIGHT...
IT'S BEEN TWO WEEKS NOW, AND IT HASN'T HELPED A BIT.

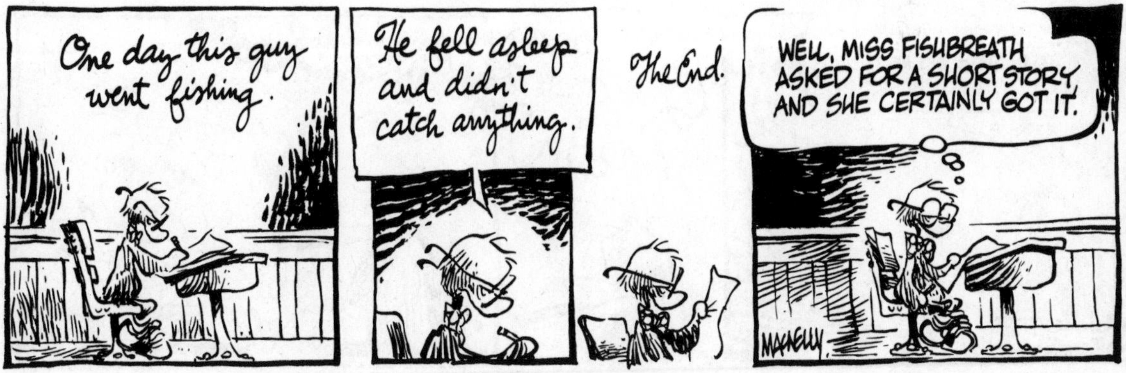
One day this guy went fishing.
He fell asleep and didn't catch anything.
The End.
WELL, MISS FISHBREATH ASKED FOR A SHORT STORY AND SHE CERTAINLY GOT IT.

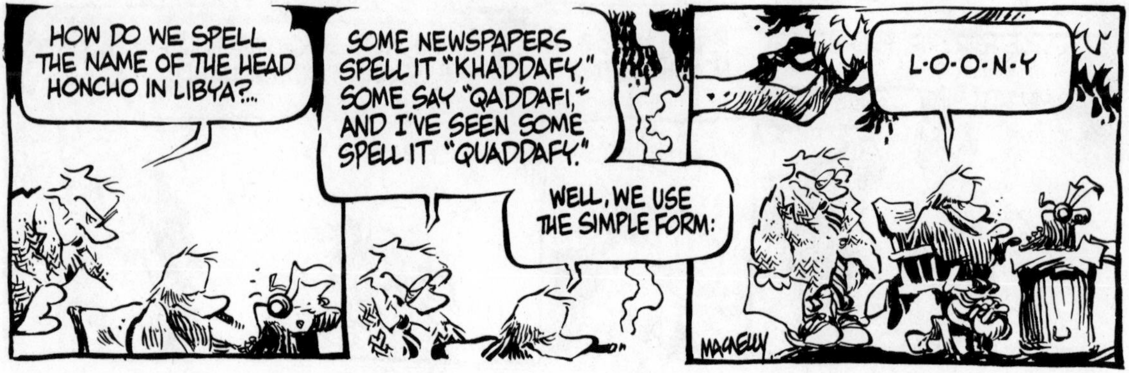
HOW DO WE SPELL THE NAME OF THE HEAD HONCHO IN LIBYA?...
SOME NEWSPAPERS SPELL IT "KHADDAFY," SOME SAY "QADDAFI," AND I'VE SEEN SOME SPELL IT "QUADDAFY."
WELL, WE USE THE SIMPLE FORM:
L-O-O-N-Y
MACNELLY

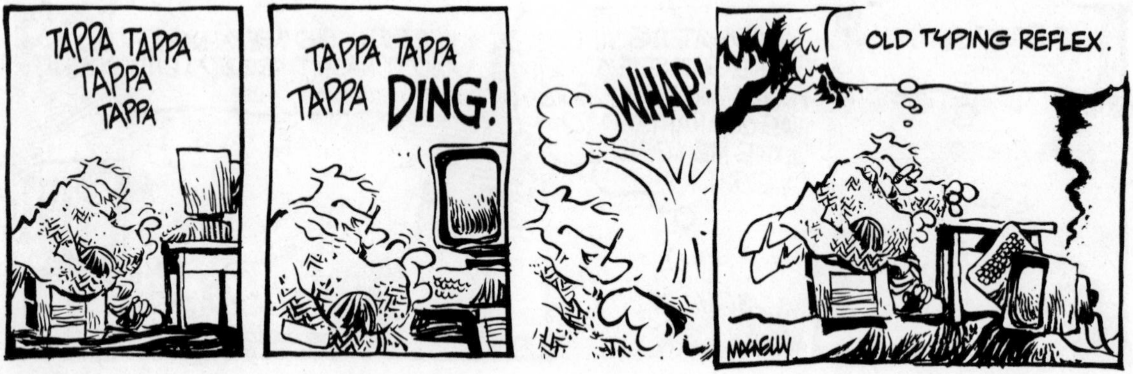
TAPPA TAPPA TAPPA TAPPA
TAPPA TAPPA TAPPA DING!
WHAP!
OLD TYPING REFLEX.
MACNELLY

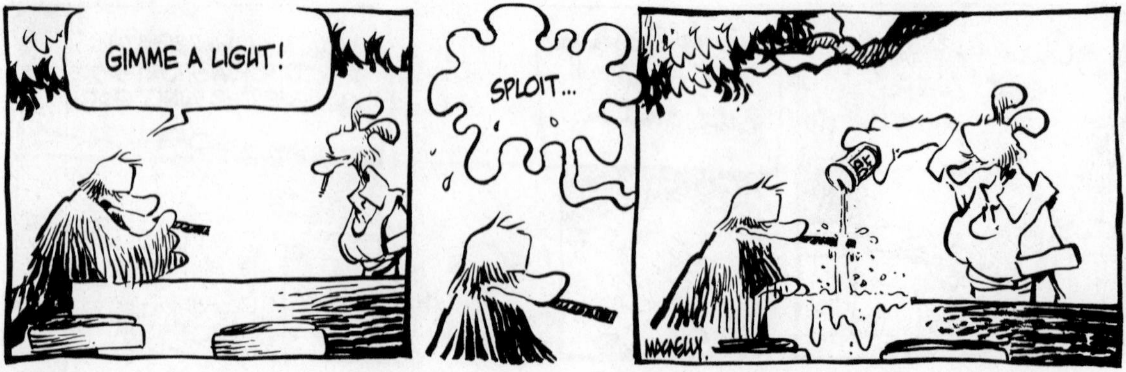
GIMME A LIGHT!
SPLOIT...
MACNELLY

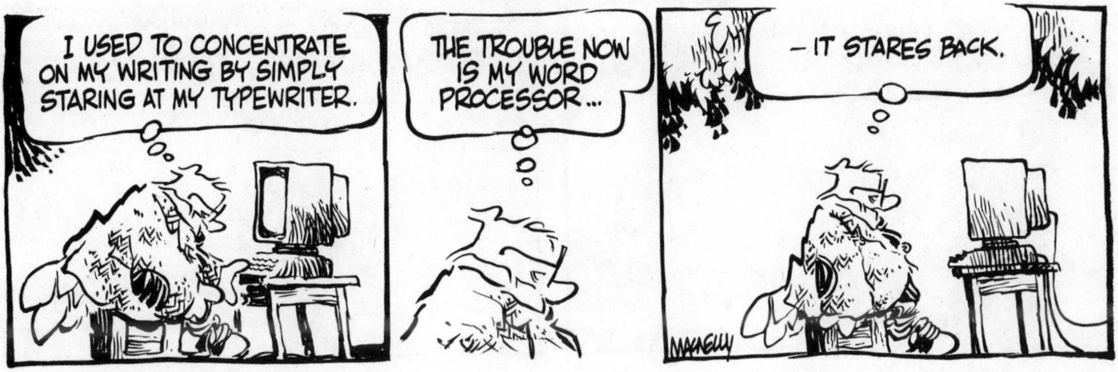
I USED TO CONCENTRATE ON MY WRITING BY SIMPLY STARING AT MY TYPEWRITER.
THE TROUBLE NOW IS MY WORD PROCESSOR...
– IT STARES BACK.

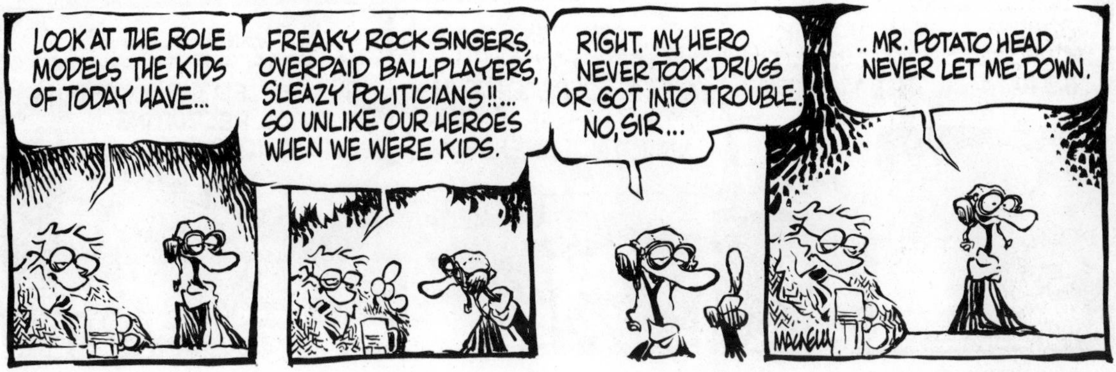
LOOK AT THE ROLE MODELS THE KIDS OF TODAY HAVE...
FREAKY ROCK SINGERS, OVERPAID BALLPLAYERS, SLEAZY POLITICIANS !!... SO UNLIKE OUR HEROES WHEN WE WERE KIDS.
RIGHT. MY HERO NEVER TOOK DRUGS OR GOT INTO TROUBLE. NO, SIR...
.. MR. POTATO HEAD NEVER LET ME DOWN.

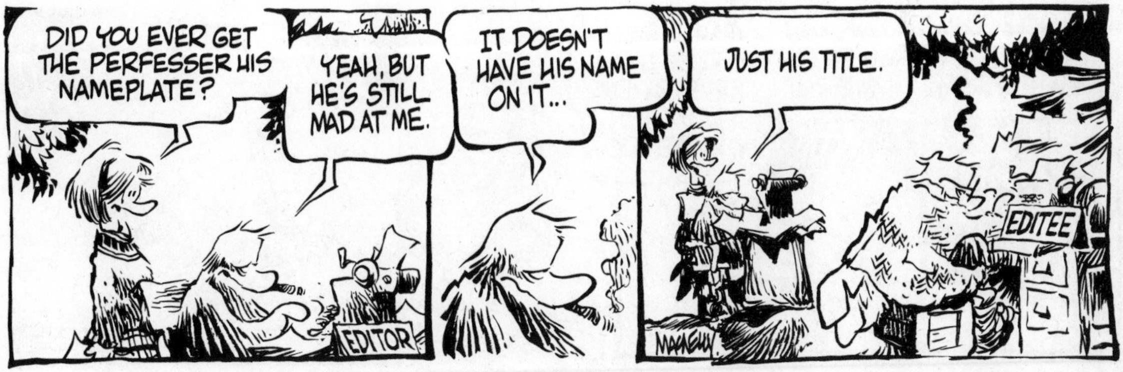
DID YOU EVER GET THE PERFESSER HIS NAMEPLATE?
YEAH, BUT HE'S STILL MAD AT ME.
EDITOR
IT DOESN'T HAVE HIS NAME ON IT...
JUST HIS TITLE.
EDITEE

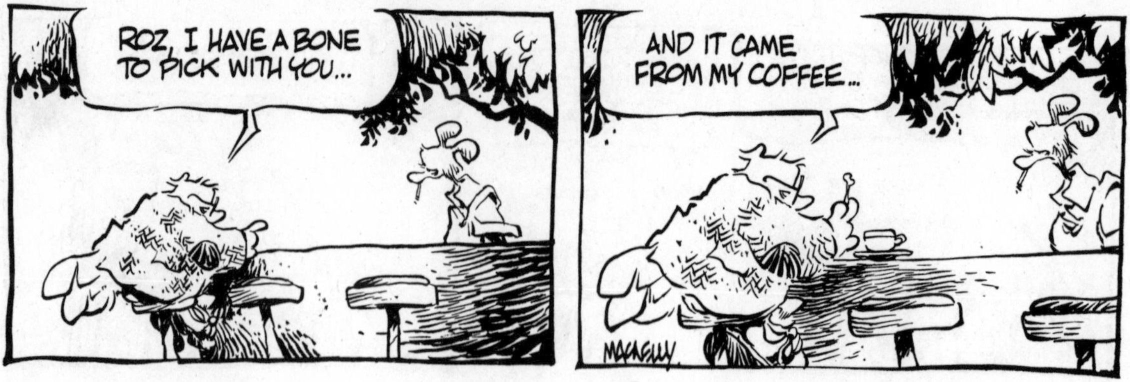
ROZ, I HAVE A BONE TO PICK WITH YOU...
AND IT CAME FROM MY COFFEE...

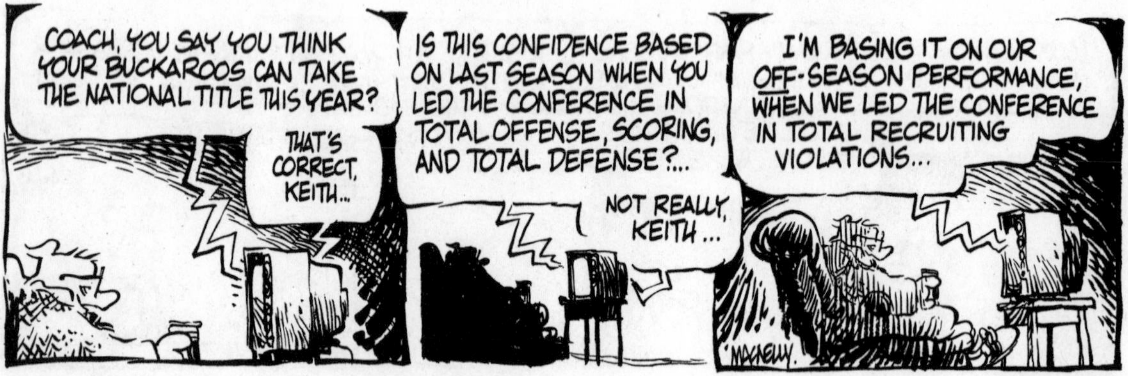
COACH, YOU SAY YOU THINK YOUR BUCKAROOS CAN TAKE THE NATIONAL TITLE THIS YEAR?
THAT'S CORRECT, KEITH...
IS THIS CONFIDENCE BASED ON LAST SEASON WHEN YOU LED THE CONFERENCE IN TOTAL OFFENSE, SCORING, AND TOTAL DEFENSE?...
NOT REALLY, KEITH...
I'M BASING IT ON OUR OFF-SEASON PERFORMANCE, WHEN WE LED THE CONFERENCE IN TOTAL RECRUITING VIOLATIONS...

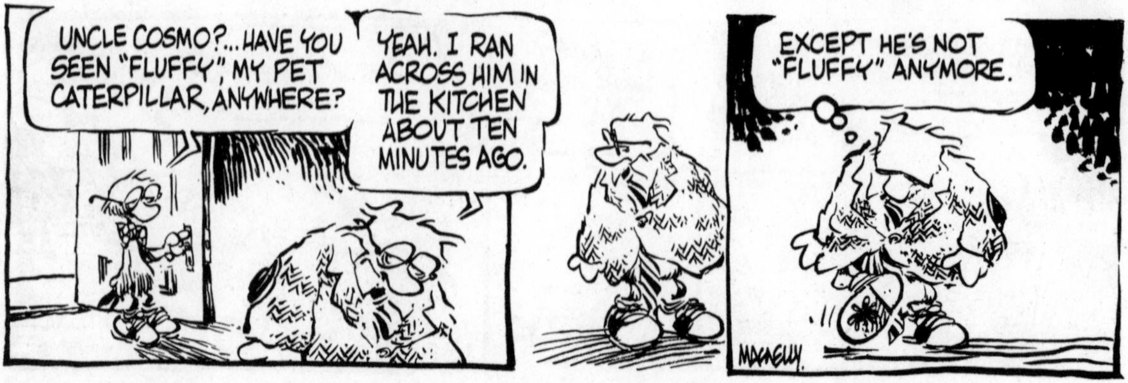
UNCLE COSMO?... HAVE YOU SEEN "FLUFFY", MY PET CATERPILLAR, ANYWHERE?
YEAH. I RAN ACROSS HIM IN THE KITCHEN ABOUT TEN MINUTES AGO.
EXCEPT HE'S NOT "FLUFFY" ANYMORE.

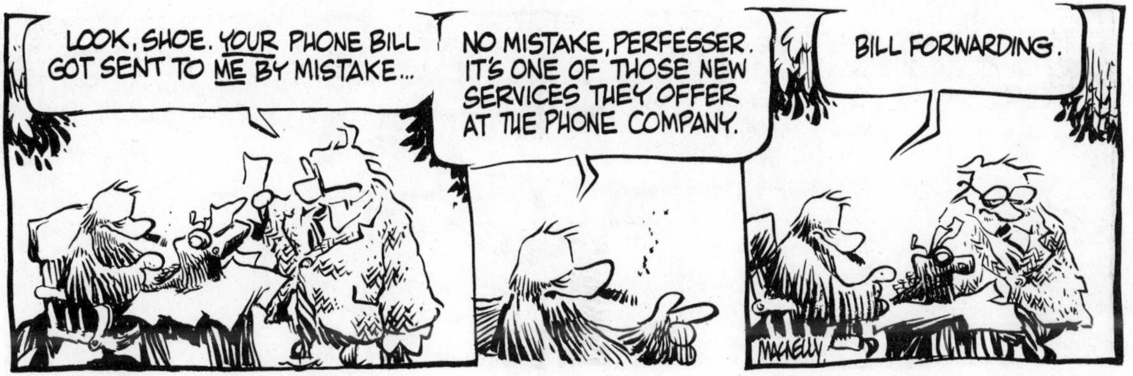
LOOK, SHOE. YOUR PHONE BILL GOT SENT TO ME BY MISTAKE...
NO MISTAKE, PERFESSER. IT'S ONE OF THOSE NEW SERVICES THEY OFFER AT THE PHONE COMPANY.
BILL FORWARDING.
MACNELLY

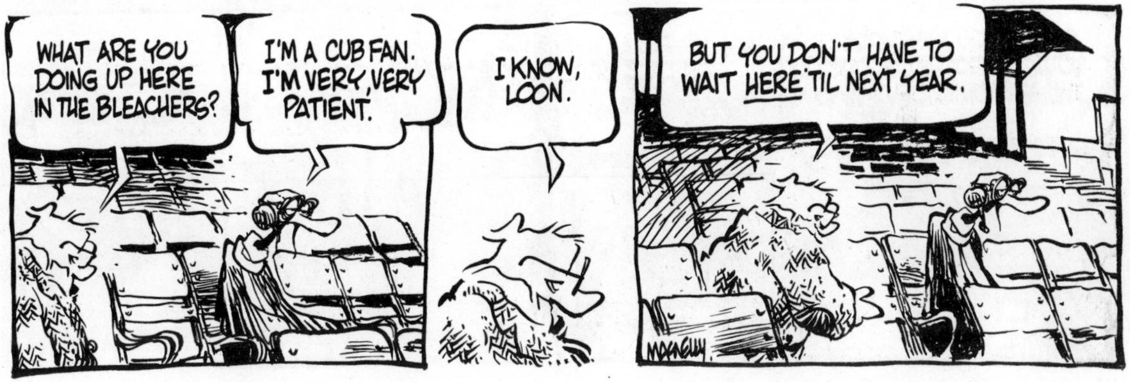
WHAT ARE YOU DOING UP HERE IN THE BLEACHERS?
I'M A CUB FAN. I'M VERY, VERY PATIENT.
I KNOW, LOON.
BUT YOU DON'T HAVE TO WAIT HERE 'TIL NEXT YEAR.
MACNELLY

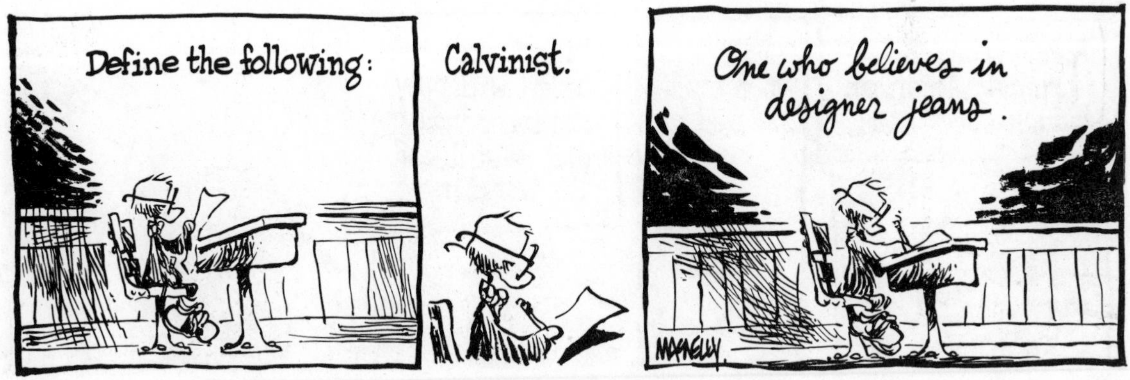
Define the following:
Calvinist.
One who believes in designer jeans.
MACNELLY

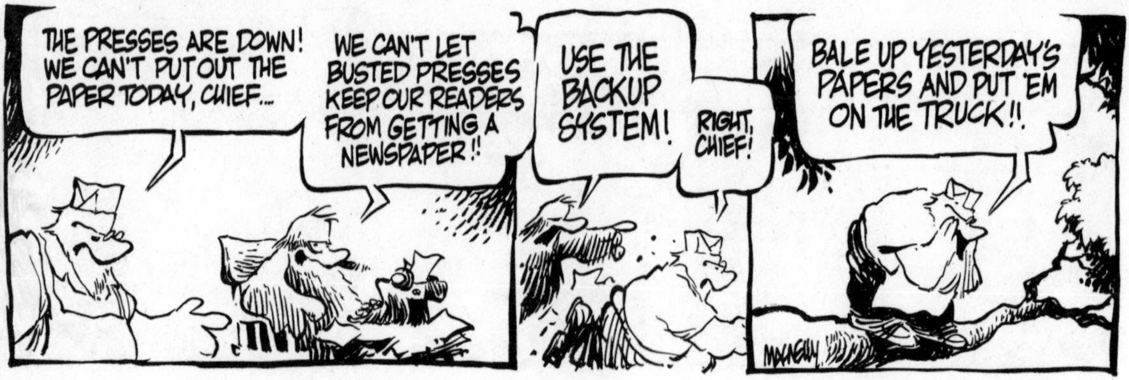
THE PRESSES ARE DOWN! WE CAN'T PUT OUT THE PAPER TODAY, CHIEF....
WE CAN'T LET BUSTED PRESSES KEEP OUR READERS FROM GETTING A NEWSPAPER!!
USE THE BACKUP SYSTEM!
RIGHT, CHIEF!
BALE UP YESTERDAY'S PAPERS AND PUT 'EM ON THE TRUCK!!

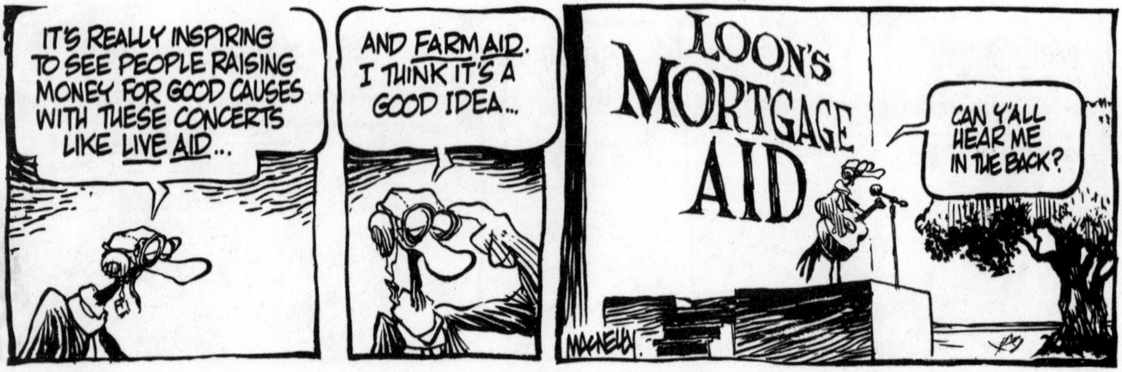
IT'S REALLY INSPIRING TO SEE PEOPLE RAISING MONEY FOR GOOD CAUSES WITH THESE CONCERTS LIKE LIVE AID...
AND FARM AID. I THINK IT'S A GOOD IDEA...
LOON'S MORTGAGE AID
CAN Y'ALL HEAR ME IN THE BACK?

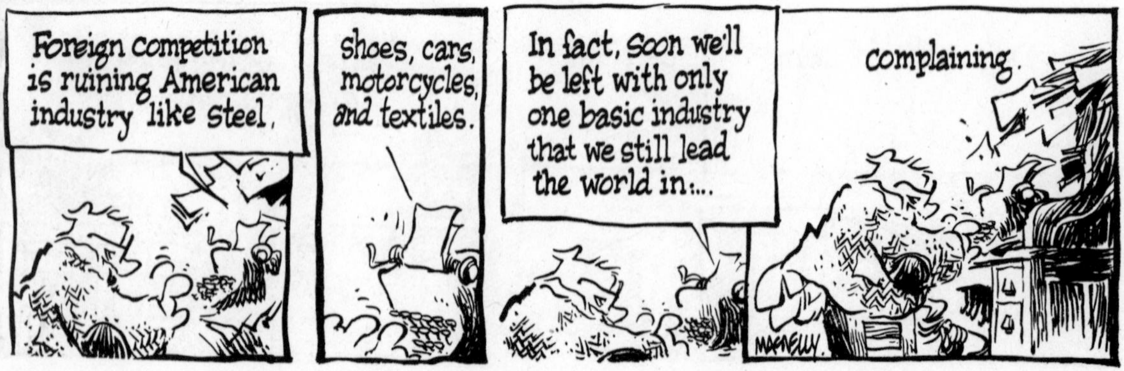
Foreign competition is ruining American industry like steel,
shoes, cars, motorcycles, and textiles.
In fact, soon we'll be left with only one basic industry that we still lead the world in:...
complaining.

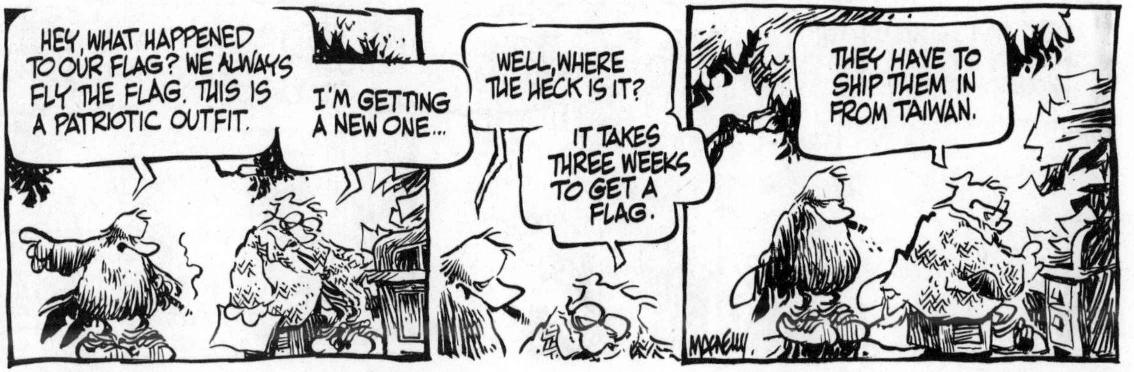
HEY, WHAT HAPPENED TO OUR FLAG? WE ALWAYS FLY THE FLAG. THIS IS A PATRIOTIC OUTFIT.
I'M GETTING A NEW ONE...
WELL, WHERE THE HECK IS IT?
IT TAKES THREE WEEKS TO GET A FLAG.
THEY HAVE TO SHIP THEM IN FROM TAIWAN.
MACNELLY

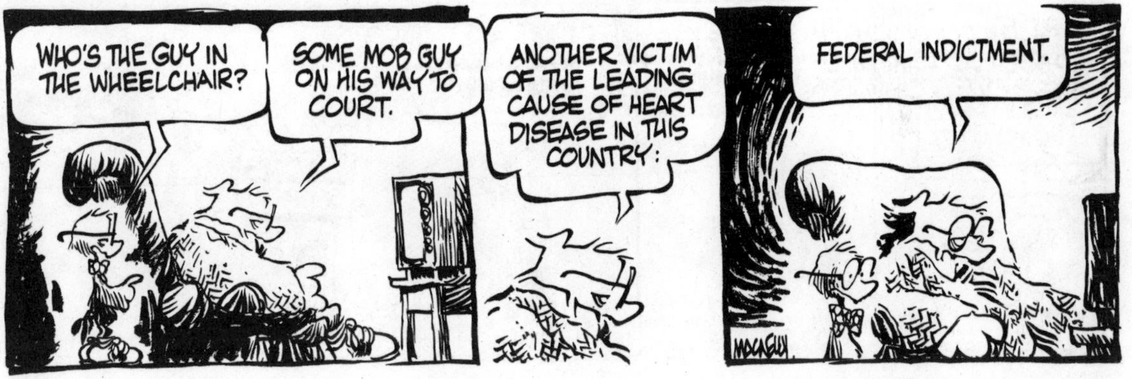
WHO'S THE GUY IN THE WHEELCHAIR?
SOME MOB GUY ON HIS WAY TO COURT.
ANOTHER VICTIM OF THE LEADING CAUSE OF HEART DISEASE IN THIS COUNTRY:
FEDERAL INDICTMENT.
MACNELLY

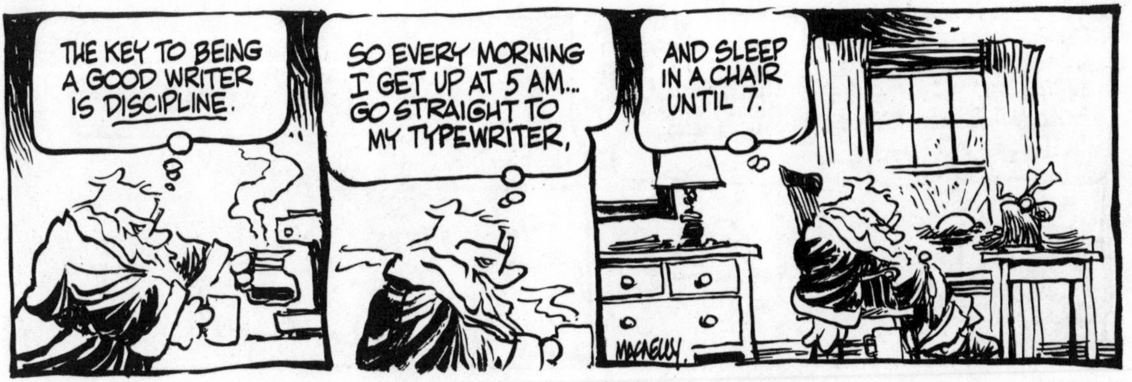
THE KEY TO BEING A GOOD WRITER IS DISCIPLINE.
SO EVERY MORNING I GET UP AT 5 AM... GO STRAIGHT TO MY TYPEWRITER,
AND SLEEP IN A CHAIR UNTIL 7.
MACNELLY

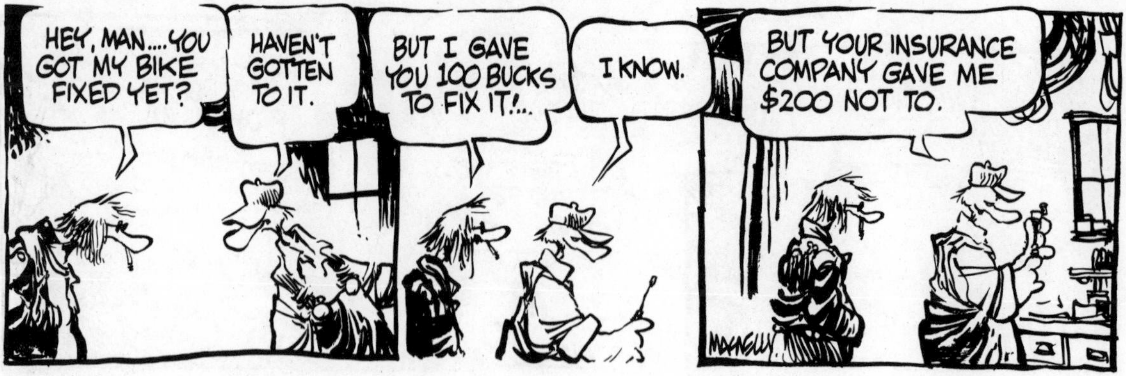
HEY, MAN....YOU GOT MY BIKE FIXED YET?
HAVEN'T GOTTEN TO IT.
BUT I GAVE YOU 100 BUCKS TO FIX IT!..
I KNOW.
BUT YOUR INSURANCE COMPANY GAVE ME $200 NOT TO.
MACNELLY

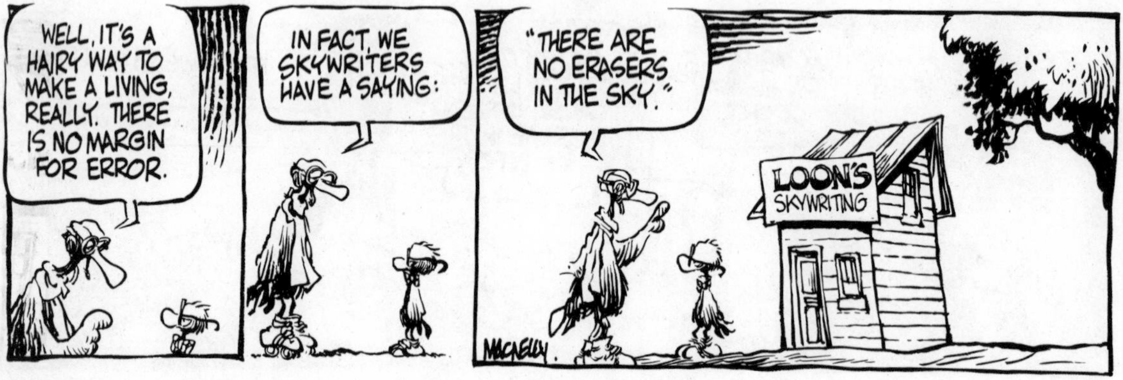
WELL, IT'S A HAIRY WAY TO MAKE A LIVING, REALLY. THERE IS NO MARGIN FOR ERROR.
IN FACT, WE SKYWRITERS HAVE A SAYING:
"THERE ARE NO ERASERS IN THE SKY."
LOON'S SKYWRITING
MACNELLY.

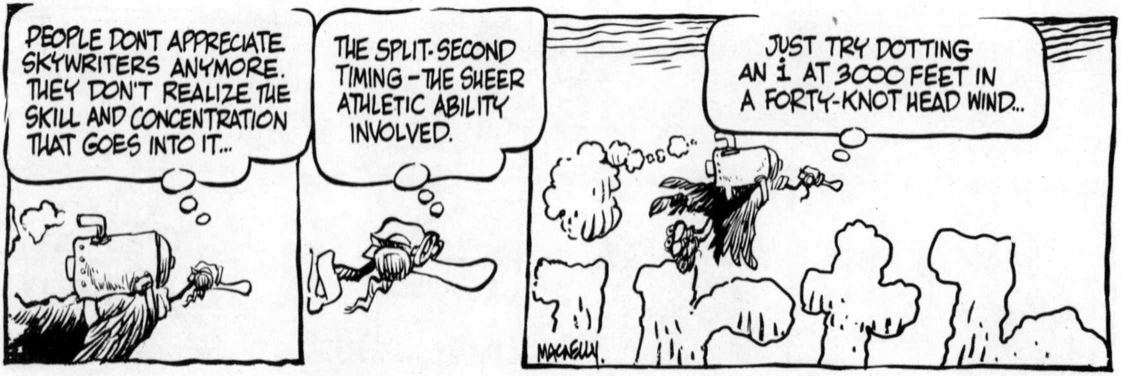
PEOPLE DON'T APPRECIATE SKYWRITERS ANYMORE. THEY DON'T REALIZE THE SKILL AND CONCENTRATION THAT GOES INTO IT...
THE SPLIT-SECOND TIMING—THE SHEER ATHLETIC ABILITY INVOLVED.
JUST TRY DOTTING AN i AT 3000 FEET IN A FORTY-KNOT HEAD WIND...
MACNELLY.

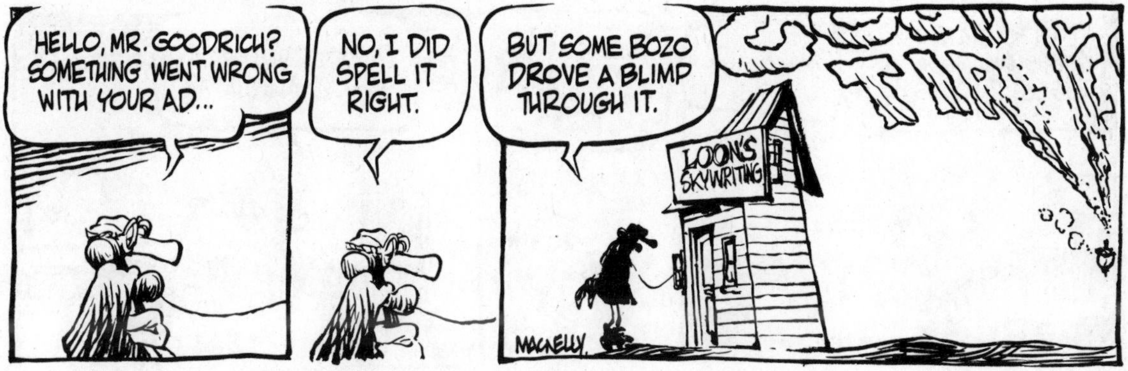
HELLO, MR. GOODRICH? SOMETHING WENT WRONG WITH YOUR AD...
NO, I DID SPELL IT RIGHT.
BUT SOME BOZO DROVE A BLIMP THROUGH IT.
LOON'S SKYWRITING
MACNELLY.

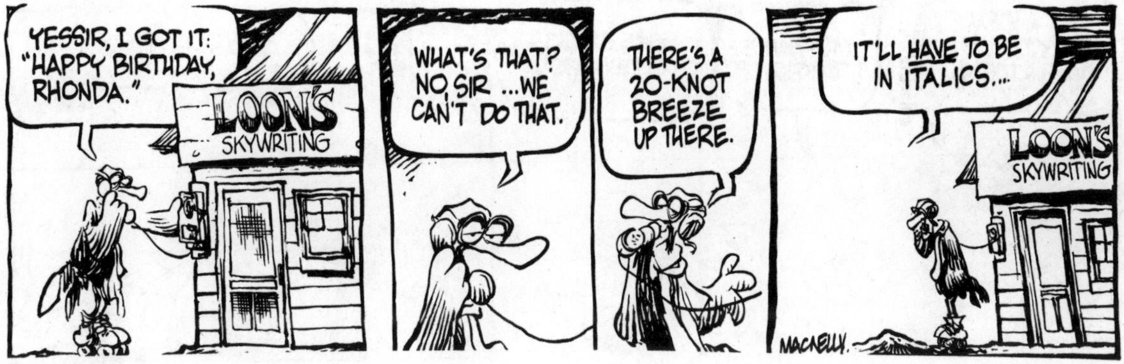
YESSIR, I GOT IT: "HAPPY BIRTHDAY, RHONDA."
LOON'S SKYWRITING
WHAT'S THAT? NO, SIR ...WE CAN'T DO THAT.
THERE'S A 20-KNOT BREEZE UP THERE.
IT'LL HAVE TO BE IN ITALICS....
LOON'S SKYWRITING
MACNELLY.

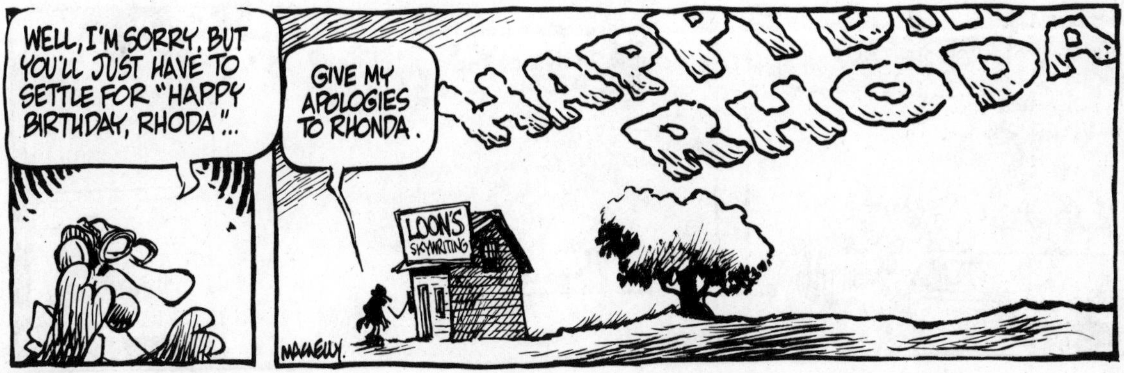
WELL, I'M SORRY, BUT YOU'LL JUST HAVE TO SETTLE FOR "HAPPY BIRTHDAY, RHODA"...
GIVE MY APOLOGIES TO RHONDA.
RHODA
LOON'S SKYWRITING
MACNELLY.

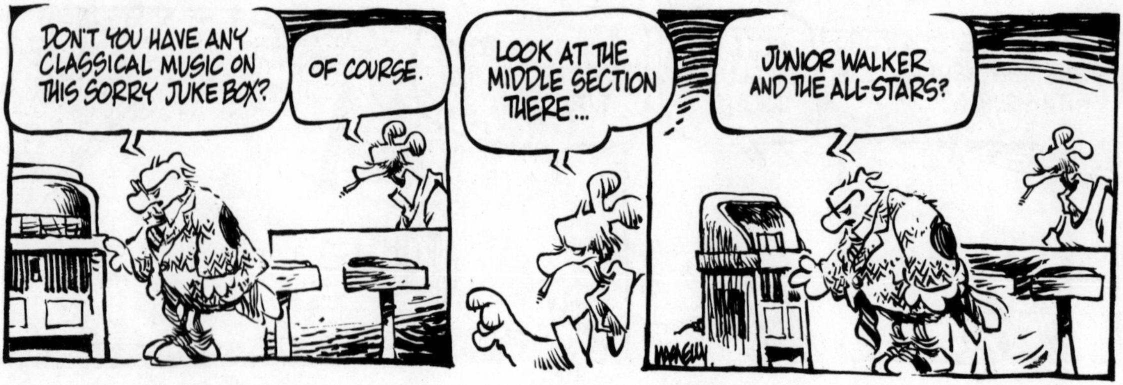
DON'T YOU HAVE ANY CLASSICAL MUSIC ON THIS SORRY JUKE BOX?
OF COURSE.
LOOK AT THE MIDDLE SECTION THERE...
JUNIOR WALKER AND THE ALL-STARS?
MACNELLY

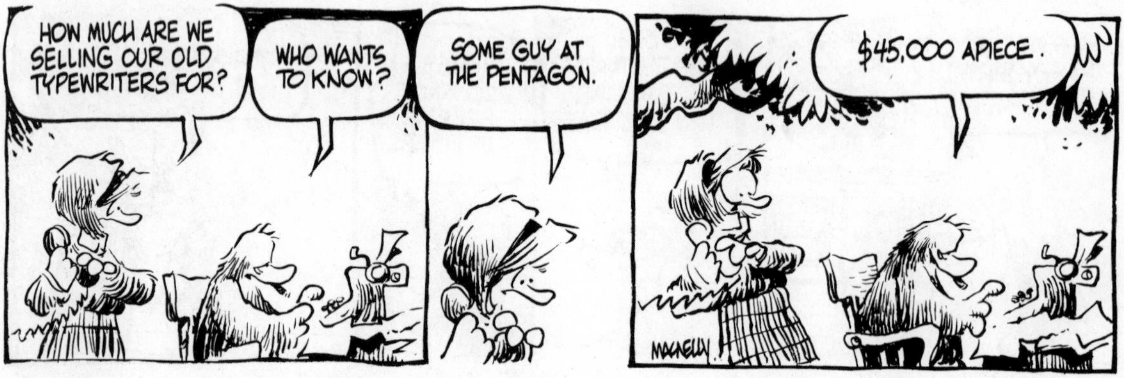
HOW MUCH ARE WE SELLING OUR OLD TYPEWRITERS FOR?
WHO WANTS TO KNOW?
SOME GUY AT THE PENTAGON.
$45,000 APIECE.
MACNELLY

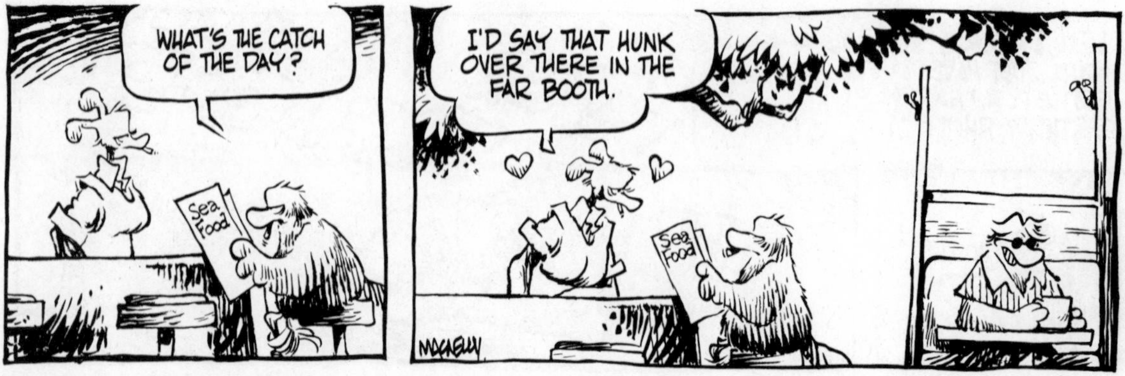
WHAT'S THE CATCH OF THE DAY?
Sea Food
I'D SAY THAT HUNK OVER THERE IN THE FAR BOOTH.
Sea Food
MACNELLY

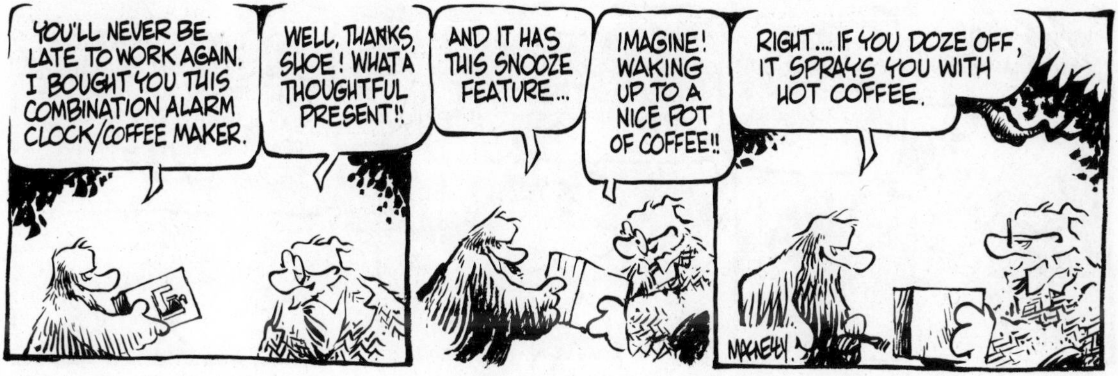
YOU'LL NEVER BE LATE TO WORK AGAIN. I BOUGHT YOU THIS COMBINATION ALARM CLOCK/COFFEE MAKER.
WELL, THANKS, SHOE! WHAT A THOUGHTFUL PRESENT!!
AND IT HAS THIS SNOOZE FEATURE...
IMAGINE! WAKING UP TO A NICE POT OF COFFEE!!
RIGHT.... IF YOU DOZE OFF, IT SPRAYS YOU WITH HOT COFFEE.
MACNELLY.

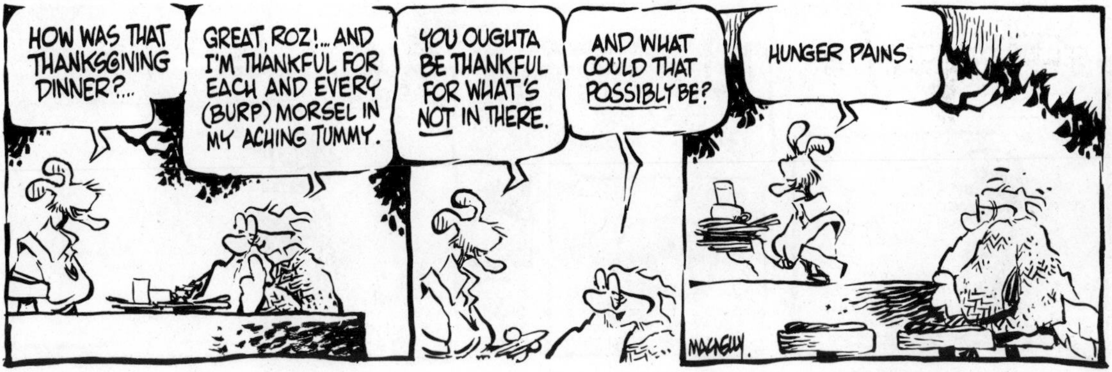
HOW WAS THAT THANKSGIVING DINNER?...
GREAT, ROZ!... AND I'M THANKFUL FOR EACH AND EVERY (BURP) MORSEL IN MY ACHING TUMMY.
YOU OUGHTA BE THANKFUL FOR WHAT'S NOT IN THERE.
AND WHAT COULD THAT POSSIBLY BE?
HUNGER PAINS.
MACNELLY.

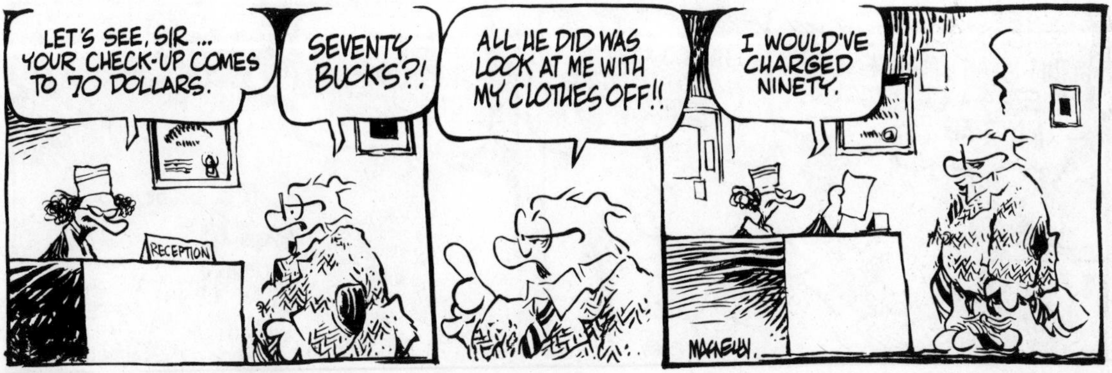
LET'S SEE, SIR ... YOUR CHECK-UP COMES TO 70 DOLLARS.
SEVENTY BUCKS?!
RECEPTION
ALL HE DID WAS LOOK AT ME WITH MY CLOTHES OFF!!
I WOULD'VE CHARGED NINETY.
MACNELLY.

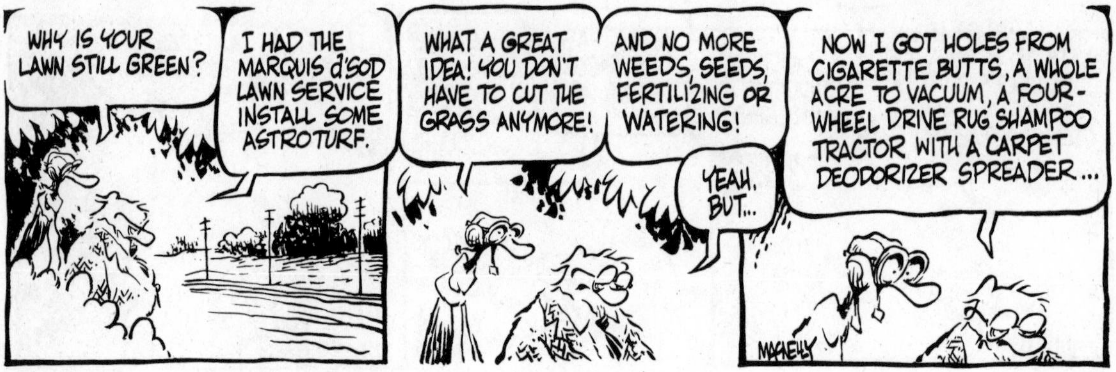
WHY IS YOUR LAWN STILL GREEN?
I HAD THE MARQUIS d'SOD LAWN SERVICE INSTALL SOME ASTROTURF.
WHAT A GREAT IDEA! YOU DON'T HAVE TO CUT THE GRASS ANYMORE!
AND NO MORE WEEDS, SEEDS, FERTILIZING OR WATERING!
YEAH, BUT...
NOW I GOT HOLES FROM CIGARETTE BUTTS, A WHOLE ACRE TO VACUUM, A FOUR-WHEEL DRIVE RUG SHAMPOO TRACTOR WITH A CARPET DEODORIZER SPREADER...
MACNELLY

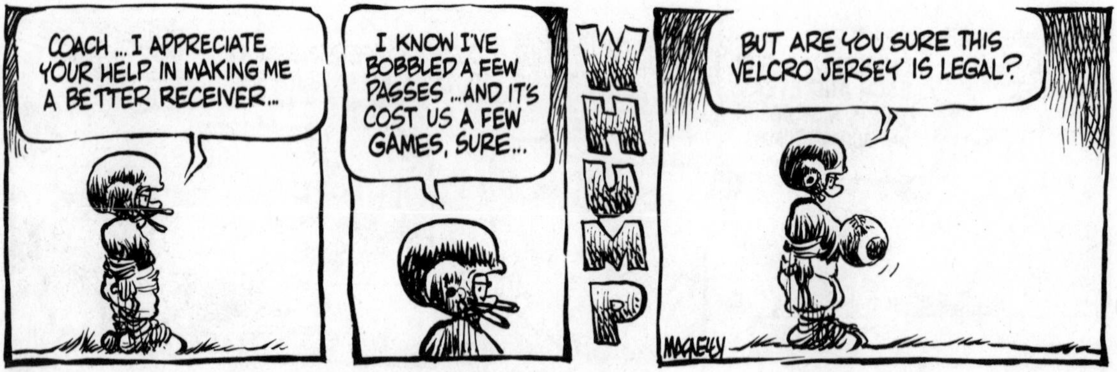
COACH ... I APPRECIATE YOUR HELP IN MAKING ME A BETTER RECEIVER...
I KNOW I'VE BOBBLED A FEW PASSES ...AND IT'S COST US A FEW GAMES, SURE...
WHUMP
BUT ARE YOU SURE THIS VELCRO JERSEY IS LEGAL?
MACNELLY

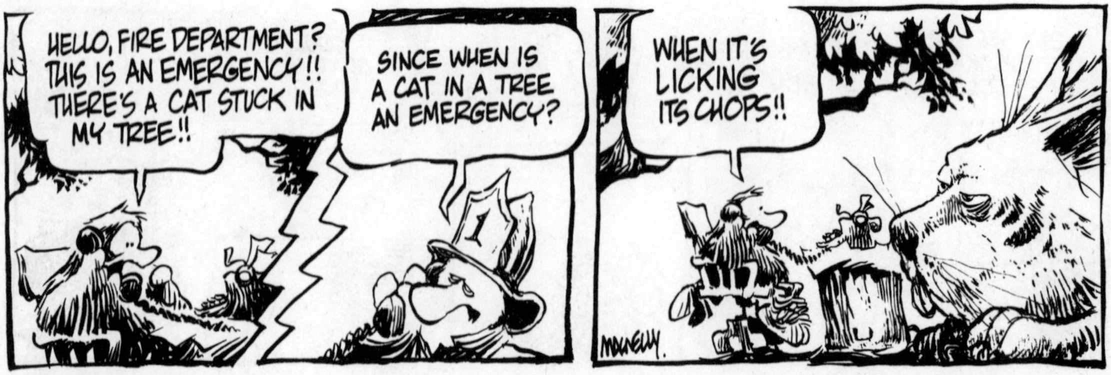
HELLO, FIRE DEPARTMENT? THIS IS AN EMERGENCY!! THERE'S A CAT STUCK IN MY TREE!!
SINCE WHEN IS A CAT IN A TREE AN EMERGENCY?
1
WHEN IT'S LICKING ITS CHOPS!!
MACNELLY.

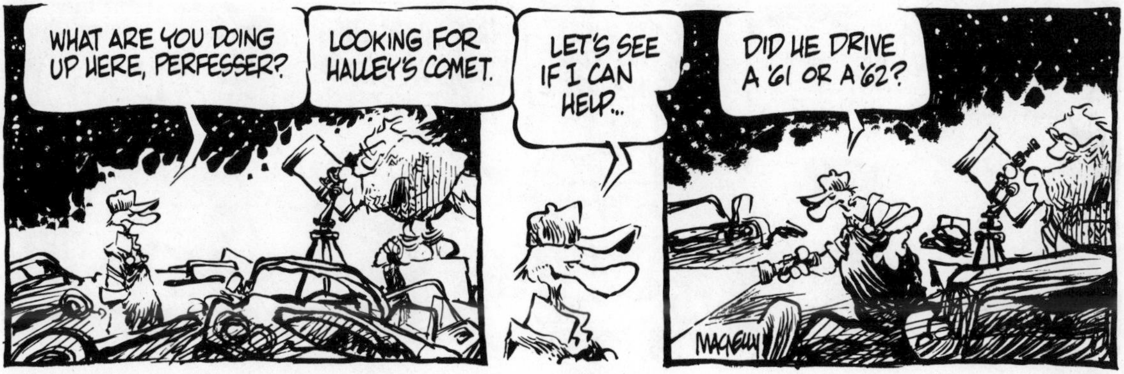
WHAT ARE YOU DOING UP HERE, PERFESSER?
LOOKING FOR HALLEY'S COMET.
LET'S SEE IF I CAN HELP...
DID HE DRIVE A '61 OR A '62?
MACNELLY

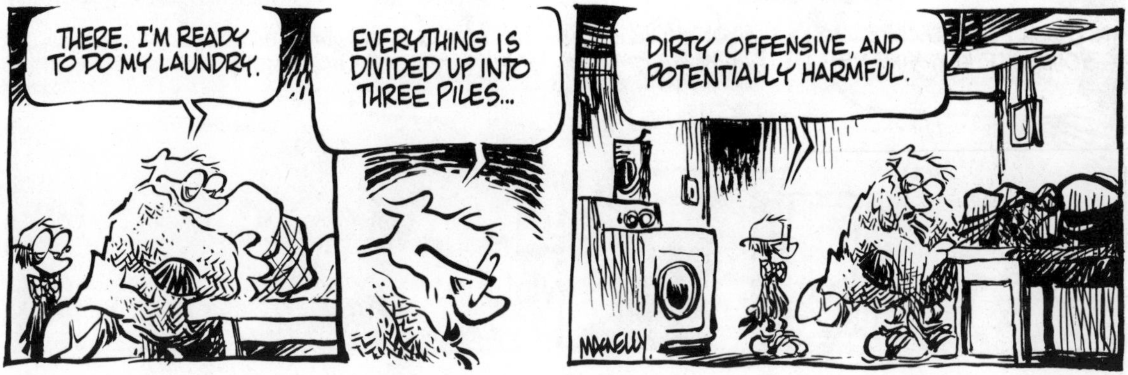
THERE. I'M READY TO DO MY LAUNDRY.
EVERYTHING IS DIVIDED UP INTO THREE PILES...
DIRTY, OFFENSIVE, AND POTENTIALLY HARMFUL.
MACNELLY

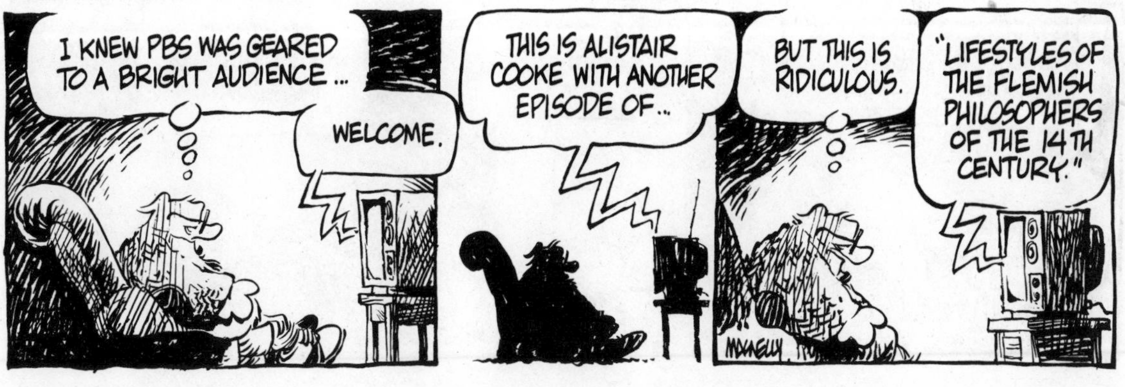
I KNEW PBS WAS GEARED TO A BRIGHT AUDIENCE ...
WELCOME.
THIS IS ALISTAIR COOKE WITH ANOTHER EPISODE OF...
BUT THIS IS RIDICULOUS.
"LIFESTYLES OF THE FLEMISH PHILOSOPHERS OF THE 14TH CENTURY."
MACNELLY

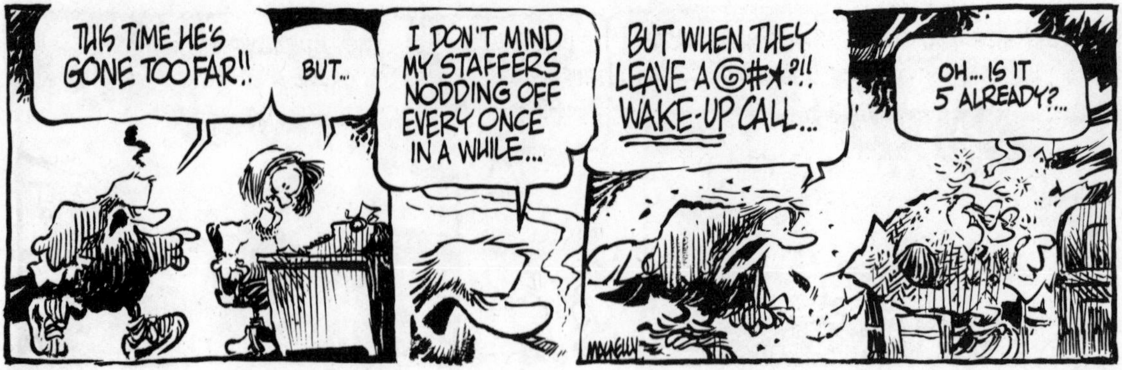
THIS TIME HE'S GONE TOO FAR!!
BUT...
I DON'T MIND MY STAFFERS NODDING OFF EVERY ONCE IN A WHILE...
BUT WHEN THEY LEAVE A @#*?!! WAKE-UP CALL...
OH... IS IT 5 ALREADY?...
MACNELLY

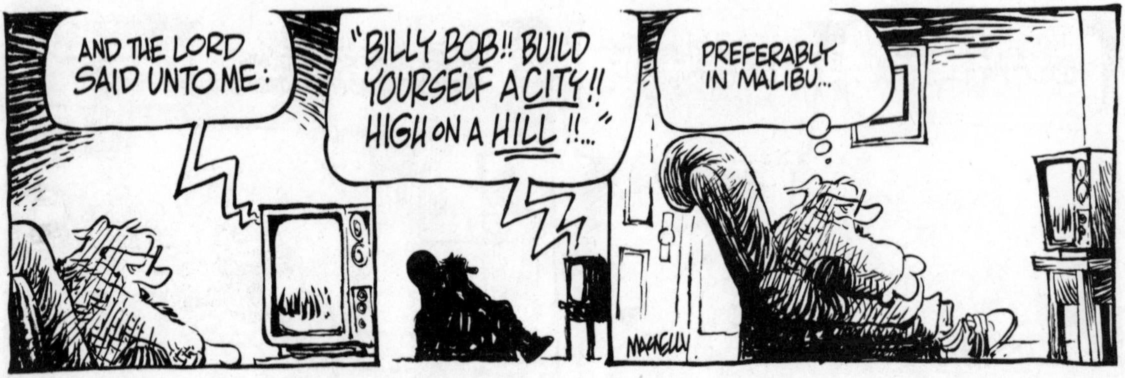
AND THE LORD SAID UNTO ME:
"BILLY BOB!! BUILD YOURSELF A CITY!! HIGH ON A HILL!!..."
PREFERABLY IN MALIBU...
MACNELLY

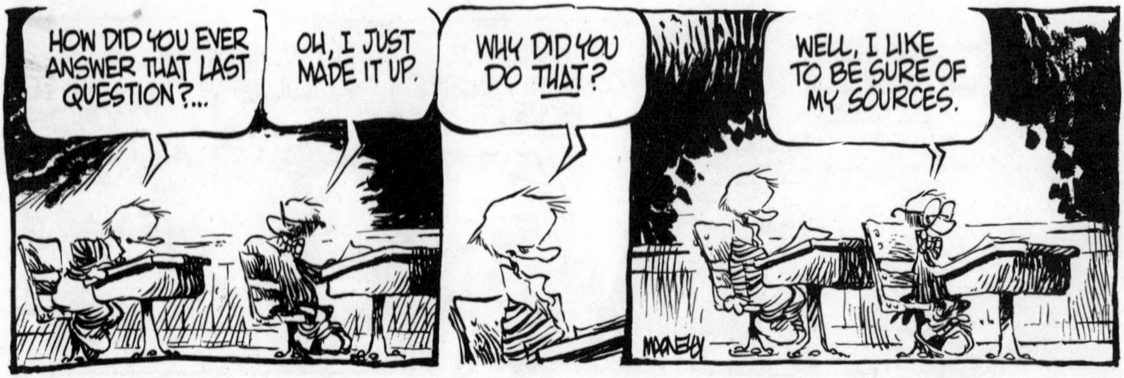
HOW DID YOU EVER ANSWER THAT LAST QUESTION?...
OH, I JUST MADE IT UP.
WHY DID YOU DO THAT?
WELL, I LIKE TO BE SURE OF MY SOURCES.
MACNELLY

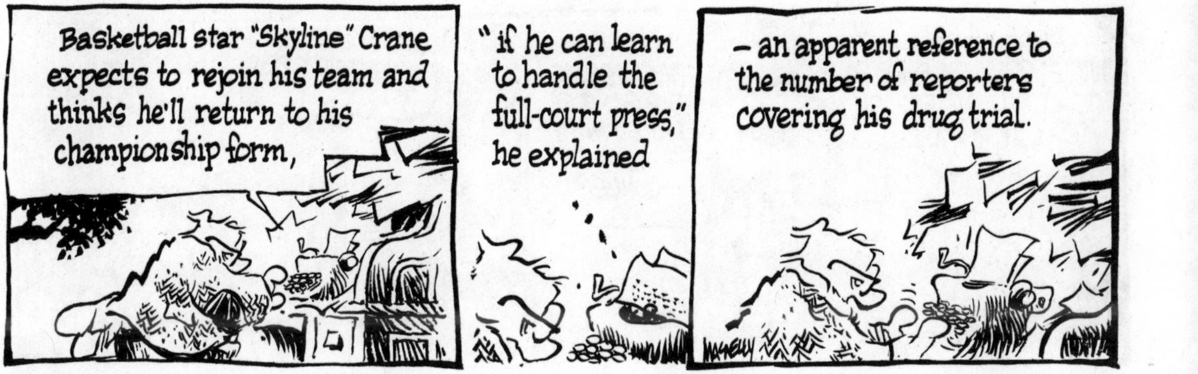
Basketball star "Skyline" Crane expects to rejoin his team and thinks he'll return to his championship form,
" if he can learn to handle the full-court press," he explained
– an apparent reference to the number of reporters covering his drug trial.
MACNELLY

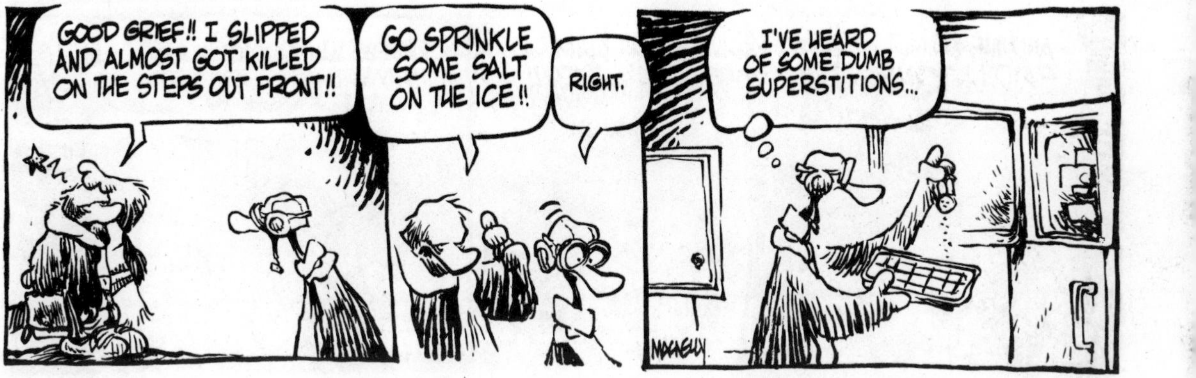
GOOD GRIEF!! I SLIPPED AND ALMOST GOT KILLED ON THE STEPS OUT FRONT!!
GO SPRINKLE SOME SALT ON THE ICE!!
RIGHT.
I'VE HEARD OF SOME DUMB SUPERSTITIONS...
MACNELLY

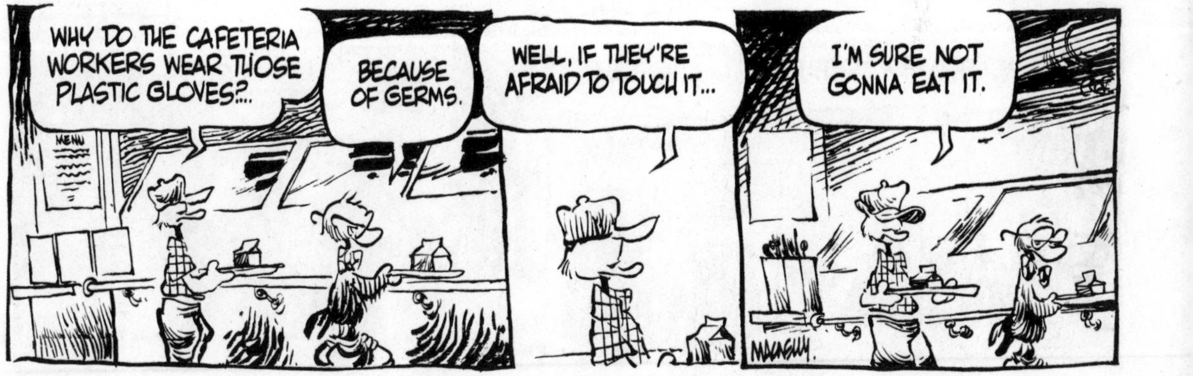
WHY DO THE CAFETERIA WORKERS WEAR THOSE PLASTIC GLOVES?...
BECAUSE OF GERMS.
WELL, IF THEY'RE AFRAID TO TOUCH IT...
I'M SURE NOT GONNA EAT IT.
MENU
MACNELLY

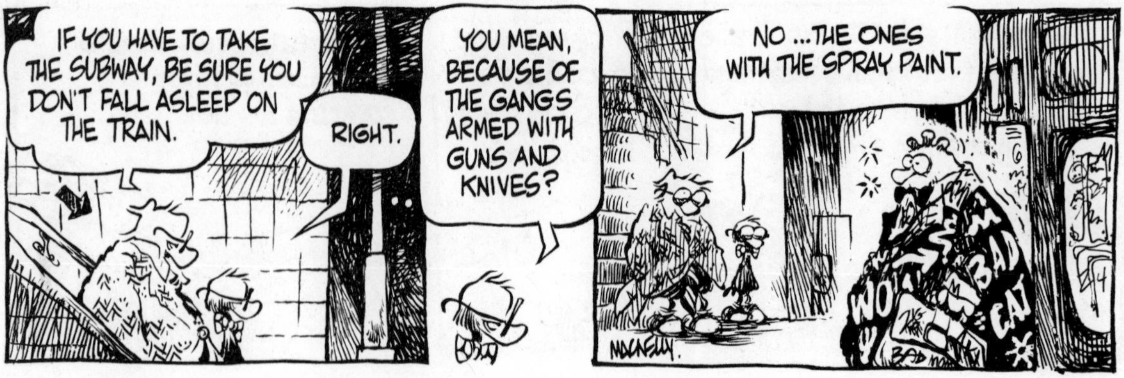
IF YOU HAVE TO TAKE THE SUBWAY, BE SURE YOU DON'T FALL ASLEEP ON THE TRAIN.
RIGHT.
YOU MEAN, BECAUSE OF THE GANGS ARMED WITH GUNS AND KNIVES?
NO ...THE ONES WITH THE SPRAY PAINT.
MACNELLY

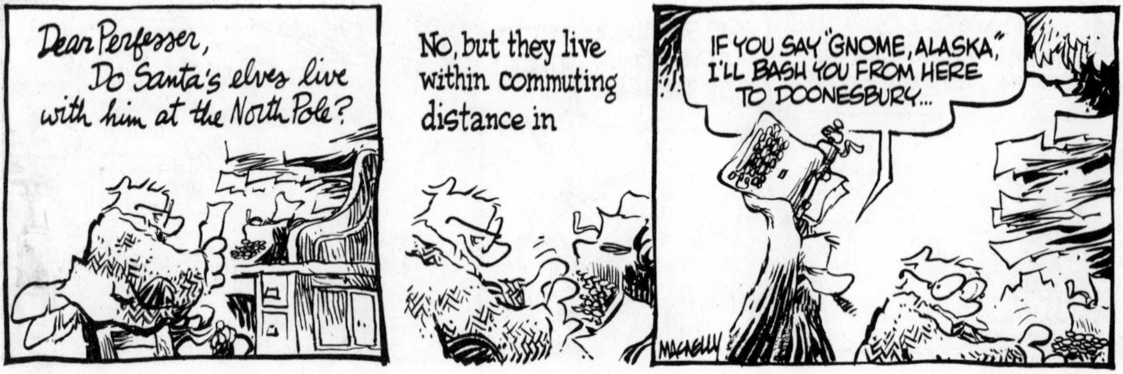
Dear Perfesser,
Do Santa's elves live with him at the North Pole?
No, but they live within commuting distance in
IF YOU SAY "GNOME, ALASKA," I'LL BASH YOU FROM HERE TO DOONESBURY...
MACNELLY

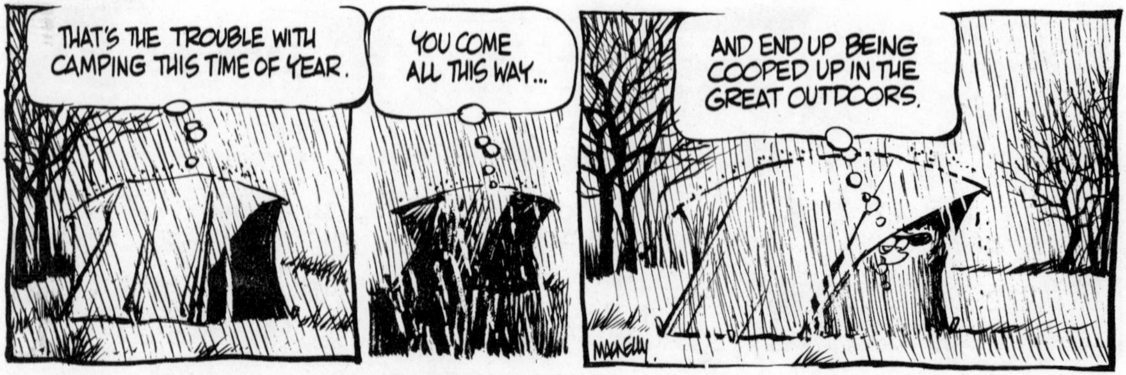
THAT'S THE TROUBLE WITH CAMPING THIS TIME OF YEAR.
YOU COME ALL THIS WAY...
AND END UP BEING COOPED UP IN THE GREAT OUTDOORS.
MACNELLY

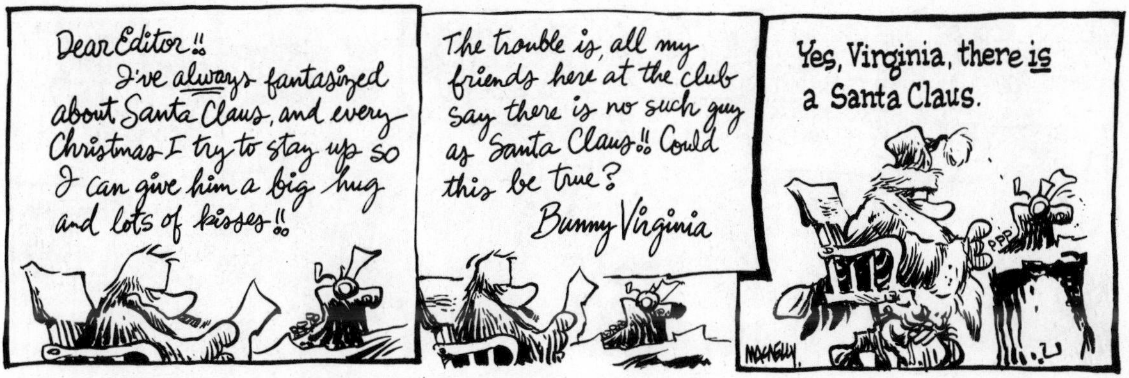
Dear Editor!!
I've always fantasized about Santa Claus, and every Christmas I try to stay up so I can give him a big hug and lots of kisses!!
The trouble is, all my friends here at the club say there is no such guy as Santa Claus!! Could this be true?
Bunny Virginia
Yes, Virginia, there is a Santa Claus.
PPP
MACNELLY

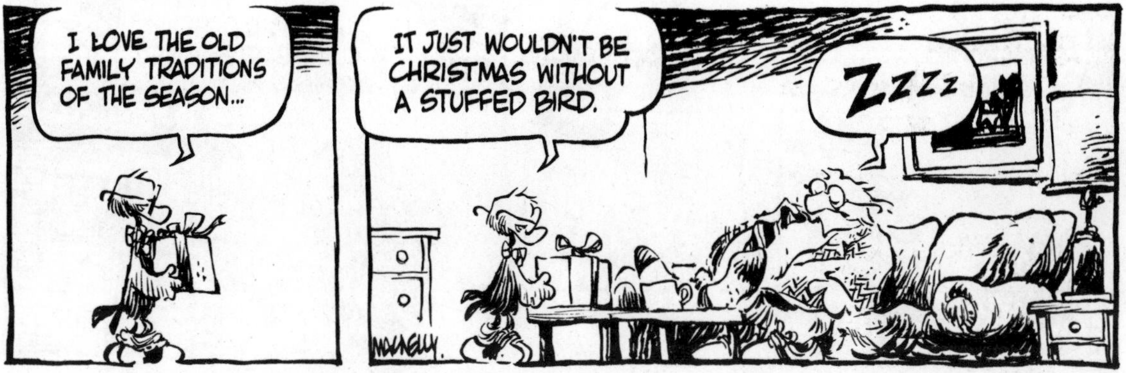
I LOVE THE OLD FAMILY TRADITIONS OF THE SEASON...
IT JUST WOULDN'T BE CHRISTMAS WITHOUT A STUFFED BIRD.
ZZZZ
MACNELLY

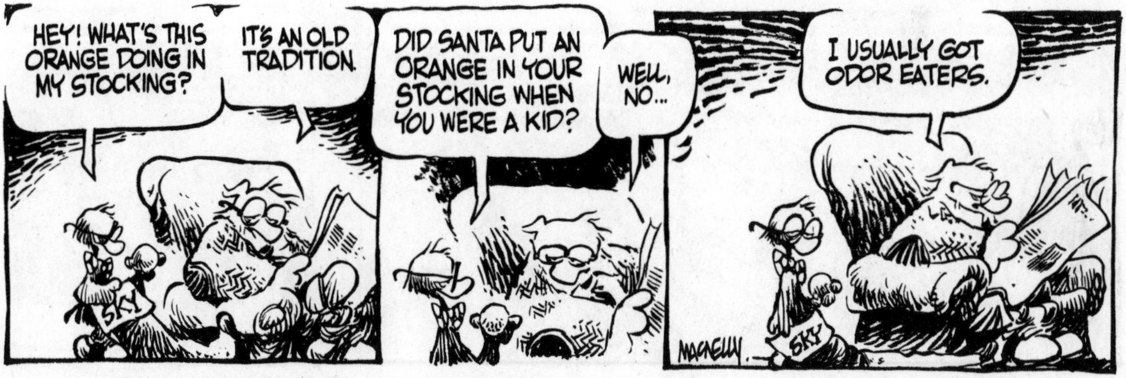
HEY! WHAT'S THIS ORANGE DOING IN MY STOCKING?
IT'S AN OLD TRADITION.
DID SANTA PUT AN ORANGE IN YOUR STOCKING WHEN YOU WERE A KID?
WELL, NO...
I USUALLY GOT ODOR EATERS.
SKY
MACNELLY

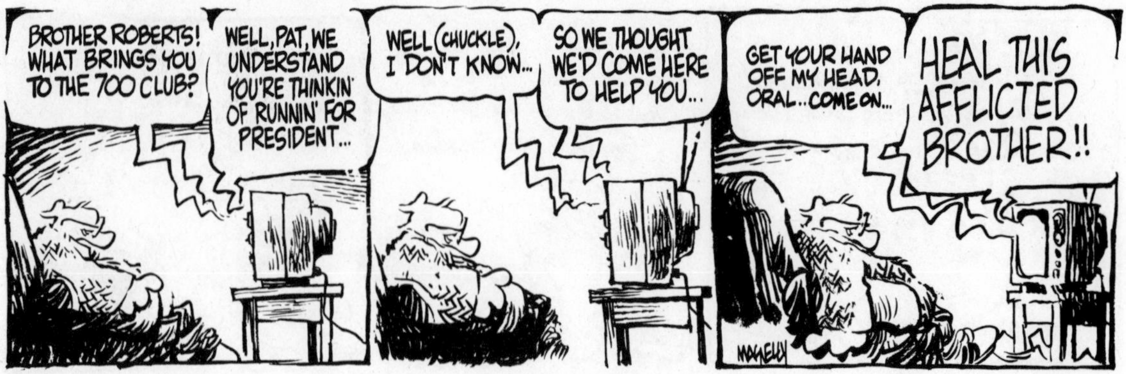
BROTHER ROBERTS! WHAT BRINGS YOU TO THE 700 CLUB?
WELL, PAT, WE UNDERSTAND YOU'RE THINKIN' OF RUNNIN' FOR PRESIDENT...
WELL (CHUCKLE), I DON'T KNOW...
SO WE THOUGHT WE'D COME HERE TO HELP YOU...
GET YOUR HAND OFF MY HEAD, ORAL...COME ON...
HEAL THIS AFFLICTED BROTHER!!
MAGELLY

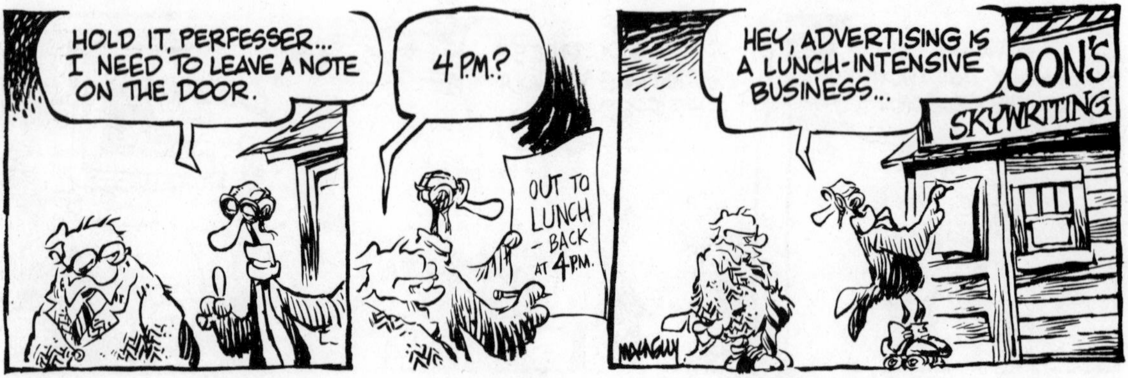
HOLD IT, PERFESSER... I NEED TO LEAVE A NOTE ON THE DOOR.
4 P.M.?
OUT TO LUNCH - BACK AT 4 P.M.
HEY, ADVERTISING IS A LUNCH-INTENSIVE BUSINESS...
OON'S
SKYWRITING
MAGELLY

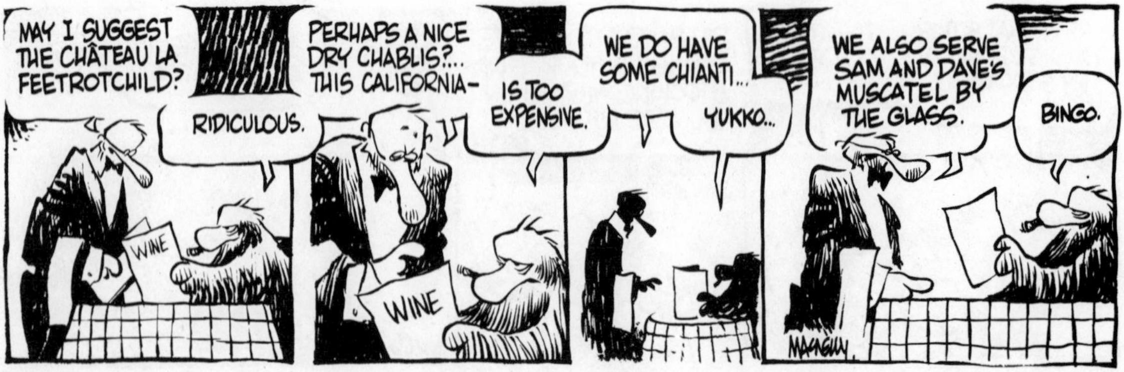
MAY I SUGGEST THE CHÂTEAU LA FEETROTCHILD?
RIDICULOUS.
WINE
PERHAPS A NICE DRY CHABLIS?... THIS CALIFORNIA-
IS TOO EXPENSIVE.
WINE
WE DO HAVE SOME CHIANTI...
YUKKO...
WE ALSO SERVE SAM AND DAVE'S MUSCATEL BY THE GLASS.
BINGO.
MAGELLY